American-Japanese
Security Agreements,
Past and Present

American–Japanese Security Agreements, Past and Present

THOMAS A. DROHAN

McFarland & Company, Inc., Publishers
Jefferson, North Carolina, and London

LIBRARY OF CONGRESS CATALOGUING-IN-PUBLICATION DATA

Drohan, Thomas Alan.
   American-Japanese security agreements, past and present /
Thomas A. Drohan.
      p.   cm.
   Includes bibliographical references and index.

   ISBN-13: 978-0-7864-2890-8
   (softcover : 50# alkaline paper) ∞

   1. National security — United States.   2. National security —
Japan.   3. United States — Military relations — Japan.   4. Japan —
Military relations — United States.   5. United States — Military
policy.   6. Japan — Military policy.   I. Title.
UA23.D735   2007
355'.03109730952 — dc22   2006037127

British Library cataloguing data are available

©2007 McFarland & Company, Inc., Publishers. All rights reserved

*No part of this book may be reproduced or transmitted in any form
or by any means, electronic or mechanical, including photocopying
or recording, or by any information storage and retrieval system,
without permission in writing from the publisher.*

Cover photograph ©2007 Corbis Images

Manufactured in the United States of America

*McFarland & Company, Inc., Publishers
   Box 611, Jefferson, North Carolina 28640
      www.mcfarlandpub.com*

To Madeline

Security is a value, then, of which a nation can have more or less and which it can aspire to have in greater or lesser measure. It has much in common, in this respect, with power or wealth, two other values of great importance in international relations. But while wealth measures the amount of a nation's material possessions, and power its ability to control the actions of others, security, in an objective sense, measures the absence of threats to acquired values, in a subjective sense, the absence of fear that such values will be attacked.

— Arnold Wolfers

Contents

Preface 1

1. Security Alliance Dynamics 5
2. Pre-War Origins 22
3. Post-War Security Bargain 42
4. Security Treaty Revision 71
5. Division of Military Roles 91
6. Co-Development of Military Technology 110
7. Allied Military Commitment 130
8. Past Patterns, Future Options 152

Chapter Notes 179
Bibliography 199
Index 209

Preface

My journey to understand and explain the U.S.–Japan security relationship began nearly two decades ago when I was an Air Force officer entering graduate school with a follow-on position to teach political science at the Air Force Academy. By that time, my military career had registered a pattern of academic and operational assignments that would repeat itself over the years. From this vantage point, I observed that the two worlds of academic and military service frequently yielded different insights to the security issues of the day.

First of all, the assumptions were often different. Those which academia generated were more varied, and competed for tenure in a marketplace of scholarly approaches. Military assumptions tended to frame worst case scenarios against which soldiers, sailors, airmen and marines repeatedly planned and practiced operations.

The second key difference had to do with what was generally regarded and rewarded as learning. Academic rigor, at least in the dominant international security literature, involved building and then tearing down arguments that essentially simplified the complex—*using a little to explain a lot*. Military rigor meant knowing essential doctrinal frameworks and training to execute them in detail. This was more a process of *using a lot to explain a little*.

Each approach to inductive and deductive learning was useful in its own way, so I committed to a process of reconciling both types of experiences. Princeton University's Department of Politics and the Woodrow Wilson School were productive places to discover approaches to this dual task.

As I explored academic perspectives on security relations, it seemed to me that disciplinary approaches to critical security issues, taken singly, were of limited use in the real world. The international security literature was littered with respectable theories which deliberately ignored details that I knew mattered in the competitive arena of military operations. Comparative studies tended to embrace more details, but often created their own ponderous vocabulary, remote from practical concerns. Historical works often got the details right, but shunned theories that might explain rather than describe phenomena. Military doctrine addressed operational particulars with useful analytical frameworks, but there were scant connections to academic approaches and then only in a general sense, at a strategic level of abstraction.

The more I learned about the U.S.–Japan security relationship through available frameworks, the more I sought an integrative approach that sufficiently captured the nature of the relationship, how it was changing, and why. American scholars seemed driven by simplistic theories or mired in impractical jargon. Their counterparts in Japan largely preferred to begin discussions about security either in the postwar period, or as if the Pacific War started on August 6, 1945.

My initial response to the challenge of creating a more useful framework was to develop the central idea of this book: "security bargain." These two words appeared to capture the strategic and tactical realities of the U.S.–Japan relationship quite well. My dissertation advisors, Kent Calder and Aaron Friedberg, rightfully posed difficult questions and supported my efforts to develop the concept. I remain grateful for their intellectual tolerance because the concept was too descriptive for elegant international relations theorists and too theoretical for purist historians.

As I wrapped up dissertation research and interviews in Japan in 1990, Iraqi forces invaded Kuwait. I watched U.S. and Japanese government officials respond in mutually beneficial yet polar opposite ways to this act of aggression. These different reactions fit nicely into the security bargain framework, so I concluded the dissertation with pretty much the 1987 case you see in Chapter 6.

I returned to the Air Force Academy to teach cadets political science and how to fly. For four years, I thought about the security bargain, but dutifully inflicted familiar frameworks of analysis on cadets enrolled in my political science classes. Next came a three-year operational flying assignment that sent me to Central America, Europe and the Middle East. During this time, my observations and experiences far from Japan validated the usefulness of the framework in this book. Our airlift missions routinely required negotiating with a number of host country agencies up, down and across chains of command and webs of coordination. Bargaining over the terms of security cooperation seemed very much alive and well in the world.

Back to the academic and research world, where I had the chance to refocus on the U.S.–Japan relationship in light of the intervening operational experiences. A Hitachi-sponsored Council on Foreign Relations fellowship allowed me to work at two research institutes, the International Institute of

Policy Studies (*Seikai Heiwa Kenkyujo*) and the National Institute of Defense Studies (*Boei Kenkyujo*). As I studied the new U.S.–Japan Defense Guidelines, I watched Japanese reactions to North Korea's launch of a multi-stage missile over Japan. Nine months later, I had drafted basically what you will read as Chapter 7.

Returning to the Air Force Academy, this time to teach military strategic studies, I began to focus more on the dynamic context of military strategy and operations. In this regard, too, the U.S.–Japan security relationship was changing at a fast pace, but the scholarly literature still seemed stuck in traditional views of alliance and military security. Military transformation outpaced doctrinal publications, but this stimulated great debates over how to organize, train and equip post–Cold War armed forces.

On September 11, 2001, I watched with a class of freshman cadets as terrorists attacks and their aftermath unfolded in New York, Washington, D.C., and a field outside of Pittsburgh. Our lesson for that day was on ethics in warfare. The subsequent and ongoing war on terror led us to explore more integrated approaches to intelligence, interagency coordination, and special operations, as well as how to reorganize and re-train in support of national goals and strategies.

Now it was time for a sabbatical, which for military faculty at the Air Force Academy means "re-bluing" one's academic mindset with operational or staff duty. The subsequent assignment to the U.S. and South Korean Antiterrorism and Force Protection Division in Seoul yielded insights into the multiple aspects and manifestations of security in an evolving threat environment. This timely experience expanded my view of regional perspectives on the U.S.–Japan security relationship, and led me to review and further update this manuscript.

My hope is that you find the resulting book a useful alternative to traditional approaches to security.

The objectives of this book are twofold. First, I examine the puzzling historical origins of U.S.–Japan security relations. How can we characterize the beginning of a chronically controversial relationship lauded as the cornerstone for regional stability? Several works have related the story of the American occupation of Japan and the ensuing security framework, but none addresses the question of what realistically provided the basis for postwar security cooperation. Alliance theory based on common threat or the exigencies of military occupation cannot explain why such bitter enemies in 1945 became genuine security partners so rapidly. What, in fact, has been the nature of "alliance?" Rather than presuming the overriding priority of a common threat, I answer these questions by using a comparative perspective of security relationships that allows for differences in security priorities among alliance partners.

Second, I explore the neglected question of alliance change. What has the original relationship evolved into, and what will it become? Furthermore, I introduce a conceptual frame of reference, the security bargain, as a realistic way to think about alliances in their broader political-military-economic contexts. By analyzing four historical cases of significant alliance change as new security bargains negotiated in 1960, 1981, 1987, and 1997, I search for answers to the question of how and why this critical security relationship has evolved since its inception in the mid-twentieth century.

The structure of the book serves these dual aims. Chapter 1 poses the central questions, considers relevant scholarly literature, and sets forth the argument and organization. Chapters 2 and 3 analyze the prewar roots and postwar institutionalization of the original security bargain framework. Chapters 4 through 7 use the organizing concept of the security bargain to understand how the four structural changes to the original framework occurred. The concluding chapter summarizes the origins and transformation of the security bargain, explains why the major changes occurred, then draws strategic policy implications for the relationship into the next century. The quality of the security bargain approach introduced here should be judged in terms of its usefulness in thinking about continuity and change in various alliance relationships, and in offering ideas for security cooperation and legitimate competition.

The views expressed in this book are those of the author and do not necessarily reflect the official policy or position of the U.S. Air Force, the Department of Defense, or the U.S. government.

1

Security Alliance Dynamics

Central Questions

The transformation of U.S.–Japan security relations from its mid–19th century origins and into the 21st century is as important as it is contentious. Given the combined economic and military potential of the United States and Japan, harmonious security relations between the world's two leading industrialized democracies are essential for global stability. The original postwar framework for U.S.–Japan security cooperation has evolved politically, militarily and economically — but specifically how and why, and what kind of future relationship is emerging? While policy makers in both nations describe the bilateral relationship as fundamental to security in East Asia, its direction is uncertain. Some experts view U.S.–Japan security relations in terms of inexorable progress toward alliance; others prescribe larger changes to forestall alliance breakdown due to domestic politics, fears of militarism, trade or economic disputes. Alarmist literature competes for our attention with more scholarly examinations of the changing security relationship. In the process, the nature of the security relationship itself has become the key issue in U.S.–Japan relations.

Enduring issues have plagued the relationship: is a passive Japan using American military strength to avoid security responsibilities commensurate with its democratic commitment and economic status? Or is a resurgent Japan bolstering mutual regional security interests through financial support, military basing rights, and a growing defense capability? Is the United States using its military preeminence to retain Japanese security dependence, preventing Japan from being able to defend itself or becoming a threat to surrounding states? Or is the United States providing a credible military guarantee while accepting domestic and international limits on Japan's security strategy? What will Japan's regional security role be, given domestic constraints and emerging security challenges?

These questions have been sharpened by a series of developments: the rise of Chinese power and Taiwanese nationalism; Russian military decline and domestic discord; nuclear proliferation by strategic rivals India and Pakistan and unstable North Korea; simmering territorial disputes in the Spratly Islands and throughout Southeast Asia; Asian financial dynamism; and the U.S.-led global war on terrorism following the 9/11/01 attacks on the United States. These factors intensify fundamental questions about the nature and future direction of the U.S.–Japan security relationship.

It is difficult to address these policy questions and concerns without an historical appreciation of where the relationship started, and a theoretical understanding of how and why the alliance has changed. To accomplish this, fundamental questions about the nature of the alliance need to be addressed. That is what this book sets out to do.

This inquiry seeks to present alliance dynamics as they have unfolded so far, to explain continuity and change, while also drawing implications for future scenarios. The central questions are: *how did the U.S.–Japan security relationship originate historically? Since its formative period, how and why has the relationship been transformed? What have been the political, military, and economic parameters of change? What have been the sources of alliance change?* In order to offer useful strategies for future U.S.–Japan relations, an understanding of previous options is crucial. By posing basic questions, I hope to offer useful theoretical insights for the management of complex security relationships.

Theoretical Considerations

Obstacles to explaining security aspects of U.S.–Japan relations are plentiful — most often noted are differences in language, cultural misunderstandings, and perception gaps. Problems of miscommunication and mutual misperception can be significant, but they are to a degree unavoidable. Even among culturally similar allies, differences in personalities, policy, and orders of priority tend to produce "muddled perceptions."[1] More importantly, preoccupation with misunderstanding can mask differences of interest central to the notion of national security. In the case of U.S.–Japan security relations, explaining the basis of cooperation is complicated by national differences that affect security objectives and shape the state's role in economic and military affairs. Although mutual misperception certainly exists, the prime obstacle to understanding U.S.–Japan security relations is absence of an intellectual framework that illuminates how security alliances actually behave in the dynamic, real world of competition and cooperation. This book treats the question of U.S.–Japan alliance change as a theoretical and analytic challenge rather than a cultural or communicative problem.

The theoretical challenge of explaining the U.S.–Japan security relationship becomes clear when attempting to either make sense of the alliance's historical origins, or trace the course of U.S.–Japan security relations since the Pacific War. The main problem has been that the two leading alliance theories, balance of power theory and public goods theory, do not explain the dynamics of U.S.–Japan security relations. Force levels of military personnel, equipment and weapons systems, and the relative proportion of allied force contributions, are basic elements of an alliance that merit explanation. Yet neither theory accounts for the persistence of Japanese military force levels, or the stability of the American and Japanese military contributions to collective security.

Balance of power theory suggests that as the common threat increases, increases in military force structure follow. However, Japanese Ground Self-Defense Force (GSDF) troop levels, Maritime Self-Defense Force (MSDF) naval flotillas and ships, and numbers of Air Self-Defense Force (ASDF) groups, squadrons and aircraft have been stable over the years. In spite of periodic increases in external military threats by China, North Korea and the Soviet Union, Japanese force levels have not similarly adjusted. Remarkably static, they have not been low by international standards. As early as 1955, Japan's defense expenditures ranked eighth in the world, and have progressively risen since. (See Table 1.1 on page 8.)

Japanese defense spending increases have been particularly steady since the late 1970's, averaging 6.4 percent a year, including 2 percent increases in the late 80's while U.S. defense spending declined. In contrast to the American post–1991, pre–September 2001 drawdown which have averaged 3 percent annual decreases in defense expenditures, Japan's defense budgets have maintained an average increase of 2.6 percent.[2] The dramatic increase in U.S. defense spending since the terrorist attacks of 2001 and subsequent military operations in Afghanistan and Iraq has not been reciprocated in Japan, despite North Korea's demonstrated ability to reach Japan with long-range missiles and nuclear threats.

Public goods theory suggests that states which would benefit most from a public good (such as collective security from attack) and which have the greatest ability to provide it, will bear higher costs of providing the good.[3] The good must be non-excludable to be a public good, that is, neither ally is excluded from receiving the benefits of the good when the good is provided. Security from attack is generally agreed to be a non-excludable good since deterring or countering a threat does so for both alliance partners. Free riding by the weaker ally is likely because it is assumed that the larger ally (size measured by national income) values the alliance more. This dispropor-

TABLE 1.1—GLOBAL DEFENSE EXPENDITURES 1955–2005

	1955	1960	1965	1970	1975	1980	1985	1990	1995	2000	2005
1	USSR	US	US	US	US	US	US	US	US	US	US
2	US	USSR	USSR	USSR	USSR	USSR	USSR	USSR	Russia	Russia	UK
3	UK	UK	UK	France	UK	UK	UK	Saudi Arabia	Japan	Japan	Japan
4	France	FRG	FRG	FRG	FRG	FRG	France	UK	France	China	France
5	FRG	France	France	UK	France	France	FRG	France	Germany	UK	Germany
6	Italy	Italy	Italy	Italy	Iran	Japan	Saudi Arabia	Germany	UK	France	China
7	Netherlands	Netherlands	Japan	Japan	Japan	Italy	Japan	Japan	China	Germany	India
8	Japan	Japan	Canada	Nigeria	Italy	Iran	Italy	China	Italy	Italy	Saudi Arabia

tion is expected to diminish as the weaker ally experiences relative economic growth. However, the Japanese contribution to alliance force structure has hovered around 1 percent of the GDP, even during times of meteoric economic growth, while U.S. expenditures have varied from a high of 10 percent in 1955 to a low of 3 percent in 2000 just before the attacks of 9/11/2001.

Instead of conforming to the expectations of public goods theory, the U.S.–Japan relationship exhibits just the opposite tendency. In the face of manifold increases in the Soviet Pacific Fleet, and more recently, sharp rises in Chinese naval capability in the South China, an increase in alliance military capability would seemingly benefit Japanese security more than American security.[4] Japan's total dependence on foreign sources of oil and the need to ensure its secure transit from the Persian Gulf suggest this should be the case. Yet, during the 1991 United Nations eviction of Iraq from Kuwait, Japanese officials were unable to dispatch even unarmed C-130 transport aircraft to evacuate war-zone refugees, and Japan's minesweeping ships were sent well after hostilities ended. In response to the Al Qaeda 9/11/2001 attacks on the United States, however, Japan has provided unprecedented air, naval and ground support for U.S. military operations in Afghanistan and Iraq, even though Japanese public opinion disagrees such support benefits Japan.

Furthermore, with only one percent of GNP devoted to defense, Japan would seem more capable of providing the public good than the United States, which typically spends three to six percent of GNP on defense. In contrast to significant increases in U.S. defense spending during the Korean conflict (1950–1953) and early years of the Vietnam conflict (1965–1969), Japanese defense spending as a percentage of GNP actually declined during these periods. Yet both of these conflicts were closer to Japan than the United States, and occurred while both American and Japanese policy makers declared communist regimes as the common enemy. In this period, Japanese GNP growth outstripped that of the United States by an average of seven percent. During the period of most rapid Soviet military growth and in times of regional armed conflict, Japanese spending on defense only marginally increased. Curiously, it has been in the late 1970s–1980s, after the slowdown in Japanese economic growth approached American levels of GNP growth, that Japanese defense spending as a percentage of GNP increased, then leveled off. Public goods theory suggests the opposite tendency. Despite the 1993–4 North Korean nuclear crisis, the 2001 terrorist attacks and ensuing Japanese military support of U.S. forces in the Middle East, and the simmering North Korean nuclear standoff, Japan's defense expenditures have either risen modestly or declined in real terms. Public goods theory would point to the chronic recession in Japan during the 1990's and well into the new millennium to explain these modest levels, with U.S. defense expenditure and force increases presumably countering these threats for both allies.

Both balance of power theory and public goods theory assume an alliance is defined by a common military threat. Fixated on the notion that bilateral behavior is driven by the presence of an overriding common adversary, traditional alliance theory does not adequately address the question of change. Instead, alliances have been largely conceptualized as "on-off" switches. Even recent alliance theorists who focus on alliance formation and wartime performance assume a common rival as the basis for cooperation.

The failure of balance of power theory and public goods theory to explain these enduring dynamics of U.S.–Japan security relations suggests a need to loosen some assumptions. Interactive approaches to international relations lead to other bases of cooperation.

Rational choice theory suggests domestic and international bargaining is an important aspect of alliances. Two-level games involve negotiators reaching feasible international agreements by satisfying key national constituents. Policy officials attempt to reach agreement on a win set that achieves bilateral goals and appeases influential domestic groups.[5]

Other studies focus on the decisions states face in an anarchic international system. The security dilemma[6] explains how a state's pursuit of security can increase the insecurity of its neighbors, therefore producing a less secure environment. Scholars have used the security dilemma concept to analyze patterns of cooperation,[7] and to describe alliance and adversary games as elements of alliance politics.[8] Allies not only concern themselves with how firm or conciliatory to be toward an adversary, but also perceive fears of abandonment (fear that one's ally will defect) and entrapment (fear that one will become embroiled in an unwanted conflict due to an ally's recklessness) toward an ally. Studies on declining powers have considered how states assess power, view threats, and create strategies to achieve security.[9] Internal state characteristics and decisions vary in their reactions to changes in the international balance of power.

These works support the need for a contextual approach to security relations; one that considers how external situations interact with domestic characteristics and coalitions to produce different conceptions of threat. In a bilateral relationship where significant differences of domestic structure and process exist, a comparative approach is needed to allow for important differences in state concepts of security.

The Value of Comparative Studies

Comparative works illustrate the importance of factors other than common threat in explaining bilateral cooperation and conflict. In the British-American alliance, policy makers' failure to recognize mutual national constraints has ignited crises.[10] Misunderstanding national constraints has disrupted U.S.–Japan trade negotiations as well, exacerbating broader relations.[11] Foreign policy models such as the rational actor, organizational process, and bureaucratic politics have also been applied to alliances.[12] Empirically rooted studies of alliance politics suggest that combinations of all three models are needed to explain security relations. Even the NATO alliance, traditionally assumed to be based on a common threat, has seen cooperation frustrated by the lack of common priorities.[13] Comparisons across numerous contemporary defense policies have identified many international and domestic variables that explain defense policy differences, illustrating the need to admit nuanced threat assessments and allied competition.[14]

Support for an alternative to common threat as the basis for security cooperation is found among Japan specialists. Within this diverse group, there is remarkable conformity about the trans-war continuity of Japanese economic security concerns.[15] Given the strident ideological battle between the class-based approach and pluralist approach, and the tendency for both sides to simplify and exaggerate the other side's claims, their convergence is noteworthy.[16] Apart from ideological debates and methodological issues, controversies center on the sources, not the fact, of Japan's pursuit of economic security.[17]

Many postwar studies have pointed to deep-seated Japanese perceptions of economic vulnerability among elites and bureaucrats interested in maintaining access to raw materials, or in avoiding commercial instability.[18] Intellectual debates have not questioned the pursuit of economic security itself; divergence has been on why it has been persistently pursued. To some scholars, organizational structure and a cultural expectation of continuous adaptation have given rise to an effective Japanese industrial policy that responds well to national economic challenges.[19] Another interpretation argues that cultural norms favoring social, economic, and political stability, and cultural assumptions about the need to adapt security policy to broader changes, explain Japan's post–1945 non-violent approach to national security.[20] Still another perspective accounts for the periodic "clashes" between the United States and Japan as rooted in two different forms of capitalism, accompanied by deep societal differences.[21] United by a common economic purpose or cultural preferences, commercial and industrial competitiveness has become a method to achieve security, just as belief in a common threat can support military alliance as the prime method.

Vulnerability to economic instability has been used to explain Japan's governmental intervention in energy markets.[22] One scholar has listed the causes of Japanese economic vulnerability as: (a) lack of raw materials, (b) geographic isolation, (c) prewar trauma, (d) fear of unavailability of foreign technology, (e) integration into the international economy, (f) industrial latecomer status and the imperative of postwar economic reconstruction. Debates over national security priorities have tended to be over the relative importance of these multiple causes.[23] Some have viewed these multiple causes as systemic,[24] while less pessimistic scholars have used the concept of crisis,[25] political parties,[26] or individual incentives[27] as analytic points of departure.

The Regional Context of Security

Such differences in the scope and judgment of what constitutes threats to security are not unique to the U.S.–Japan relationship. Broadly speaking, what states conceive as matters of national security is important in complex regions where actors struggle to establish priorities against perceived threats. In Northeast Asia, states deliberate over relatively broad concepts of security that frame strategic issues in terms of how they affect their vital interests. Although terrorist groups are on the rise today, the major security actors in this region remain its states: China, Taiwan, the Koreas, Russia, and Japan. A review of the contemporary challenges facing Japan's closest neighbors illustrates some of the diverse aspects of security in this competitive region. The core considerations of security in this region are: protecting one's political survival, preserving national sovereignty, advancing economic development, and maintaining a level of military capability to support these goals.

China

China's post-revolutionary pursuit of the "four modernizations" has required balancing often competing interests. Given the pressures of comprehensive modernization, political survival and regime legitimacy are crucial. China's grand strategy sets domestic and international priorities. Domestically China's party elites intend to lay low, bide their time and focus on sustaining economic growth.[28] The plan is to preserve domestic stability with a single-party regime (Communist Party) while achieving great power status. Democracy will come later, in time. This is in turn requires maintaining good relations with the United States and surrounding powers, and expanding contacts to promote external stability in the region.[29] Internally China will have to enact serious market reforms to maintain long-term economic growth and political stability among its 1.3 billion people, if only to provide employment opportunities in an increasingly open competition.

Economic development is the domestic priority that fuels military modernization and enables stable political change. Yet economic development also is altering the content and role of the revolution's communist ideology in order to maintain regime legitimacy. Vapid Party slogans increasingly are less convincing to China's citizens than practical methods for market success. Perceived threats to economic development are taken seriously. Initial American opposition to China's accession to the WTO, for instance, was seen as an attempt to keep China down. The imperatives of global capitalism and the Party's need to recruit entrepreneurs into its ranks are forcing incremental reforms in political and economic sectors. As the Party attempts to manage modernization, the parameters of non-threatening domestic change are likely to widen as long as economic growth can be maintained. If China can adapt to WTO incentives and rules, to include intellectual property rights and telecommunications agreements, the creation of a middle class from an expanding services sector could build social stability.[30] If political reforms do not occur quickly enough, unemployment can lead to widespread discontent and open opposition.[31] As Chinese leaders focus on economic development, they tend to regard value-laden American rhetoric about individual freedom and democracy as attempts to stir up internal opposition against Beijing's authority.

China's legitimacy of rule also rests on preserving national sovereignty due to China's sense of historical victimization. The government apparatus promotes hyper-sensitivity to territorial and national identity threats in order to build loyalty. China is already surrounded by a dozen states including nuclear India, Pakistan and Russia, and faces ongoing separatist movements in Taiwan, Xinjiang and Tibet. As ideology wanes, national sovereignty remains an uncompromised interest as articulated in the Five Principles of Peaceful Coexistence.[32]

Unfavorable resolution of Northeast Asia's strategic issues could add to China's list of challenges a fourth nuclear border (Korea), a resurgent predator (Japan), an irredentist rogue province (Taiwan), and traditional territorial and economic competitor (Russia). Rival military capabilities in Asia threaten China the most when they increase the risks to Chinese sovereignty. For instance, U.S. missile defense capability that could cover Taiwan, U.S. counter-terrorism bases in Central Asia, and a U.S. counter-terrorism policy that contains the right of "preemptive action"[33] exacerbate a "siege mentality"[34] perspective among conservative Chinese leaders.

Chinese military modernization is oriented outward in the direction of Taiwan, Japan, Korea and a contested "line of actual control" with India.[35] China's 300-year old border dispute with Russia was frozen in 1997 but remains unsettled after nine years of negotiations. Toward Taiwan, China's military response to the threat of independence has been to develop offensive air, missile, and naval capabilities to deny U.S. forces local access and display the will to invade, even at high cost. Japan's world-class naval surface combatants and air force complete with air refueling capability and space-based reconnaissance spur the need for a Chinese blue water navy and effective air defenses. South Korean military improvements that shift from peninsular defense to regional air and naval power projection are yet another threat from a U.S. security partner. Expanding Japanese and South Korean roles inhibit Chinese freedom of maneuver. The prospect of Korean nuclear weapons or significant conventional power projection capability counsels further development of China's nuclear and conventional arsenal. India's nuclear and conventional capability, while directed primarily at Chinese-supported Pakistan, threatens Chinese territory due to a border dispute and a Tibetan independence movement based in India.[36]

China's growing interest in securing border areas are illustrated by its short and medium-range ballistic missiles opposite Taiwan, purchase of 50-plus Russian Su-30MK fighter bombers, development of new fighter-bomber and air-to-air fighters, and attempts to purchase advanced early warning aircraft. American bases in Japan and South Korea and the U.S. presence throughout Northeast Asia present China with the need for an area denial capability to prevent forcible entry particularly in a Taiwan independence scenario. Any U.S. deployable missile defense system for South Korea or Japan, if regarded as a useable umbrella for Taiwan, will threaten all of China's vital interests and likely provoke increased missile production to overcome it. Consistent with expanding economic interests, China's desire to assert national sovereignty and assure territorial integrity calls for increased military capabilities.

Taiwan

The main priority for Taiwan's leader is securing its political identity as a democratizing state, having moved away from the pre–1991 KMT claim of national sovereignty over all of China. As political parties compete for the votes of various ethnic groups, public opinion runs against unification if China were to remain an authoritarian state. If China were to become a democracy, Taiwanese support for unification is expected to rise. Without serious Chinese reforms, Taiwanese support for independence increases even as China's sensitivity to separatism rises.[37] Political leaders risk a Chinese military response if independence were declared, but fear authoritarian China as a threat. Taiwanese views of China as a threat primarily depends upon democratic reforms in China but is also affected by economic relations.

Taiwan's strategy to achieve its security priorities is one of globalization to attract investment and create capital. However, Taiwan's economy is fast becoming integrated with arch-adversary China. Although Taiwan formally allows only indirect trade with China, cross-strait trade has expanded 100-fold since 1979. Taiwan has become China's fifth-largest trading partner and has the highest trade surplus ($120 billion) of any country trading with China. In the year 2000, 5000 Taiwanese businesses relocated to China where labor and land costs are lower, portending a hollowing out of Taiwan's economy.[38] Bilateral trade more than doubled in the past five years.[39] Taiwan sends one-quarter of its exports to China, its biggest export market. Taiwan's capital investments in China comprise four percent of GDP, a high enough figure to raise concerns that Taiwan is too reliant on China's economy.[40]

Chinese economic dominance threatens Taiwan as long as China's economic expansion is seen as predatory rather than the outcome of market competition. As a result, Taiwan has vital interests in preserving key industries and capital as it competes in the lengthening shadow of an already large Chinese economy. If Taiwan's economy can thrive and if China narrows the gap in per capita income, Taiwanese sentiment for independence is likely to erode as business incentives for unification increase.

Taiwan's interest in a robust military capability is to exact unacceptably high costs on China in case of a Chinese attack. The presence of such a capability encourages independence rather than unification. However, Chinese intentions and capabilities are relentless. Besides China's insistence that Taiwan is its province, China's 1992 Law of Territorial Waters and their Contiguous Areas claims sovereignty over the entire South China Sea. China's subsequent fortification of disputed islands and improvements in air and naval power projection capabilities intensify Taiwan's vulnerability to intimidation. Taiwan's military interest is to gain and retain qualitative advantages over China's massive forces. Since the institution of civilian control of the military, Taiwan's military has become more externally-oriented. Civil-military reform was accelerated in March 2002 with the National Defense Law and the Organization Law of the Ministry of National Defense, which directs the military to secure its territory, national lifestyle, and prevent external aggression.[41] The military's mission now includes not only protecting Taiwan from physical attack, but also from intrusions upon its democratic capitalist identity.

The Koreas

The prime interest of the North Korean regime is to prevent the collapse of its authoritarian and ideological political system. The requirements of domestic legitimacy, enshrined in the *juche* concept of self reliance, consign economic development efforts to uncompetitive methods. Hard currency and economic aid are must haves. Arms sales and in particular missiles generate hard currency. The plan for a Sinuiju Special Administrative Region, a capitalist enclave on the Chinese border and walled off from the rest of North Korea, may be an attempt to test capitalism outside of a hermetically sealed society and extract its material rewards for the state. Unwilling to embrace individual freedom-oriented political or economic reforms, North Korea's authoritarian bureaucrats levy on its starving population double the percentage of any other East Asian state's GDP for military expenses to extort external economic aid, stave off internal social unrest, and wield an offensive doctrine. Any U.S., South Korean or Japanese policies or capabilities that block North Korean food or energy supplies, encourage domestic instability, or neutralize North Korean military capability threaten the Pyongyang regime. The possession of what is suspected to be a small number of nuclear weapons would provide minimum deterrence against the threat of U.S. nuclear or high tech conventional attack. Constitutional changes in 1998 (after the death of Kim Il-sung) continued the Kim political dynasty by placing Kim Jong-il in charge of the military and the only permitted political organization, the Korean Worker's Party. North Korea hopes to achieve a unified sovereign peninsula under its control by extracting enough foreign aid, domestic labor, and quarantined business wealth to maintain political stability and equip its million-man military.

South Korea's overarching interest is to build an economically vibrant democratic state in a unified or confederated peninsula capable of playing a regional role with respected military power. Recent economic and political reforms are being joined by unprecedented military reforms designed to guarantee national survival.[42] Peninsular reunification is seen both as a goal and a threat. The Ministry of Unification advocates unification in terms of economic effectiveness, racial reunification and a desire to play a role of regional "balancer" due to Korea's geopolitical position.[43] However public opinion is deeply divided over reunification. The majority desires unification in principle, but expresses apprehension about how to get there. Former President Kim Dae-jung's "sunshine policy" of offering North Korea economic inducements and political accommodation in exchange for warmer attitudes requires patience and is controversial in light of the facts on the ground. More than two-thirds of North Korea's military forces are forward deployed between Pyongyang and the Demilitarized Zone, less than 30 miles north of Seoul's 15 million inhabitants. South Koreans tend to be content with the status quo of a divided Korea because of the North's economic liability, political backwardness, and predatory intent.

The threat of a North-South conflict over peninsular sovereignty hides complementary interests in resisting Chinese and Japanese influence and establishing an independent Korean role in Northeast Asia. It is not clear that a North Korean nuclear weapons program would run counter to the interests of a unified Korea. Similarly, a confederation might enable peaceful coexistence as economic integration encourages political accommodation. The core clash of North-South interests is about the type of political-economic rule in a unified peninsula or the terms of a confederation. If an agreeable bargain can be struck, it is conceivable that mutual interests could produce Korean economic, political and military competition against historic antagonists Japan and China.

Russia

Above other interests, Moscow elites seek to retain Russia's dominant position among the Soviet Union's former republics. This struggle began as an economic problem after Soviet implosion led to a shrinking Russian GDP for five years in a row. Russia's across-the-board decline in its economic performance, ability to govern, military capabilities, social well-being, and environmental quality prevents any administration from focusing on one policy area. A decade of continuous population decline adds to the sense of urgency and strengthens the tendency to see challenges as threats.

The National Security Concept of the Russian Federation outlines Russian interests and threats rather frankly.[44] Stable economic development is acknowledged to be the foundational vital interest which enables other interests to be balanced among individual, societal, and state levels. Numerous national interests are specified but priorities are most clear at the state level. State interests are separated out as domestic or international in nature. Domestically, maintaining the political survival of the constitutional regime, sovereignty and territorial integrity, and democratization are at the top of the list. International priorities are the maintenance of Russian sovereignty, great power status, and beneficial relations with other states.

Military modernization is critical as a symbol of state strength and as a tool to assert Russian sovereignty. While nuclear deterrent forces are expected to shrink in accordance with the Bush-Putin agreement, improvements to the offensive nuclear force such as the Topol-M ICBM intend to counter a growing Chinese nuclear capability and maintain parity with the United States. Russia's deteriorated conventional forces and economic constraints on large-scale equipment upgrades push military planners to consider using nuclear weapons in war fighting contingencies to protect vital interests.

The National Security Concept's comprehensive specification of threats bluntly describes an ambitious grand strategy of strength in all instruments of power to arrest national decline. Domestic economic threats are stagnant growth and investment, growing debt, dependence on energy and raw material exports, and reduced indigenous research and technological advances. Social threats include endemic crime, corruption, disparities in income distribution, declining health and social services, and terrorism. Solutions to domestic threats emphasize strengthening federal power to enforce regulations and controls.

International threats are no less omnipresent; they are nearly any condition or agent that could weaken Russian political, economic, or military influence. NATO's eastward enlargement and U.S. counter-terrorism bases in Central Asia are seen to strangle Russia with western influence even as former Soviet republics and religious extremists claim Russian territory. China and Japan complete the encirclement. Russia's cooperation with NATO, the United States, and China against terrorist groups in Central Asia and the Southern Caucasus requires balancing common interests and diverse motives with former adversaries. Solutions to external threats stress the need for Russian economic integration and a full range of military capabilities in any situation.

This broad definition of what constitutes a matter of national security contains basic inconsistencies between its domestic and international components, most importantly in the foundational vital interest of stable economic development. The call for strong domestic economic controls and increased liberalization of Russian trade and finance is contradictory and indicate traditional Russian political values are at odds with economic integration. In addition, the goals of economic growth and democratization are incompatible with the view that the sources of Russian decline are simply threats to be countered. Such contradictions point to ambivalence about western style democracy, resistance to outside interference, and sensitivity about Russia's relative decline.[45] As a result of this strategic outlook, the tendency is to see any diminution of Russian influence as threatening.

Russian leaders are seeking national recovery with a broad, perhaps paranoid, concept of interests and threats. As Russian leaders look toward Northeast Asia, they see modernizing China and remilitarized Japan as challenges to Russian influence. An independent Taiwan would create a dangerous precedent for Russia's dozens of ethnic republics and provinces, especially separatist Chechnya and Dagestan. A nuclear Korea or unified conventionally armed Korea could restrict Russian freedom of action near critical Russian Far East ports. The multitude of challenges facing Russia leaders explains the broad official concept of security, but it is less clear how Russian leaders might employ their declining instruments of power against specific threats.

Japan

Japan's consistent post–World War II security goal has been to ensure its political survival by carving out an acceptable role based on diplomatic and economic power. Neighbors occupied by Imperial Japan still harbor uncertainty about the intent of Japan's military potential, a distrust fed by Prime Ministers' frequent forays to Yasukuni shrine which commemorates Pacific War criminals, and standardized government textbooks for school children that blame external events for the war.

Japan's contemporary quest may be to earn the respect and influence expected of the world's second largest economic power. However the tangibles of international leadership, such as gaining a permanent seat on UN Security Council, is limited by failure to accept full responsibility for the Pacific War and by constitutional constraints on military power.

National sovereignty is not a hot issue at the moment, although the Northern Territories/Kurile Islands dispute with Russia, the Senkaku Islands/ Diaoyutai dispute with China, and the Dok-do/Takeshima dispute with Korea simmer among ultranationalists, fishermen and groups interested in offshore mineral rights. The inability of Japan and Russia to resolve the dispute over four islands (Etorofu, Kunashiri, Habomai, and Shikotan) seized from Japan by Russia in 1945 still prevents a Japan-Russia peace treaty that would lead to deeper economic ties and perhaps defense cooperation. Exclusive economic zones declared by both Japan and China do not specify boundaries, leaving the Senkaku/Diaoyutai issue to future negotiations. In 1996, the Japanese Maritime Self-Defense Force conducted a landing exercise near the two islets that comprise Tok-do/Takeshima, but South Korean coastal forces continue to occupy them. Given the reach, lethality and precision of modern military power, these territories are not as strategically important as they are convenience issues for domestic political gain.

Economic development is nominally Japan's first priority, represented by an official policy of comprehensive security which includes food, energy, other protected markets, and increasingly, military security. Japan's recovery from its chronic recession requires serious reforms to the banking industry that politicians so far have proven unwilling to implement. Non-performing loans are being addressed by a Financial Services Agency plan more concerned about a safety net for businesses than in allowing bad debt holders to fail. Japan's ability to maintain political stability and expand its foreign policy role in a decade of economic decline suggests overall economic growth is less important than maintaining conservative domestic control. The main threat to Japan's economy is the inflexibility of its collective management.

Japanese military self-restraint has been loosened by global crises which have increased the priority of equipping and employing the Self-Defense Forces in support of national interests. Closer training and operations with U.S. forces lessen the fear of Japan's isolation but revives controversy about Japanese intentions. Despite possessing the means to become a nuclear power and develop the most sophisticated conventional weaponry, Tokyo downplays its defense capabilities as low priority necessities.

The possibility of a strike from North Korea has increased with the improved range of Pyongyang's missiles. South Korean military expansion that could exceed Japan's allowable offensive capabilities is an intermediate concern, particularly if Japan's economic recovery is not forthcoming. A reunified Korea with nuclear weapons is perhaps Japan's worst nightmare, particularly if Korea were to tilt toward an undemocratic or revengeful China. The Russian Pacific Fleet based at Vladivostok, even in the absence of peace treaty, is not a major concern and does not justify the large Ground Self-Defense Force in northern Japan. The Cold War threat of a Soviet military presence and the competition to control vital sea lanes south of Japan has been replaced by Chinese capabilities and intrusions into Japan's exclusive economic zone.

Japan's national priorities could change relatively quickly in the presence of a clear threat. The top dozen defense industrial firms account for almost all of the Japan Defense Agency's acquisition budget and because of the government's ban on weapons exports, are a small sector of their parent companies. As a result, incentives to research and develop leading military technologies with dual-use prospects are high. Military end-use projects such as ballistic missile defense will depend on technology transfer agreements and U.S.–Japan partnerships. Given incrementally relaxed policy constraints and a growing arms market, a defense industrial surge could be in Japan's economic interests if the downturn continues.

The Security Bargain Framework

The value of comparative approaches to security and the rich regional context of security in Northeast Asia lend support to using a framework introduced here as a security bargain. In the real world, national security policy makers often emphasize different relative security priorities and reach bilateral agreement through a strategic exchange of different military, economic and political interests. Different values within and among societies can affect how interests are defined, to be sure. But instead of tracing interests back to different cultures with presumably discrete values, values are reflected when states set priorities among competing interests. Each security partner is presumed to have something to offer that the other partner lacks. The presence of a military threat does not require both allies to agree this threat is more important than economic performance or political stability. Underlying this differentiated exchange are differences among national decision makers about external vulnerability and the best means to protect the state. For a variety of reasons, economic competitiveness, rather than military inferiority, may matter more to one set of security policy makers than to the other.

The security bargain is conceptualized as an institutionalized framework of agreements and formal expectations by which security policy makers seek to achieve national advantage in various ways. Security, an ambiguous symbol[46] and relative concept, is defined from the state's perspective, both as a value and as a process. As a value, security is an ideal condition and goal—

the absence of threat to one's values.[47] Typical national values are stability, freedom, prosperity, and health. Security is also a realist process — the state's pursuit of relative advantage over threat conditions or threat agents. Common threat conditions are military vulnerability, political instability, economic recession, and high crime; common threat agents are predatory states, terrorist organizations, and individual tyrants.

Using this realist ideal and threat-based definition of security, it follows that states pursue security by creating relative advantage over conditions or agents that threaten national values. The tools that states use to seek relative advantage are the military, economic, and political instruments of national power. The state consists of relevant institutional actors that define matters of national security. The assumption of a common threat among state policy makers and between states is relaxed. Alliance dynamics, therefore, involve different national mixes of military and economic security goals and unequal, unlike contributions to mutual security.

In addition to allowing for a more realistic explanation of alliance origins, this organizing concept of the security bargain serves as an historically accurate point of departure for analyzing subsequent changes in the actual basis for cooperation. The assumption that the original security bargain strongly affects how the relationship transforms over time seems reasonable, as differences in relative security priorities are set in arrangements and institutions that benefit from them. In this conception of alliance, the political, economic and military forces for change are perceived and filtered by two domestic systems of different relative security priorities. In actual alliances, each partner gets a mix of economic, political, and military benefits, which is more complex and useful than existing models of alliances.

Using this analytical framework, Chapters 2 and 3 relate the prewar origins and postwar institutionalization of the original security bargain. These are largely stories of contrasting threats and different national security priorities. Chapters 4 through 7 explain postwar security alliance relations in terms of the four main adjustments to the founding bargain: the 1960 Security Treaty, the 1981 division of military roles and announcement of an alliance, the 1987 co-development of leading technology aircraft, and the 1997 Defense Guidelines. Each chapter presents the adjustment in terms of historical development, terms of the new bargain, and aftermath. Summarized and extended into the future in Chapter 8, these sequential bargains reflect the continuity and change in American and Japanese security priorities as the relationship adapts over time to new regional and global conditions.

2

Pre-War Origins

The pleasure I feel in having made the treaty [the U.S.–Japan Treaty of Amity and Commerce] is enhanced by the reflection that there was no show of coercion, nor was menace in the least used by me to obtain it. There was no American man-of-war within one thousand miles of me for months before and after the negotiations ... all I wished was that they would listen to the truths that I would lay before them.[1]
— Consul-General to Japan Townsend Harris, 1858.

The course which lies now before the Japanese empire is plain. Both ruler and ruled should apply their efforts smoothly and harmoniously to preserve tranquility; to elevate the status of the people; to secure the rights and promote the welfare of each individual; and finally by manifesting abroad the dignity and power of Japan, to secure and maintain her integrity and independence.[2]
— Prime Minister Ito Hirobumi, 1889.

The history of U.S.–Japan security relations did not start with Imperial Japan's surprise attack on Pearl Harbor in December 1941; nor did the record begin with wartime America's atomic attacks on Hiroshima or Nagasaki in August 1945. The relationship's roots are in the pre–Pacific war period, where it originated as a collision of contrasting threat perceptions and national security concepts. As relations developed, differences in how national leaders perceived foreign threats and conceptualized the scope of national security defined the basis for cooperation.

By the mid–1800s, Japan's very survival as a sovereign entity was at stake as contact with the West after 200 years of self-inflicted isolation evoked feelings of national economic and military vulnerability.[3] At the turn of the 18th century, Russian naval expeditions seized Tsushima Island in an attempt to force trade. In 1808 and 1813, British warships enforced "trading rights" in Nagasaki, and in 1824 skirmished in Kagoshima Bay. China's defeat during in Opium Wars in the 1840s only reinforced Japanese fears of weakness and foreign penetration. So in 1854, when American Commodore Matthew C. Perry arrived with President Fillmore's instructions to secure "friendship, commerce, a supply of coal and provisions, and protection for our shipwrecked people," Japan's leaders feared more of the same. American interests in coaling stations for refueling steamships and benevolent treatment for shipwrecked whalers had led to the U.S. government authorizing the Perry mission.[4] Although Perry's instructions were to use force only for self-defense, his armed fleet of four warships[5] and request for humanitarian treatment of shipwrecked American sailors was manifestly threatening[6]:

> If your country should persist in its present practices and fail to mend them, it will surely be looked upon with hostility. If your country becomes an enemy, we will exhaust our resources if necessary to wage war. We are fully prepared to engage in a struggle for victory. Our country has just had a war with a neighboring country, Mexico, and we even attacked and captured its capital. Circumstances may lead your country to a similar plight. It would be well for you to reconsider.

This ultimatum succeeded in producing the first commercial treaty between Japan and a foreign power, the Treaty of Kanagawa.[7] The American-Japanese Treaty of Amity and Commerce of 1858, although less restrictive than British, Russian and Dutch treaties, won Japanese acceptance by warning of a greater threat, British intolerance[8]:

> When the British ask for trade, they say they will come with men-of-war and demand that ports be opened at once. If opened, well; if not, war will at once be declared. There will be a great difference between granting their demands and making a treaty with me, who am consulting the advantage of both countries. It will be greatly to the honor of Japan to do as I say.

Seventy percent of the Japanese *daimyo* (feudal lords) continued to oppose opening trade relations with foreigners.[9] Subsequent treaties with Britain, Russia and Holland extracted humiliating terms of extraterritoriality. Japanese clans fearing foreign penetration clashed with Western powers enforcing their right to trade. In 1863, British warships bombarded Kagoshima for the murder of a British citizen. The following year, an allied force of 17 warships (9 British, 4 Dutch, 3 French and 1 American) attacked Japanese shore batteries to gain free passage through the Straits of Shimonoseki.[10] From the farsighted perspective of the Western powers, the advance of civilization and commercial liberty clearly were at stake. But from the nearsighted viewpoint of Japanese leaders, foreign contact and its unequal treaty terms codified Japan's inequality with respect to other states and threatened the ruling Tokugawa shogunate's tenuous hold over domestic factions. Later in 1868, anger over the unequal treaty terms helped unify four rival clans, toppling the House of Tokugawa.

To these samurai leaders who ousted the Tokugawa and began reforms that launched the Meiji Restoration, military might and economic development were rightly regarded as matters of national security. The sudden external threat of a powerful foreign menace and breakdown of Japan's internal political order demanded a modern military and active government involvement in the economy. The new Meiji government remained an unstable amalgam of feudal principalities,[11] reinforcing a siege attitude as the great powers competed among themselves to secure the most advantageous treaty terms.[12]

Threat Perceptions

Japan's initial contact with powerful Western states presented a dual problem to Meiji authorities. Newly installed state leaders had to contend not only with economic and military inferiority, but also with the prospect of internal instability as they labored to consolidate domestic rule. Traditional Tokugawa manufacturing methods proved inadequate to stem the influx of British cotton or to produce military armaments on a par with British, French, German and American industries. As foreign warships visibly anchored near the capitol clarified the military threat to Japan's security, economic upheavals intensified fears of foreign investment and goods. The influx of foreign goods displaced less efficient local industries such as cotton and sugar, disrupting basic commodity prices. Between 1860 and 1866, the price of rice increased thirteen fold and the number of rebellions more than doubled.[13]

The Meiji government countered mounting demands for expanded political participation by centralizing political and economic power with reforms and institutions such as the Charter Oath (1868), Constitution and bicameral Diet (1889), Ministry of Industry (1870) and Ministry of Education (1871).[14] In the first decade of Meiji rule, government enterprises expanded without serious opposition from private entrepreneurs.[15] The ring of external envelopment by superior powers and severe internal flux led Japanese to conclude that national trade disadvantages and military vulnerability threatened domestic welfare and stability. National priorities seemed obvious — to catch up with the West both militarily and economically.[16]

Japan's economic security dilemma was that foreign commerce served both as a channel for undesirable foreign influence and a potential foundation for building a modern, powerful state. From this close-in view, the threat of foreign capital seemed best deflected by protectionist policies, cartels and mercantilist expansion. State fear of foreign capital was so great that despite the shortage of capital in Japan, an imperial rescript was issued against foreign loans. Only two foreign loans were taken out in the 19th century.[17] As Japan's isolationism ended, many Japanese viewed economic openness as the path to collective insecurity.[18] With fewer natural resources, limited territorial space, and beset by starkly superior Western military power, Japan relied on the export of manufactured goods to pay for imports needed for modernization. This required active protection of domestic markets from foreign penetration, and the acquisition of foreign technology.

To this end, Meiji oligarchs sought and received French, German and British instructors and engineers to build a modern military. In 1868 the Naval School, forerunner of Etajima Naval Academy, opened with 63 cadets under French instruction. Later, the British Gunnery School was modeled there. In 1871, the first of many missions to the United States and Europe was dispatched in an effort to understand the sources of Western modernization and trade, industrial organization, and military power.[19] The following year, French-engineered naval dockyards in Yokosuka were underway, and by 1876 Japan had acquired its first steam-driven warship. In 1888, Home Minister Yamagata Aritomo declared rapid armament as the number one national priority, popularized by the slogan, *fukoku kyohei* (rich country, strong army). Japan's strategic response to the outside world was to pursue a dual track. Militarily, policy consisted of foreign-assisted modernization and accommodation to the predominant regional power, Great Britain. Economically, the state centralized control over strategic industries such as shipbuilding, mining, railroad, and communications to counter the foreign menace.

During distant Japan's Meiji Restoration, American foreign policy makers also deemed economic expansionism and commerce as vital to national survival, but the role of the state in achieving security was fundamentally different. A tradition of political and economic liberalism limited the state's involvement in the economy to pursue national security. Conspicuously absent in the United States was a Department of Industry that might define the collective economic good and lead national economic policy. A century of democratic institution-building and federalism had enabled individual citizens increasing influence over economic affairs, so by the end of the nineteenth century, economic liberalism had emerged as an alternative to state mercantilism. While Japanese authorities viewed the Perry mission as commercial aggression, American policy makers saw the advance of free trade and individual liberties.

Insulation from the machinations of European-style continental balance of power politics and lack of major external military or economic threats encouraged such ideals. The European national security system of state-led industrialization and colonies to wrest advantages over other states had not been embraced by a primarily isolationist America. A military strategy of "naval isolationism"[20] seemed sufficient to protect American national security and promote free trade. Absence of imminent intervention by other states contributed to the U.S. government's passivity in external security concerns. The role of military technology was key.

In contrast to the 17th century level of Japanese military technology, the ability of American military technology to stay abreast of developments in the early period of industrialization kept foreign powers at bay.[21] From the mid–1800s on, rapid European improvements such as the iron-clad steamship, breech-loading rifle and armor-piercing naval artillery began a revolution in military organization and weaponry that states ignored at their own peril. U.S. rifle manufacturing processes were ahead of the British, French and Prussians, and U.S. companies exported automatic milling machines for the mass production of firearms. In matters of "internal" security such as the forced expulsion of native American Indians from their traditional homelands, the state was quite active in providing land, promoting the western expansion of railroads, and extending military protection for invading American settlers. But in external matters the Monroe Doctrine, which in 1823 warned European monarchs against "any attempt on their part to extend their system to any portion of this hemisphere," defined a foreign policy seen as passive, declaratory and isolationist.

Concepts of National Security

These differences in Japanese and American perspectives of foreign threat affected the scope of activity defined as matters of national security. A relatively broad Japanese definition of security included active state intervention in achieving economic and military advantage over other states. A narrower American concept considered security limited to military matters. American economic activity was not deemed to be a matter of national security, but rather the proper domain of private entrepreneurs and consumers.

Two characteristics of the Japanese state encouraged the relatively broad definition of national security that accompanied perception of the foreign threat: (a) the dominance of military concerns over private civilian interests, and (b) the nature of state involvement in the economy. Military dominance in civil-military affairs was aided by the timing of its institutionalization, which came before the Meiji Constitution of 1889[22]:

1871: the creation of a national armed service
1872: conscription system

1878: formation of an autonomous General Staff with "the right of direct access" to the Emperor

1882: Imperial Rescript of supreme command over the armed services, as well as the special relationship to Japanese troops and sailors

Within this civil-military framework, the ability of Meiji leaders to control regional military chiefs was weakened by internal instability and the presence of the powerful external threat. The desires of the predominant Satsuma, Choshu and Tosa clans to diminish the influence of lesser factions coincided with the new Meiji government's need for order in the face of foreign threats. Needing the support of the powerful clan chiefs to build a credible national military, Meiji leaders abandoned civilian control of the military.

State involvement in the economy, ranging from direct control of industries to guarantor of markets for national firms, also contributed to Japan's broad definition of national security. The textiles industry was the first key sector actively promoted by the Meiji state to earn foreign specie to pay for imported raw materials.[23] In order to stem the flow of superior European cotton fabrics into the home market, the Ministry of Agriculture directed the development of better fibers through research institutes as early as the 1860s. Entrepreneur Toyota Sakichi's adaptation of the oil engine to the cotton loom spread to other domestic firms. Other government initiatives included sponsoring national trade fairs beginning in 1877, importing spinning equipment, and financing of local business loans. In the chemical, mining and heavy industries, even privately-owned firms relied on the state for procurements, technical assistance and laboratories. Ministry of Industry officials' alarm over Japanese dependence on foreign sources of iron and steel led to state-initiated projects such as the Kamaishi (1885) and Yawata (1897) Steel Mills, which replaced less efficient domestic handicraft, iron and steel producers.[24]

Although intimate business-government interaction did not always ensure state dominance, the process itself fused separate interests to pursue economic and military advantage over foreign competitors. Business leaders seeking international advantage and state bureaucrats pursuing security goals interacted in traditional group forums that sought protection from economic shocks and military strength during times of crisis. Consensus-building broadened the scope of security matters by incorporating more groups into the decision-making process.[25] Even when the Japanese state did not nationalize an industry, as in coal, policy makers acted as the guarantor of private firms. In the electric power and oil industries, where private leaders resisted government controls, the state intervened in market conforming actions or played a role of market guarantor and risk eliminator.[26]

In contrast to the Japanese approach, the American government's view of foreign capital inflows was a generally benign one, so the prevailing definition of national security excluded economic activities as a state policy arena to achieve national advantage. Although industrial lobbyists were able to protect certain markets, the large size of the domestic market thwarted the development of a siege attitude against foreign capital. Even before the American economy achieved international prominence, the United States was a major borrower and porous recipient of foreign direct investment.[27] In the absence of either an external economic predator or serious domestic unrest, America's conception of national security was largely one of externally directed military protection.

That security was defined largely in terms of military threats rather than economic threats to the nation is quite evident in American foreign policy of the period. Expansion across the Great Plains was justified in terms of individual freedom, individual economic opportunity, and national manifest destiny instead of national economic security. Regional interventions were portrayed and justified by evoking images of individual rights and economic openness, rather than the need for stable markets and secure sources of raw materials. Presidents and security policy makers emphasized preventing European colonization rather than the protection of national markets.[28] When penetration of foreign markets followed the use of force to protect the rights of U.S. citizens overseas, American liberal principles were validated rather than questioned.

American leaders espoused liberal values and defined security in terms of the absence of threats to them. U.S. security interests derived from regional concerns in Mexico and the Caribbean, and were still unspecified in distant Asia. The principal fear was the prospect of European colonization of the Western Hemisphere, which could inhibit free trade. In the 1860s, Secretary of State Seward promoted a policy of Mexican self-determination to obstruct French and Spanish imperial expansion in Mexico. Later, American economic penetration of Mexico was initiated by private American citizens and encouraged by the liberal policies of the Mexican Diaz government.[29] In Caribbean affairs, U.S. Secretaries of State showed only intermittent interest until the decision to build an isthmian canal had been made. Building the Panama canal was supported by the Department of State and ratified by the Senate in 1850 to exclude British colonies and protectorates in Central America.[30] Later in 1902, President Roosevelt enjoined an isolationist Congress to accept the increased responsibilities the canal would bring[31]:

> The events following the war with Spain and the prospective building of the Isthmian Canal render it certain that we must take in the future a far greater interest than hitherto in what happens throughout the West Indies, Central America, and the adjacent coasts and waters.

The Taft administration continued the geographical expansion of American strategic thinking within the rhetoric of progressive economic liberalism. William H. Taft was the first civilian governor of the Philippines, America's colonial possession won in a foreign war. His Secretary of State Henry Knox saw the promotion of economic progress and competition as the best means to prevent European intervention in the western hemisphere. Knox advocated the use of force after diplomatic methods failed, to protect American property rights and lives rather than to build a collective sense of U.S. economic security.

While Meiji leaders adopted a broad approach to achieving state security, U.S. policymakers defined and pursued national security interests by non-economic means, focusing on the military balance of power. U.S. interest in maintaining an Asian balance of power was minimal and confined to the sporadic efforts of private individuals. In 1882, for instance, thirteen years before the Sino-Japanese War in Korea, Commodore Shufeldt persuaded the State Department to authorize an attempt to open Korea as a matter of personal ambition. A previous expedition in 1871 had failed.[32] Although he succeeded in securing a Treaty of Commerce with Korea, his accomplishment was dismissed by Secretary of State Blaine, who saw no strategic value in the treaty.[33] Not until the Russo-Japanese War did security planners in Washington divert their attention from British-German naval rivalry to a potential security threat from imperial Japan[34]:

1860: beginning of Japanese Navy: feudal lords privately acquire 93 foreign vessels, confiscated after Meiji Restoration

1876: 10 capital ships (1 steam-driven)

1894: 19 destroyers (15 built in Great Britain and 4 of British design)

1902: Japan builds British-designed destroyers; dispatches naval mission to Great Britain, France and U.S. to study submarines

1904–5: Russo-Japanese War: first use of armored cruisers and 12-inch naval guns; Japan's modern ships and tactics prevail

1907: U.S. Navy Orange Plan developed for a Far East contingency involving Japan

U.S. Navy Outlays in Thousands of Dollars

Year	Outlays
1870	21,780
1875	21,498
1880	13,537
1885	16,021
1890	22,006
1895	28,798
1900	55,953
1905	117,550
1910	123,174
1915	141,836

Alliance and Accommodation

Security policies reflected these national differences of threat perception and concepts of security. The first major policy divergence involved the issue of revising the unequal treaties in 1872, which was followed by Japan's policy decision to expand its holdings by force. The solution offered by the American Minister-Residence in Japan called for Japan to initiate a complete opening to foreign trade. Meiji authorities, however, proposed increased restrictions on foreign trading rights, fearing that opening the Japanese market to foreign trade under an unequal treaty system would permit Japanese commercial capital to be overwhelmed by the great trading nations of Europe. In addition, trading restrictions on foreign powers could be used as a means to finance the building of a modern, powerful state. But restrictions such as duties on goods brought in at treaty ports and taxes on Japanese employed by foreigners were treaty violations. Seen from a frame of reference that sought collective economic security and political order, Japan's choice was to accept increased dependence on foreign powers disinterested in treaty revision, or follow the predatory practice of acquiring colonies. The nearby Korean peninsula, comparatively rich in raw materials and arable land, was a tempting target. Having repulsed earlier English, Russian, French and American attempts to force commercial relations, Korea subsequently became the first object of Japan's security policy expansion.

The use of Japanese military force to achieve national economic and military parity with the West was pursued in accordance with established practices of great powers in the Far East. Korea's own 250-year isolation had recently ended with a French expedition in 1866, followed five years later by an American excursion. Five years later, a Japanese mission accompanied by two battleships and three troop ships extracted from Korea an unequal treaty modeled after the Anglo-Chinese Treaty (1842) and the American-Japanese Treaty of Commerce (1858).[35] The treaty's effects on Korea included many of the foreign evils from which the Meiji and successive Japanese governments had sought to free themselves.[36] Treaty terms included the opening of three ports to Japan, paving the way for an influx of Japanese goods that wiped out native Korean industries. In 1882, Japanese troops were dispatched to Korea to extract a new treaty after Korean veterans rebelled against pro–Japanese policies and destroyed the Japanese consulate.[37] Other foreign powers soon negotiated similar treaties of commerce with Korea, although the presence of Japanese troops ensured the bulk of Korean concessions would flow to Japanese businesses.

Japan's intervention in Korea culminated in the Sino-Japanese War of 1894–1895, a clash between traditional Chinese interests and Meiji-initiated economic expansionism. No American security interests in Korea were articulated which might have deterred the use of military force to achieve national economic objectives. For Japan, the colonization of Korea served not only to gain raw materials and markets, but also denied them to rival powers at a time when the Japanese economy was shifting from agricultural exports to manufactured goods.[38] The utter failure of other powers' probes emboldened Japan's Meiji nationalists to claim Japan's intervention was designed to prevent foreign domination of Korea. Japan's dissatisfaction with disorder in Korea led to demands for Korean political reforms to maintain the stability of bilateral trade relations.[39] Tokyo also issued an ultimatum that Seoul break its trade agreements with China. When the Korean royal court requested and received Chinese troops to quell domestic uprisings,[40] Japan sent troops, triggering the Sino-Japanese War. The subsequent Japanese victory secured economic advantages in rice production, cotton and wool. Thereafter, Japanese control of the Korean peninsula became an essential element of Japanese national security. The economic and military definitions of national security had merged to produce a broad national security policy.

The United States government made no official pronouncement of national security interests in Asia during the Sino-Japanese War. Instead the American government claimed neutrality as a peaceful trading nation. After the outbreak of hostilities, the President instructed the American Minister in Japan to attempt a peace settlement[41]:

After driving Chinese forces from Korea and securing Port Arthur on the Liaotung Peninsula, Japanese authorities accepted the U.S.–mediated agreement in 1895.[42] The terms ceded both Korea and Taiwan to Japan. Three years later, a Russo-Japanese Treaty formalized Russian acceptance of Japanese hegemony in Korea in exchange for Japan's consent to Russia's 25-year lease of Port Arthur and Ta-lien in China.

Japan's colonization of Korea seemed to be rewarded by the first agreement on equal terms between a Western power and an Asian power, the Anglo-Japanese alliance of 1902. Apart from collective security aims, the alliance with the predominant regional military power allowed Japan to pursue national economic objectives. In fact, Japan's failure to send military forces to Europe in support of its British "ally" during World War I may has been cited as the main reason the British abrogated the alliance.[43] Prior to the outbreak of war, however, Japanese interests appeared quite compatible with British aims of preserving a global naval presence while concentrating forces in European waters.

Internally the alliance satisfied the disparate security interests of three influential cabinet groups that shaped Japanese policy — the Foreign Ministry, Army and Navy. British approval of Japan's free hand in Korea met the Foreign Ministry's concerns for political stability there. A pliable Korean peninsula provided secure access to Manchurian and Mongolian timber and mineral imports for Japan's manufacturing industry. To accomplish this, Tokyo actually encouraged a larger British presence in the Far East than London was willing to maintain.[44] In 1921, Foreign Minister Uchida lauded the British naval presence as stabilizing the region for trade:

> Japan is naturally anxious to strengthen the ties of friendship and loyal cooperation between herself and the British Empire, which she regards as of the utmost importance to the stability of the Far East.

For the Imperial Army, the alliance neutralized France in the event of a war with Russia, the chief ground threat to Japan's economic control of Korea and expansion in Manchuria. The Foreign Ministry was also deeply concerned with Russian strategic intent, but was more willing to compromise on the establishment of separate Japanese and Russian spheres of interest in order to avoid conflict.[45]

By 1900, Russian military forces in the Far East had substantially increased. Besides the Russian fleet anchored at Port Arthur, 180,000 Russian troops were stationed in Manchuria, having been dispatched during the Boxer Rebellion on the pretext of guarding railways. To counter this threat to Japanese economic interests, British naval forces (roughly equivalent to the Russian and French fleets combined) provided a prudent counterweight. For its part, the Imperial Navy recognized its weakness relative to the British and American forces, and initially sought to balance naval powers. Later though, as oil-burning fleets replaced coal-burning steamships, oil requirements would vastly increase. This development would consume naval leaders with the problem of oil access to support wartime operations, creating an interest in exclusive economic expansion.[46]

Overall, the Anglo-Japanese Alliance served to accommodate British naval preeminence and Japanese economic interests in China. The security arrangement reduced Japan's requirements for a costly naval buildup, permitting the stable pursuit of economic interests. The Russian threat to Japanese economic interests in Korea and Manchuria was then eliminated by the Russo-Japanese War of 1904–1905, launched in a preemptive Japanese strike at Port Dairen.[47] With the Russian military threat removed, the next logical outlet for economic expansion was China. As in the Korea acquisition, part of the public rationale was to prevent a weak state from being dominated by another power. As long as regional power interests could be appeased or balanced, foreign resources and markets were secure.

At the time, U.S. security policy toward China was nearly non-existent. The Open Door Notes of Secretary of State John Hay proclaimed the ideals of China's territorial integrity and state rights of free trade in the face of real foreign spheres of influence in China. The Open Door Notes, characteristic of American policy toward East Asia up to December 1941, were not even a government initiative. They simply stated what had been the activities of early American traders in China, who had not been controlled (as had been their European counterparts) by state-sponsored trading companies. While leaders in Japan moved forward with plans to ensure secure colonies for economic expansion, American security policy makers emphasized principles of free trade and focused on military capabilities as threats to national security. Only a few mid-level naval officers and Asian experts in the State Department regarded Japan's intervention in China as threats to American security interests.[48]

Over the issue of relations with China, the Japanese Foreign Ministry's pursuit of national economic objectives became linked with the Army's desires for secure access to an expanding list of materials to project military power.[49] Avoiding entanglement with its British ally in Europe's World War, Japanese observers brought back lessons of economic and military modernization. By 1925, Japan shouldered the heaviest burden of military expenditures in the world, measured by percentage of national wealth spent on armaments[50]:

TABLE 2.1—NATIONAL WEALTH AND ARMAMENTS

State	National Wealth ($)	Armaments Appropriations ($)	Armaments % of National Wealth
United States	320,803,862,000	553,861,346	.17
United Kingdom	159,802,400,000	904,354,270	.56
Germany	84,157,700,000	107,705,903	.13
France	74,037,673,000	254,485,150	.34
Japan	**32,178,725,000**	**218,500,000**	**.68**
Soviet Union	30,876,000,000	190,694,000	.62
Italy	29,747,763,000	159,349,200	.52

In the 1920s Imperial Army strategists developed action plans to mobilize resources during wartime, including the use of Shantung territory in China, gained from Germany after World War I. In 1925, the Army General Staff planned the construction of railroads in China, and two years later dispatched Japanese troops to protect interests during the Chinese civil war. In spite of disagreement within the army over the timing of continental expansion, there was consensus that the Soviet Union was Japan's main military threat, and Manchurian raw materials were needed for an eventual war.[51] The policy linkage of economic and military means to achieving national security was not yet complete. Although the Foreign Ministry shared the Army's view that the Anglo-Japanese Alliance was needed to protect Japanese commercial interests in China, it did not yet advocate military means to pursue them[52]:

Japan fully realizes that any such venture of aggression would be not only hopeless but destructive of her own security and welfare. She sincerely wishes for China an early achievement of the peace, unity, and stable government. Her vast commercial interests alone, if for no other consideration, point unmistakably to the wisdom of such a policy. This is a basic principle of the Anglo-Japanese Alliance.

Later in 1925, however, Foreign Ministry Official Yoshida Shigera reaffirmed Japan's legal claims on the Asian continent, justifying the Sino-Japanese War (1894–5) and Russo-Japanese War (1904–5) in terms of an economic menace to Japanese security through the Korean peninsula[53]:

The economic problem of Japan's future consists in obtaining from China and Siberia her supplies of food and raw materials and seeking to dispose of her goods in the great market on the east.

The Japanese invasion of China followed failed economic measures to preserve Japanese markets, seeking to suppress "communist-inspired" Chinese movements which threatened those markets. By 1927, the Foreign Ministry's expressed preference for fiscal and economic methods to ensure economic access and Chinese stability gave way to what had worked in Korea — the use of the Army to secure economic interests.[54]

Conflict

Initially, U.S. policy makers ignored these national differences in Japan's approach to security. Japan's quest for economic security was met by a U.S. policy that tolerated the shipment of war supplies to Japan while simultaneously condemning Japanese militarism in China. American leaders continued to oppose economic sanctions, clinging to liberal principles of the Open Door as Japanese troops marched through it in 1928. The Washington Naval Conference of 1921–1922 had ostensibly achieved security in its proper military domain, and the Nine-Power Treaty had announced Chinese territorial integrity.[55] When Japanese military intervention in the 1931 Mukden Incident led to the establishment of a Japanese puppet state (Manchukuo) the following year, American policy makers blamed it on a few militarist conspirators. Less considered was the effect of the Great Depression on domestic definitions of security in Japan. Unemployment in 1930 Japan had reached one million. The price of silk, a good that comprised 30 percent of Japanese exports, plummeted. Activism by military and right-wing intellectuals increased as the state's pursuit of national rights seemed choked by external forces. The Capital Flight Law of 1932, followed in 1934 by the Industrial Association Law and the creation of the Cabinet Investigative Bureau, centralized state control over the military and economic means to achieving security. In 1934 at the London Disarmament Conference, Japan expressed displeasure with the 10:6 ratio of the 1921 Washington Naval Conference. Meanwhile, the Imperial Navy was committed to an ambitious naval construction program. Diplomats abroad peddled the drive toward security as legitimate competition in the form of economic expansion. Many Japanese saw little difference between the Japanese actions in China and American intervention in its southern sphere of interest. Ambassador to Great Britain Yoshida Shigeru, who would later become Japan's most influential postwar Prime Minister, consistently attempted to persuade Western powers to condone Japanese actions in China. Citing Japan's overpopulation and need for raw materials and markets, Yoshida hoped Western appeasement would mollify rather than encourage militarists in Japan.

Japan's pursuit of security started up well with an American approach that separated military interests from commercial interests. Conflict between the broad Japanese and narrow American approaches to security was delayed by U.S. unwillingness to consider Japan's militarist economic policy as a threat to national security. Even after the Mukden Incident, American acceptance of Japan's military pursuit of economic security was intact. The following year, Depression-President Hoover, hardly an advocate of government intervention in the economy, opposed an arms embargo against Japan. Secretary of War Stimson opposed economic sanctions until Japan's military campaign in China led him in the clutch to conclude that Japanese leaders really did mean to establish an exclusive economic bloc.[56] Finally in 1934, when Japan abrogated the unequal naval arms limitation treaty, President Roosevelt and Secretary of State Hull pressed for an arms embargo. By 1935, Hull countered Yoshida's calls for appeasement with a frank characterization of Japanese objectives in China[57]:

> The impression among many persons in this country was that Japan sought absolute economic domination, first of eastern Asia, and then, of other portions as she might see fit; that this would mean political as well as military domination in the end; that the upshot of the entire movement would be to exclude countries like the United States from trading with all of those portions of China thus brought under the domination or controlling influence so-called of Japan.

As an alternative to Japan's economic exclusionary practices, Hull proposed trade reciprocity among the economic powers, complaining of countries exporting "abnormal quantities of highly competitive products to the extent of 20 or 40 or 50 percent of our domestic production."[58] Yoshida stressed that excessive barriers to trade unnecessarily constrained Japanese business opportunities, and emphasized Japan's national security requirement for outside trade. Ambassador to the United States Saito Hiroshi defended Japanese vital interests in Manchuria as trading interests that directly meshed with Japan's survival.[59]

Hull and Yoshida agreed that international free trade did not exist, but differed over the appropriate national response. The narrow American definition of national security excluded trade competition and heralded free trade as an objective, if not an ideal. Free trade meant unencumbered access for all market participants, and reciprocal trade agreements were seen as a practical approximation of that ideal. In contrast, the broader Japanese definition of national security expected that the state pursue national economic advantage. Reciprocal "free" trade with the United States did not appear to be a prudent security policy when the rest of the world did not afford similar commercial opportunities. Even managed reciprocity was deemed unacceptable — it simply supported the intolerable status quo that denied Japan its fair share and sphere of economic advantage. If free trade were not possible through peaceful interactions, then security policy makers would seek a secure share of world trade through military and economic means.

Increasing Japanese involvement in China effectively merged the military and economic means to achieving state security. The domestic formula that enable this venture was the convergence of objectives among the Foreign Ministry, Army and Navy. The Konoe cabinet was powerless to stop the dispatch of army troops when national security seemed to require it.[60] Population pressures, the need for external markets and natural resources, and the overriding objective of catching up with predatory western powers led the Foreign Ministry to advocate national economic security. The military correlates of economic security were broad indeed, leading to expanded roles and missions designed to secure resources. In both the Foreign Ministry and the armed forces, the absence of economic liberal ideas and political controls over the cabinet facilitated the linkage of economic and military security policies.[61]

American reluctance to impose economic sanctions allowed Japan's economic and military security objectives to be regarded as feasible. When the United States finally froze Japanese assets and announced the oil embargo in the summer of 1940 — in effect implementing a broad security definition toward Japan — Japanese officials responded by welding together the economic and military definitions of security. The means advocated by the Foreign Ministry and the armed forces now converged; divisiveness among the Army, Navy and Foreign Ministry evaporated in the heat of the foreign economic threat. The historic Japanese peace proposals to Secretary of State Hull on September 6, 1941, reflect the uncompromising nature of Japan's broad definition of national security. In the proposal, Japanese leaders demanded the restoration of full economic relations with the United States and freedom from American interference with Japanese activities in China.[62] When Hull rejected the proposal invoking principles of territorial integrity to demand Japan's military withdrawal from China, Japanese leaders realized there was no basis for a settlement.[63] The only option compatible with Japan's broad national security concept was to forcibly expand markets and eliminate military threats to that expansion.

The American government viewed Japan's security dilemma quite differently. Within the State Department in particular, economic liberalism ruled out including economic affairs as matters of national security. National security was the proper domain of the military, a separation reinforced by liberal democratic structures. From this perspective, the answer to Japan's dilemma was to work toward the ideal of free trade — "if and as such free trade was realized, Japan would receive her substantial share without any effort or contribution on her part, as would other trading countries."[64] Short of somehow changing the illiberal international system, Americans viewed Japan's only rational recourse to be to support free and open trade. After all, in the September 6th note, Prime Minister Konoe had indicated full support of President Roosevelt's four principles of international relations.[65]

The reluctance of American policy makers to adopt a broader definition of security was encouraged by belief in the desirability of a liberal economic order. In June, 1940, U.S. Ambassador Joseph Grew noted a relationship between inter-state conflict and an illiberal economic order[66]:

> Fundamental policy of Japanese Empire based upon mission as stabilizing force East Asia. Obviously Japan concerned not only with China continent but also with South China Seas. Economic relations between Japan and other countries East Asia very close. These countries' territories mutually dependent for prosperity. Japan has deep concern not only for political status quo Netherlands East Indies but also for economic resources, trade, industry, and development of those islands. Can nations avoid conflict friction when there exist tariff walls, immigration restrictions, other barriers preventing smooth interchange of goods between nations which are complementary in economic sense? Construction of new world order to come after present European war will require basic settlement of this issue.

Non-Resolution

The fundamentally different Japanese and American conceptions of national security persisted to the end of the Pacific War. During the war, both sides disagreed over what constituted legitimate matters of national security. Despite ominous military setbacks and inadequate resources to prosecute planned wartime operations, Japanese leaders remained gridlocked over security interests. On the U.S. side, the policy of unconditional surrender policy held fast. As military victory seemed inevitable, there was no particular incentive to entertain differences in Japanese and American definitions of security. Late wartime internal debates over how to achieve security would shape the new basis for postwar cooperation.

The inability or unwillingness of American national security policy makers to understand, satisfy or stop Japan's pursuit of economic security is evident in American debates over the origins of Japanese aggression, appropriate terms of surrender, and postwar objectives. Most policy makers agreed later that they had misread Japanese intentions, failing to realize, in Secretary of State Dean Acheson's words, "...that he (General Tojo) and his regime regarded the conquest of Asia not as the accomplishment of an ambition but as the survival of a regime. It was a life-and-death matter to them. They were absolutely unwilling to continue in what they regarded as Japan's precarious international position surrounded by great and hostile powers."[67]

On the question of the origins of the Pacific War, two lines of thought emerged. One emphasized the assumption of power by militarists whose capable and spirited forces had to be thoroughly defeated. The Japanese threat to regional security was seen to be limited to the militarist element of Japanese society, which needed to be purged forever. The other explanation saw the origins of Japanese aggression as imbedded in a feudalistic society that permitted the militarists to seize power in the first place. The task, therefore, was to democratize society and allow Japan to reenter the international economy as a peaceful trader. Both explanations agreed on the necessity to purge militants, democratize Japanese society and promote non-military industrialization. It seemed that only unconditional surrender would allow for such sweeping objectives to be implemented in Japan.

FDR's unconditional surrender policy was not only the only politically acceptable option in the United States after Pearl Harbor; it also was seen to be a practical requirement for correcting the Japanese security problem. Post war demilitarization and democratization of Japan required comprehensive control. This was particularly the view of the Office of War Information, which had been generating a stream of reports to the President. Its publication, *Japan's Unconditional Surrender*, defined the Japanese *gunbatsu* [military faction] problem so broadly that anything less than complete American military victory would be insufficient to extricate militarism from Japan.[68]

In 1944, as military victory seemed assured, the U.S. government created the State-War-Navy Coordinating Committee (SWNCC) to plan postwar policies. By the spring of 1945, the debate over the details of unconditional surrender was well underway. Chief among the concerns was the securing of an early unconditional surrender to prevent Soviet territorial expansionism in Manchuria.[69] Complicating this objective was the discovery of the bargain struck at Yalta while preparations for the invasion of Japan (set for 1 November 1945) were in full swing — before the atomic bomb had been developed. In February of 1945, FDR reached accords with Stalin and Churchill, but failed to inform the SWNCC or State that Russia would soon enter the war and was promised economic privileges in Manchuria and Sakhalin. FDR's postwar plans were heavily influenced by Treasury Secretary Henry Morganthau. Morganthau headed the Informal Policy Committee on Germany and advocated dismantling heavy industry, removing domestic political authority and dividing the country into zones of occupation. FDR's death and Truman's opposition to Morganthau's punitive plan reinvigorated the debate over what unconditional surrender would attempt to achieve.

The military and State members of SWNCC focused on different aspects of unconditional surrender. Army and Navy leaders emphasized the total military defeat of Japanese forces on the battlefield. Impressed by the stiff resistance encountered in Pacific battles, most military planners assumed an invasion was necessary to obtain unconditional surrender. The Joint Chiefs recommended against making any commitment regarding the issue of whether to eliminate the Emperor system:

> From a strictly military point of view consider it inadvisable to make any statement or take any action at the present time that would make it difficult or impossible to utilize the authority of the Emperor to direct a surrender of the Japanese forces in the outlying areas as well as in Japan proper.[70]

Department of State officials emphasized political means and looked for liberal forces within Japan that might preclude the necessity for invasion.[71] Secretary of State Byrnes also favored ambiguity with respect to the Emperor system, although Secretary of War Stimson and former ambassador to Japan Grew favored guaranteeing the Emperor's survival to ease surrender and promote order in Japan. Stimson and Grew were excluded by FDR from participating at Potsdam.

Despite these differences, there was consistent agreement on one point characteristic of the prewar American approach to national security. The cause of the Pacific War was not viewed as Japan's pursuit of economic security. Japanese militarism, whatever its origins, was the cause. To correct the Japanese departure from legitimate security relations, Japan's political system would need to be democratized and its war-making ability removed. This policy consensus was evident in the Potsdam Declaration of 26 July 1945, signed by the United States, Great Britain and China. The Potsdam Declaration was ambiguous regarding the Emperor system but clearly demanded unconditional Japanese surrender. The chief reason was the timely development of the atomic bomb, news of which reached Truman during the Potsdam negotiations. This guaranteed there would be no compromise or conditional surrender.

During the war, Japanese leadership persisted in the problematic pursuit of achieving an empire that would bring Japan economic security. The desirability of a Greater East Asian Co-prosperity Sphere was never in doubt. Even the Emperor's surrender announcement on 15 August 1945 to the Japanese people, upheld Japan's declaration of war based on a "sincere desire to ensure Japan's self-preservation and the stabilization of East Asia."

Neither did the Emperor's address agree with the American version of the origins of the war. Instead, the statement rationalized non-achievement of the war's objectives in terms of:

> ... the general trends of the world [which] have all turned against her interest, ... and due to the fact that the enemy has begun to employ a new and most cruel bomb, the power of which to do damage is indeed incalculable, taking the toll of many innocent lives. Should We continue to fight, it would not only result in an ultimate collapse and obliteration of the Japanese nation, but also it would lead to the total extinction of human civilization.[72]

During the initial stages of the war, there was no reason to scale down the ambitious wartime objectives of national security broadly defined. As Singapore and the Philippines were captured, and the oil fields of Borneo and Sumatra were seized, Japanese objectives in Southeast and East Asia seemed quite attainable. On the diplomatic front, the No-Separate-Peace Treaty with Germany and Italy, a Treaty of Alliance with Thailand, and assurances of Soviet neutrality indicated further successes were likely.[73] After the shocking defeat of the Imperial Navy at the battle of Midway, however, moderates such as Yoshida began to voice disapproval of wartime objectives.[74] As the Kwangtung Army gradually became mired in Manchuria and Americans mounted military victories in the Pacific, displeasure with the Cabinet increased. Domestic initiatives to end the war short of establishing the Greater East Asian Co-prosperity Sphere objective but acceptable to the *gunbatsu* were tried. For example, four days after the Imperial Navy's pivotal defeat at Midway, Yoshida called on Marquis Kido Koichi, the Lord Keeper of the Privy Seal (with direct access to the Emperor), to send Prince Konoe to Switzerland to gather information about likely terms of peace. Later in 1943, Konoe and four of the senior statesmen attempted to get an anti-war individual into the Tojo Cabinet but also failed.[75]

Although Kido, Prince Konoe, and Foreign Minister Shigemitsu knew the war was going against Japan, the militarists' dominance sustained a broad definition of national security that legitimated military and economic means of preserving the *kokutai* (the state). The Army's broad pursuit of national security was codified within the Army Ministry and in organizations such as the National Strength Evaluation Board, Cabinet Resources Bureau, and Cabinet Planning Office. Mobilization laws established military control of civilian affairs under the aegis of national security. The domestic elite that defined security—the Minister of Foreign Affairs, Army and Navy, *jushin* (senior statesmen), and the Premier—were deadlocked by a consensus-seeking status quo.[76] Policy alternatives of the anti-war movement were rejected as too conciliatory to the Allies to appeal to the Army and Navy. Peace proposals which might have succeeded in Japan were too demanding to be acceptable to the Allies.

The deadlock ensured that there would be no coming to terms with the Allies even though the war clearly was being lost. The Potsdam ultimatum of 26 July was rejected and on 6 August, the atomic bomb was dropped on Hiroshima as an alternative to a massive invasion of Japan. The next day the Prime Minister and Foreign Minister informed the Emperor that more bombs would likely be dropped if the war were not ended. Despite the Emperor's agreement that the war be terminated promptly, a meeting of the Supreme Council failed when military members refused to participate. Even after the second atomic bomb had been dropped on Nagasaki (August 9th), the inner cabinet remained deadlocked during a meeting on August 13th. War Minister Anami and Army and Navy commanders favored a decisive battle on the Kanto plains. Foreign Minister Togo, Lord Keeper of the Privy Seal Kido, and Prime Minister Suzuki favored surrender based on the Potsdam ultimatum, which at least seemed ambiguous regarding the Emperor system. Navy Minister Yonai tacitly endorsed ending the war. The next day, the inner cabinet debated interpretations of Potsdam until the Emperor finally spoke, accepting defeat rather than face national destruction.

3

Post-War Security Bargain

Some of the things the Japanese were asking us to do in this letter we would of course do. But we could not begin the occupation by bargaining over its terms. We were the victors. The Japanese were the losers. They had to know that "unconditional surrender" was not a matter for negotiation....[1]
— President Harry S. Truman, 1945

We can never pull off the so-called rearmament for the time being.... The day we rearm will come naturally if the livelihood recovers. It may sound selfish, but let the Americans handle our security until then. It is indeed our God-given luck that the Constitution bans arms. If the Americans complain, the Constitution gives us adequate cover.[2]
— Prime Minister Yoshida Shigeru, 1956

On April 15, 1945, Emperor Hirohito accepted the unconditional surrender in the Potsdam Declaration, including the American Occupation of Japan. From the U.S. government perspective, termination of the war would occur rather unequivocally on American and Allied terms—there would be no negotiation. However, Japanese statesmen moved quickly to strike the best deal possible in order to salvage fundamental security aims, beginning with the preservation of the Emperor system.

Security Priorities During the Occupation

Japan's post-surrender priorities revolved around the maintenance of the *Tenno* (Emperor) to protect core values threatened by the impending foreign occupation: internal order, domestic identity and cultural continuity. Imperial authority and obedience underpinned the political legitimacy of conservative rule now at risk after military defeat. Indeed, public attitudes in allied countries and the United States favored elimination, if not execution, of the Emperor himself. Now the owners of a devastated state, Japanese elites' best hope for maintaining influence at home lay in negotiating details of the Occupation. In spite of the terms of unconditional surrender, several initiatives worked toward this end.

Immediately after the August surrender, Japanese leaders dispatched to U.S. authorities a message containing four conditions[3]:

1. Advance notification of Allied forces
2. Japanese troops be allowed to disarm themselves, allowed to retain and wear their swords, and evacuation to Japan be conducted speedily
3. Japanese troops in remote areas be allowed a reasonable amount of time to cease fighting
4. Allied troops speedily dispatch food and medicine to remotely located Japanese troops

Later that month, Foreign Minister Shigemitsu instituted a War Termination Office to protect Japanese sovereignty and independence.[4] Within three months of the unconditional surrender, Prime Minister Shidehara and Foreign Minister Yoshida had established a committee within the Foreign Ministry to study the terms of the Peace Treaty and the problems it presented to Japan. In the fall of 1946, Yoshida and others began compiling seven volumes of economic and political data (in English) for Occupation authorities, aiming to prepare U.S. representatives as advocates for Japan's interests in Allied discussions on the Peace Conference.[5] In May 1947 (after the Peace Constitution was instituted), the Foreign Ministry established the *Kakushorenrakukanjikai* (departmental coordinating discussion group), which presented a unified Japanese position to the Allies on various topics.

President Truman was outraged over these attempts to bargain the details of unconditional surrender. A letter to General MacArthur from the Joint Chiefs of Staff clarified the President's position that American and Allied objectives set forth in the Potsdam Declaration in fact remained the actual terms of surrender, and that there should be no intrusion of Japanese terms[6]:

> The authority of the Emperor and Japanese Government to rule the state is subordinate to you as Supreme Commander for the Allied Powers. You will exercise your authority as you deem proper to carry out your missions. Our relations with Japan do not rest on a contractual basis, but on unconditional surrender. Since your authority is supreme, you will not entertain any question on the part of the Japanese as to its scope.

This hard line became quite malleable, however, as U.S. security priorities turned toward the democratization of Japan. From the perspective of key American policy makers, Japanese economic reconstruction would be nonthreatening to other states if conducted within the context of democratic political development. Democratization implied minimal state involvement in the economy and firm civilian control of the military. But the immediate need to rebuild the Japanese economy also demanded political stability. The question of how to achieve the dual aims of democratization and economic reconstruction split Occupation authorities, opening a rift between the State and War departments.

Such internal division bode well for Japan's postwar security priorities. From the perspective of influential leaders such as Yoshida Shigeru and Ashida Hitoshi,[7] economic reconstruction was crucial to regaining national sovereignty. Poor in natural resources and having lost its colonial suppliers, Japan needed to export manufactured goods to reindustrialize. Economic independence (*keizai jiritsu*) was considered vital to national well-being, manifested by the urgent desire among Japanese conservatives and liberals alike to trade with China, no matter how "communist."[8] In addition, the threat of economic stagnation and national poverty loomed much larger than the prospect of military invasion. Accordingly, Japan's dilemma was not seen in American terms of how to simultaneously achieve democratization and economic reconstruction. Rather, the pressing problem was how to achieve some degree of national independence within the constraints imposed by the Potsdam Declaration and subsequent military Occupation.[9] The state's pursuit of economic security, a prewar policy preference, was the natural alternative.

Seen in the context of Japan's historical experience since the mid–1800s, the demolished state of the national economy and elimination of military means to pursue national security left few options. Japan's losses in heavy industrial production alone called for economic priorities. Total material losses from the war were estimated at $64.3 billion, fully one-fourth of the remaining national wealth.[10] Thirteen million people were unemployed. High inflation accompanied energy and food shortages, compounding the economic crisis. The pursuit of military security, seemingly strangled by the *Heiwa Kenpo* (Peace Constitution) of May 1947, was resuscitated later in a secret Yoshida-MacArthur agreement where Japanese military facilities were provided for American rearmament in Japan.[11] These and other agreements (discussed in detail in Section 3 of this chapter) left Japan to pursue economic security within the confines of a stabilizing alliance framework, a function provided earlier by the Anglo-Japanese alliance. American policy makers continued to produce security policies intended to promote a liberal economic order and counter illiberal military threats in accordance with traditional balance of power considerations:

> Stopping Soviet penetration (by) the development of sound economic conditions in these countries[12] ... and preventing a power vacuum into which the aggressive military power from the mainland of Asia would surely flow.[13]

War and Navy Department leaders emphasized the need for overseas bases, transit and landing rights for naval vessels and aircraft to establish a "strategic frontier"[14]:

> The Philippines were the key to Southeast Asia, Okinawa to the Yellow Sea, the Sea of Japan, and the industrial heartland of northeast Asia. From these bases on America's 'strategic frontier,' the United States could preserve its access to vital raw materials in Asia, deny these resources to a prospective enemy, help preserve peace and stability in troubled areas, safeguard critical sealanes, and if necessary conduct an air offensive against the industrial infrastructure of any Asiatic power, including the Soviet Union.

In contrast to prewar Japanese colonial designs, American plans for maintaining access to resources implied open access, at least within the ideals of liberal democratic capitalism. Strategic denial would pertain only against politically illiberal powers unwilling to abide by the rules of open access and trade. Thus, a certain continuity of national approaches to security endured in the immediate postwar period. Japan's economic security priorities, demilitarized and democratized, meshed with a traditional U.S. policy of containing military threats and promoting liberal political values and economic openness. This complement of interests enabled Japan's economic security objectives to thrive under the U.S. strategic military umbrella.

Accommodation of Economic Security

Three aspects of the American Occupation provided ample opportunity for Japanese authorities to pursue economic security: (a) the reliance on Japanese administrators by Occupation authorities, (b) the limited character of the economic purge, and (c) the minimal effect of Occupation reforms on prewar business and government elites. The broad scope of SCAP's responsibility relative to its number of personnel made American reliance on Japanese authorities a practical necessity. SCAP was organized into a dozen or so special sections, the most important of which was the Government Section that paralleled Japanese cabinet structures. The structure and flow of communication between American and Japanese policy makers allowed Occupation directives to be more interpreted than directly translated, a process aided by the low ratio of relevant SCAP personnel to Japanese administrators.[15] Of the 10,000 Americans residing and working in Tokyo in 1946, only 500 personally took part in the governing of Japan through SCAP directives.[16]

SCAP's effectiveness was hampered by the broad span of control associated with "unconditional surrender" and diluted by other factors. The paucity of Japanese-speaking Americans among U.S. officials was an obvious limitation.[17] Another constraint was the fragmented nature of U.S. intelligence services at a time when SCAP could have used objective, detailed intelligence on political and economic matters as well as military matters. Competition among Army and Navy intelligence services and the Department of State intensified almost immediately after the surrender of Japan because, in victory's rush to dismantle U.S. wartime agencies, the Office of Strategic Services (OSS) was abolished in August 1945. However, it was OSS Maj Gen William Donovan who had proposed to FDR a plan to wrest control of intelligence processes from the military services by establishing a director of central intelligence under the President. Such a director would have authority over all intelligence matters. Despite Truman's interest in transitioning from a wartime system to a peacetime system that would include heavier State Department involvement, the elimination of OSS strengthened the hand of Army and Navy intelligence agencies during the ensuing bureaucratic turf battle with State. Although President Truman did sign the letter that established a national intelligence structure in January 1946, the intervening months provided key opportunities to those who had unconditionally surrendered. As the Truman administration debated the future of U.S. national intelligence, Japan's security bargainers shaped SCAP's view of the political and economic landscape.[18]

Even more profound than American linguistic and intelligence shortcomings were to Japan's ability to pursue economic security was the American assumption that democratization was necessary to realize national security objectives in the long run. Regardless of the cause attributed to the Pacific War by American policy makers — a small band of military cliques (MacArthur's view) or the predominance of feudalistic relationships (Acheson's view) — democratization was regarded as necessary to eliminate the long-term threat of recrudescent Japanese militarism. The dual aims of promoting democratization and enacting widespread social, economic and political reforms required a transmission belt to the Japanese people. By the spring of 1946, SCAP had deliberately transformed this transmission belt into a bargaining arena when "the Section abandoned the use of directives, formal or informal, in favor of suggestion, persuasion or advice."[19] The cadre of competent Japanese administrators, most of whom were seen to have acquiesced rather than directed the war effort, assumed the role of national security bargainers.

As a result, less than one year after unconditional surrender, the ability of Occupation authorities to implement details of policy had been diluted. Although the President had given MacArthur broad authority to shape Japan's political, economic and social profile, the means to implement such changes were limited. SCAP reliance on Japanese administrators and the liberal nature of the reforms themselves mitigated the effect of Occupation policies.

Consequently, Japanese authorities of cabinet rank had direct access to the highest levels of SCAP, and lower level Japanese intermediaries had daily opportunities to question post-surrender directives and modify their implementation.

The persistence of prewar Japanese economic security goals was also a by-product of SCAP's tepid economic purge, completed by October 1949. Both the character and scope of the purge were limited in two ways that permitted Japanese economic objectives to be pursued: (1) the non-punitive nature of the purge, and (2) the minimal impact of the economic purge on financial, business, and government economic elites.

In contrast to purges conducted in postwar Germany, which sentenced offenders to jail, purges in Japan simply barred individuals from holding certain business and public offices. Even the Director of the American Civil Liberties Union, invited by MacArthur to conduct a three-month survey of civil rights in Japan and Korea, reported the purges in Japan as fair and their punishments mild.[20] The purge was harsh only to suspected war criminals, who were to be arrested immediately. War criminals were identified in the JCS Initial Post Surrender Directive to General MacArthur as (a) members of the Supreme Military Council, Board of Field Marshals and Admirals, Imperial General Headquarters, and Army and Navy General Staffs; (b) Kenpei members and other military officers who have advocated militant nationalism and aggression; and (c) high members of ultranationalistic societies. Within the confines of American liberal strategic thinking, these individuals threatened Japanese democratic reforms — reforms that would neutralize Japan as a future threat. Even so, President Truman pardoned a number of convicted war criminals whose detention had resulted in economic hardship on their families.

In addition to the war criminals, SCAP was directed to intern Japan's economic elites, to include "all persons who have played an active and dominant governmental, economic, financial or other significant part in the formulation or execution of Japan's program of aggression."[21] But in fact, the scope of the purge in financial and business circles, and among government officials, was limited. The economic purges were neither intended to retard economic growth, nor control Japanese production with the exception of munitions and armament production. In fact, the industrial production index rose 58 percent after the purge. Of the 6,951 members of economic organizations screened for dismissal, only 1,535 were purged without reinstatement.[22] Less than 2 percent of Commerce and Industry officials, 4 percent of Ministry of Finance officials and 6 percent of Ministry of Foreign Affairs officials were purged. This contrasts to the military purge, in which 1,283 of 1,287 career army officers screened were dismissed, none of whom was reinstated. Career naval officers fared only marginally better, with 792 of the 804 officers screened ultimately purged without reinstatement.[23] Within SCAP, divisiveness over whether the economic purge list should be long or short was consistent with bureaucratic responsibilities. SCAP's Finance and Industry Section urged short lists to facilitate industrial recovery, while the Anti-Trust and Price Control Section pressed for a long list to aid democratization. In the end, SCAP screened 717,415 people and purged 201,815 from government or private positions before April 1946. Of this total, the economic purge accounted for less than 0.8 percent.

Within Japanese society, organized opposition and the informal structure of power worked to weaken the effects of the purge. A Purge Appeals Committee, headed by former Minister of Justice Tanimura Tadaichiro, sought to depurge 70,000 of the 200,000 total purges. Banking and industrial officials, and non-policy makers in the government, were among the targeted categories.[24] For his part, Yoshida consistently protested to MacArthur that the purges threatened Japan's number one priority of economic reconstruction. On several occasions, the Prime Minister argued that *zaibatsu* (economic factions) such as Mitsui and Mitsubishi should be exempt from the purge as a matter of practical necessity[25]:

> In the economic world, for instance, nothing was more urgent than increased exports, and the improvement of Japan's position in world markets, but there existed a serious lack of available men experienced in such matters because of the large numbers eliminated by the purge.

The effects of the American purge on economic elites were reduced by pervasive *jinmyaku* (personal networks). Removal from office was a formality that left long-standing personal loyalties to patrons untouched. Group leaders simply continued to make key decisions through robust informal connections. The durability of old networks was demonstrated in the 1952 Diet elections, conducted just after the Occupation ended, in which 139 depurgees were elected.[26] In addition, the founder of Japan's first television station (Shoriki Matsutaro), the President of Komatsu Heavy Industries (Kawai Yasunari) and two Prime Ministers (Hatoyama Ichiro and Kishi Nobosuke) were among those once purged under the Occupation reforms.

The limited economic purge left many of the prewar advocates of economic security in the government. With regular access to SCAP authorities, influential postwar leaders advanced national priorities by directly bargaining with key definers of U.S. security interests. Even where SCAP reforms were seen as most successful, as in the military, educational, and agricultural fields, occupation reforms abetted the concentration of state influence among business and government officials. This was especially true for Yoshida, whose political ascendancy to the Premiership in 1946 was enabled when SCAP purged his main rival, Hatoyama. Yoshida's determined pursuit of economic security as Japan's immediate postwar national priority was a comprehensive policy program: forestalling Japanese rearmament until economic independence was achieved; maintaining Mutual Security Act status to receive foreign aid; suppressing labor unions and Communist influence to prevent disruptions to the economy; pushing long-term re-industrialization over short-term food supplies; and using agricultural reform to increase total production for national economic recovery. During the Occupation, Yoshida's conservative dominance was nearly continuous. He held the position of Prime Minister or Foreign Minister from the time of Japan's surrender to the year following the Peace Treaty and Security Treaty, December 1952, for all but 12 months.

Occupation reforms helped the conservatives stay in control. The removal of the military and its Constitutional subordination to cabinet ministries eliminated the most cohesive and powerful prewar opposition group. Reforms advocated by Japanese elites consolidated their dominance. Educational reforms were instigated by the Educational Reform Council, a like-minded group which according to Yoshida, aimed to increase the quality of education but also agreed on the following "pressing problems:" the decline in public morals, excesses resulting from misunderstanding the meaning of freedom, lack of respect for national traditions, and the biased political outlook of teachers.[27] Agricultural reforms, initially successful in redistributing one-third of all farmland to over 10 million people, also were subordinated to economic considerations of national security after conservatives complained that SCAP's decentralization of farmland weakened the nation's security. First, the wide distribution of land gave a firmer base of political support to right-wing militarists who traditionally enjoyed support in the countryside. Second, economic efficiency was impaired — larger concentrations of land were more conducive to high agricultural production.

The limited impact of Occupation reforms on economic elites is also attributable to questionable assumptions contained key documents, such as JCS directive 1380/15. This document contained plans submitted to the State and War Departments in March of 1946 "for dissolving large Japanese industrial and banking combines or other large concentrations of capital."[28] However, what had worked in breaking up monopolies in the United States failed to sever the personal ties at the heart of Japanese industrialist relationships. Assuming that a myriad of government laws, ordinances and regulations comprised "the means by which Japanese Commerce and Industry were controlled,"[29] JCS 1380/15 attributed the unsavory influence of financial elites to institutional defects. While cooperation among conservative government and business leaders in Japan helped unravel JCS 1380/15, further assistance came from Washington itself, where opposition to the deconcentration program had grown. Political interests focused on securing a sustained economic recovery, seen to be the foundation for political stability. By May 1948, a Deconcentration Review Board had been dispatched to Tokyo to ensure democratization did not get in the way of economic recovery. Seven months later, the Board reported the deconcentration program as complete.

Despite clamor by opposition parties directed against Yoshida's conservative coalition, there is little evidence that a different Prime Minister would have eschewed economic security as the overriding national priority. The persistence of economic security priorities among postwar cabinets is illustrated by the distribution of Japan's major security initiatives across socialist and conservative governments:

July 1947 Ashida Memorandum:	advocated a positive Japanese role in deciding terms of Peace Treaty, internal security of Japan, reparations levels and economic restrictions.
September 1947 Ashida Memorandum:	proposed U.S. military forces or UN military forces provide external security for Japan, while Japanese handle internal security.
July 1948 Ashida Memorandum:	identified U.S.–Japan security agreement as more realistic than UN–Japan security arrangement — U.S. provides external security and Japan internal security.
May 1950 Ikeda Mission:	proposes use of U.S. bases in Japan in lieu of Japan's rearmament; links Peace Treaty to Security Treaty.

U.S. Reparations Policy and Japan's Rearmament Promise

The emergence of the U.S.–Japan security bargain was not only due to the continuity of Japan's economic security policies, but also stemmed from the comparatively liberal design of U.S. security policy. Strategic issues were debated within the bounds of liberal economic assumptions of national security, and proceeded within the context of a common illiberal enemy — Sino-Soviet bloc communism. Anti-communist political considerations consistently received priority over economic definitions of national security, which provided room for bargaining by Japanese conservatives who emphasized economic priorities. U.S. national security policy toward Japan was formed in response to two immediate issues on the road to the Peace Treaty and Security Treaty: (a) the payment of wartime reparations, and (b) Japanese rearmament. Both illustrate the liberal nature of the American self-concept of security, a key ingredient in the postwar framework for cooperation.

Minimal Reparations

The American policy position that emerged on the issue of Japanese reparations favored minimizing such payments; there would be no industrial punishment of Japan.[30] The 1946 Pauley Reparation Mission's reparation plan had called for the destruction of 990 industrial units and 1476 military facilities. But in 1948, the 1948 Draper Report followed with a scaled down recommendation of removing 102 industrial and 540 military facilities. The dominant belief was that wartime damage to the Japanese economy had been substantial enough, and harsh reparations would undermine attempts to rebuild the Japanese economy. By 1945, for instance, Japan's hydroelectric power industry, the world's third largest before the war, had been reduced by bombing and lack of maintenance to 75 percent of its capacity.[31] Truman repeatedly emphasized in cabinet meetings that the ability of the U.S. economy to meet the needs of both Japanese and European recovery was not unlimited. The U.S. was spending $350 million annually in Japan for food requirements alone, in addition to the heavy financial burden of rebuilding Europe. Pressure on the U.S. capacity to meet postwar worldwide food shortages was strong. Allies who were involved in negotiating the postwar International Wheat Agreement demanded the U.S. increase its allotments as the condition for Japanese and German participation. Great Britain expressed fear of competition among wheat importers, and proposed limiting Australian wheat shipments to Japan as the price for Japan's accession to the agreement.[32] Accordingly, American policy makers sought an early resolution of the reparations issue. Agreement on this issue by the principal sub-national actors in American security policy, the otherwise divided Departments of State and Defense, occurred for separate reasons.

In the State Department, attitudes toward reparations were initially split between the Office of Far Eastern Affairs and the Policy Planning Staff. The former group, headed by Hugh Borton, emphasized the threat of resurgent Japanese militarism and favored stringent reparations. The latter group, headed by George Kennan, worried that heavy reparations would cripple the Japanese economy and increase its susceptibility to communist influence.[33] A March 1947 Department of State report emphasizing the importance of foreign trade to the Japanese economy provided timely support for Kennan's view, suggesting the United States provide external markets for Japanese economic prosperity. By May 1947, the State Department's position reflected Kennan's soft position on reparations, calling for liberal economic and political measures to counter communism. In October, Kennan publicly announced the rebuilding of the Japanese economy as top priority and urged the creation of a Japanese security police to maintain internal security.

An additional State Department initiative in 1947 attempted to deflect the damage that Allied reparations might have on the Japanese economy by maximizing Japanese exports. This plan to revive the national economy urged the development of a detailed export-import and production plan, controls on food distribution to maximize industrial production, and the revival of private trade.[34] Secretary of State Acheson spoke of the need to reconstruct Japan as a workshop of Asia, and subsequent State Department documents reflect the overriding concern with internal instability.

The War Department shared the interest in protecting the level of industry in Japan, assigning the stabilization of the economy high priority not only to counter Soviet expansionism, but also to help finance the American Occupation of Japan. Other Asian states, however, voiced concern about Japanese remilitarization. To counter these fears, Army Secretary Royall promoted the idea of an Asian Marshall plan to purchase Chinese and other states' acceptance of American stabilization of Japan's economy.[35] Later, the Mutual Security Program would begin a long-term Far East recovery program that recognized Japan's traditional need for stable South East Asian markets.[36] MacArthur, interested in preserving the democratic reforms and anti–Communist character of his Occupation legacy, favored early settlement of minimal reparations. Secretary of the Navy James Forrestal indicated that all of the military services found agreement at the top[37]:

> To get reparations settled — let the Japanese know definitely what they are to pay so that their industry can begin to survive. The Japanese economy must be set up on a basis that will enable the people to work and produce sufficient export balances to provide the exchange which will buy the balance of food and clothing which they do not themselves produce.

In NSC meetings during 1948, different economic and political interests converged, forging a consensus on minimal reparations. Treasury, Commerce and the President joined the State, War, SCAP and military service positions on low Japanese reparations. Secretary of Treasury Snyder's concerns centered on deficit financing — why should the U.S. government exact penalties on Japanese businesses to be paid to third parties, and simultaneously foot the bill for Japanese economic recovery? Commerce Secretary Sawyer voiced a similar concern over the need to reduce risks for American business. Reparations represented a sunk cost to investors and reduced opportunities for American enterprises. President Truman's fiscal frugality and pressure from Congressmen also supported minimal Japanese reparations. Truman's sensitivity to burdens on the American taxpayer during this period of global responsibility was plainly evident. In addition, John Foster Dulles' views on a non-punitive reparations policy, a reflection of his participation in the Versailles Peace Treaty, were clearly expressed.

Despite the variety of reasons for supporting minimal reparations, there was broad agreement on the need for internal stability in Japan and the necessity for economic growth to achieve it. While the State Department emphasized political threats to stability, the War Department naturally considered military threats. However, both viewed communism as inherently threatening. Against the politico-military communist threat, the fate of democracy in Japan was assessed, intimately connected to both liberal economic growth and internal stability. The reluctance of key U.S. policy makers to "Morganthau"[38] Japan was a reflection of this conception of national security.

Allies viewed the issue of Japanese reparations rather differently. Only two years after the Pacific War had ended, they considered an approach to national security that combined economic liberalism with military realism as either patently naive or self-serving. States that had been invaded or whose imperial preferences had been violated by Japanese aggression were quite intent on preventing a renaissance of Japanese economic power. The French government demanded $2 billion in reparations and a Japanese commercial agreement to protect French interests in Indochina.[39] Similar plans were unveiled at the 1947 Canberra Conference by officials from Australia, New Zealand, and Great Britain. Allies continued to demand compensation that had only been partially fulfilled. China, the Philippines, Great Britain, and the Netherlands adhered strictly to Potsdam and Canberra objectives of providing compensation to war victims, while American policies stressed Japanese economic rehabilitation. The primary threat considered by most Pacific states attacked during the war was not the more distant Soviet Union, and certainly not China — currently embroiled in a civil war, but a rearmed Japan. British members of the Far Eastern Advisory Commission became increasingly suspicious that the U.S. favored restoring Japan economically to serve as a bulwark against the Soviet Union over allied interests in reparations. British trade in Hong Kong alone constituted an interest in preventing the reemergence of Japanese economic, as well as military, power.

The American push for mild reparations became evident in drafts of and comments about the proposed Peace Treaty with Japan, which the State Department had circulated among 20 countries. One of Dulles proposals to reconcile Japan's need for raw materials with allied demands for substantial reparations was to have Japan process the raw materials of war-devastated countries free of charge.[40] As U.S. diplomats explained this soft American reparations policy, foreign resentment mounted.

Three years after dropping two atomic bombs to coerce unconditional surrender, American policy makers sought to garner Japan as an ally against communism by nourishing its devastated economy, while America's wartime Allies pursued economic and physical security against a resurgent Japanese threat. Soon the Americans would go even further, pushing for no less than the rearmament of Japan.

Limited Rearmament

In urging limited Japan's rearmament, American security policy reversed the short-term goals of the Potsdam Declaration and Initial Post-Surrender Policy for Japan, which proclaimed "irresponsible militarism" as the cause of the Pacific War. In fact, MacArthur would later (1951) apply this term to the Soviet Union to justify a democratized Japan's right to self-defense. From the liberal American perspective, Japan's militarist regime had been replaced by a benign, democratic system of government. Demilitarization seemed firmly codified in the Constitution, encouraged and largely written by Occupation authorities in January–February of 1946. By 1947, support for a prudent rearmament program had grown within a U.S. government seeking to contain a perceived global communist threat. The Truman Doctrine was announced in March. A sense of urgency and ideological threat intensified desires by U.S. policy makers to engage Japan as a strategically located ally. Navy Secretary James Forrestal's assessment reflected this sense of crisis in mid-1946[41]:

> Everywhere around the vast periphery of the Eurasian continent the situation had been the same; everywhere there was the same sense of a relentless pressure — acute in some places, latent but no less menacing in others: everywhere there had been need for firmness, action, strength and coherence of policy in meeting this extraordinary threat.

Within the foreign policy context of global containment, arguments favoring Japan's rearmament rested on considerations of military strategy, political stability, and financial burden-sharing. The first expression came in a May 1948 Department of the Army study that urged limited military armament of Japan.[42] Later, the case for armament would be made in CIA Strategic Reports and National Intelligence Estimates, and in National Security Council reports conducted from 1948 to 1952.[43] Each report echoed a common caveat, that military aid to Japan should be accompanied by economic support. This combination of separate yet related categories of security support — economic and military — became codified in the Mutual Defense Assistance Act of 1949, which tied provision of U.S. economic and military aid together under the rubric of security. Initially applied to NATO, it was later implemented toward Japan following the 1951 Security Treaty.

First, there was the geo-strategic argument. Japan was conveniently located to contain Soviet expansionism. The Soviet Union's shortage of warm water ports for naval ingress and egress included the Pacific port of Petropavlovsk on the Kamchatka Peninsula, 700 miles north of Hokkaido. Japan lies astride all three North Pacific choke points which could be mined or serve as interdiction points against the Soviet navy: (a) La Perouse Strait between Japan's northern island of Hokkaido and Soviet Sakhalin island, (b) Tsugaru Strait between the Japanese main islands of Hokkaido and Honshu, and (c) Korea/Tsushima Straits between the Korean Peninsula and Japanese main islands of Kyushu and Honshu. The Ryuukyu Islands and Okinawa in particular were important to security on the Korean peninsula, where Soviet troops had accepted Japan's surrender in the north. If Japan or perhaps Korea were to fall under Soviet influence, the Soviet Union could control Northeast Asian trade routes and threaten the string of U.S. bases (including those wrested from Imperial Japan's control) in the Western Pacific.

The second consideration was internal to Japan. The specter of an economic crisis that might spark political instability evoked real concern not only among Japanese conservatives, but also among American strategists that valued Japan's industrial potential. On May 1, 1946 ("Food May Day"), 500,000 protested in Tokyo over food shortages, reinforced by populist and communist agitation in the wake of Occupation reforms. Rearmament would at least have to address the need for a national police force to provide order. Yet, the establishment of any Japanese armed forces beyond the scope of a civilian or coastal police invited economic ruin and political opposition.

The third main concern that argued for the rearmament of Japan was that the American taxpayer was bearing the burden for its defense. Congressmen who remained sanguine about the impact of democratic political reforms in Japan emphasized the existence of trained Japanese manpower that could support rearmament for at least self-defense. Those who doubted Japanese intentions tended to keep these concerns out of the open.[44]

U.S. policy makers saw a direct link between the issues of reparations and rearmament. The desire to rebuild a democratic, economically prosperous Japan, facilitated by a low reparations policy, clearly contained the expectation of rearmament against a Sino-Soviet communist threat. American assumptions that democracy was inherently non-militaristic meant that once Japan was democratized, there was no reason to distrust Japanese rearmament. American desires of low reparations for economic growth and rearmament created a policy dilemma. Allied pressure against these policies, and the concern that an economically restored Japan eventually would seek removal of the U.S. military presence, deadlocked American policy makers on two fronts. First, Allies sought some guarantee of security from a recharged Japan, notwithstanding democratic reforms. An economically restored and rearmed Japan was seen to threaten regional states in general, rather than being narrowly directed against China and the Soviet Union. This meant that a regional security pact including Japan, which had originally been sought by Truman, was not feasible. Second, internal division between the Departments of State and Defense over the nature of the threat to Japan — political instability or military attack — prevented policy consensus.

President Truman appointed John Foster Dulles to resolve the dilemma by negotiating a peace treaty palatable to the Allies and consistent with the preferences of a divided U.S. administration. In trips to Japan in June 1950 (just before North Korea's surprise invasion of South Korea), January and April 1951, Dulles offered low reparations and aid for economic rebuilding, and insisted on rearmament within the framework of a traditional military alliance. Resistance to Japanese rearmament from the governments of Australia, New Zealand, the Philippines would be mollified by establishing separate alliances with the United States.[45] In the end, this approach ultimately obtained a Peace Treaty acceptable to 49 of the 52 states attending the September 1951 Peace Conference. The same day the Peace Treaty was signed, Yoshida signed the bilateral Security Treaty with the United States. In essence, the Security Treaty was what Japanese conservatives had to give in order to pursue economic security goals. These and subsequent agreements provided the original framework for postwar U.S.–Japan security bargain.

Formula for Cooperation

Ten agreements negotiated from 1946 to 1954 comprised the postwar bargain of security cooperation. All reflected continuities in Japanese economic security practices and the liberal democratic assumptions of American policy:

1. The Constitution of Japan (Nov 1946)
2. Ashida Memoranda (July, Sept 1947, July 1948)
3. Ikeda Proposal (May 1950)
4. The Korean War and Dulles-Yoshida Dialogues (June 1950, 1951)
5. San Francisco Peace Treaty and the Security Treaty (Sept 1951)
6. Administrative Agreement signed under Article III of the Security Treaty (Feb 1952)
7. Dodge-Suto Exchange (Feb 1952)
8. Charter Party Agreement (Nov 1952)
9. Ikeda-Robertson Communique (Oct 1953)
10. Mutual Defense Assistance Agreement & Defense Laws (March 1954)

Although important agreements continued to be negotiated after 1954, such as the Patent Rights Agreement (1956) and numerous weapon system co-production agreements (1958–present), these later agreements invariably refer to the 1954 Mutual Defense Assistance Agreement for justification. In each of the ten agreements worked out from 1946 to 1954, a complement of different security priorities, rather than simple agreement on a common threat, provided the actual basis for postwar.

November 1946: The Constitution of Japan

Japan's conservative elites did not accept the American written Constitution to democratize themselves, but rather to preserve the old order put at risk by the Occupation objectives. The Matsumoto draft of the Shidehara cabinet (Oct 1945–May 1946) had offered only marginal changes to the Meiji Constitution. Only when MacArthur threatened to take the issue to the Japanese public was SCAP's draft accepted. As a result, retention of the Tenno institution was permitted, but had to be imbedded in a democratic Constitution that reduced the Emperor's role to one of symbolism:

> Article 1. The Emperor shall be the symbol of the State and of the unity of the people, deriving his position from the will of the people with whom resides sovereign power.
> Article 4. The Emperor shall perform only such acts in matters of state as are provided for in this Constitution and he shall not have powers related to the government.

American purposes were to achieve demilitarization through the renunciation of war, democratization by creating a Parliamentary system of government, and domestic stability with the retention of the Emperor system. It was hoped these steps would cultivate a pro–Western, anti-communist Japan considered vital to U.S. security interests. The immediate need to demilitarize Japan and the longer term process of democratizing Japan reflected American assumptions about the military nature of security threats. Furthermore, an American controlled Occupation would deny future Japanese power to illiberal countries, particularly the Soviet Union. From this perspective, the repudiation of war served to allow for the preservation of a stable, yet benign Tenno system. Given the time it was expected to take to build democracy in Japan, the "no-war" Constitution would at least provide an immediate demilitarizing mechanism. These different national aims were incorporated in Article IX, the renunciation of war clause:

> Aspiring sincerely to an international peace based on justice and order, the Japanese people forever renounce war as a sovereign right of the nation and the threat or use of force as a means of settling international disputes. In order to accomplish the aim of the preceding paragraph, land, sea, and air forces, as well as other war potential, will never be maintained. The right of belligerency of the state will not be recognized.

As the first institutionalized postwar element of the security bargain, the *Heiwa Kenpo* (Peace Constitution) strongly affected the international and domestic context of Japanese security policy. By forbidding the possession of military forces and war potential, it eliminated the military option as an independent means to counter external threats. This also muzzled domestic articulation of military security priorities while democratization reforms took hold. As a result, the economic means of achieving national advantage gained added importance. Japan's only realistic security option was to seek an assurance of military security from some external source while pursuing more immediate economic security aims. Foreign Minister Ashida's two memoranda offered just that to American officials still divided over security priorities.

July 1947, September 1947, and July 1948: The Ashida Memoranda

The Ashida Memoranda are the earliest documented Japanese postwar security initiatives made to U.S. authorities. On their face (*tatemae*), the memoranda laid out Japan's strategic military security preferences — a United Nations military guarantee if regional power relations were stable, and a United States military guarantee in the event of external instability. As U.S.–USSR tensions escalated in the Cold War, the U.S. guarantee was chosen, and a division of Japanese and American roles proposed. Internal security would be handled by Japanese police forces and external security guaranteed by U.S. military forces. The desire to obtain military security from the United States was not solely intended to guard against external threats. The central aim (*honne*) was to allow Japanese resources to concentrate on the overriding national priority of economic reconstruction. Expenditures for forces to defend against external attack or intimidation was not considered as important as internal police forces needed for domestic stability. Distrust of the *gunbatsu* (military faction) who had just led Japan into its wartime failure was understandably high, and opposition groups proliferated. A few months prior to the first Ashida Memorandum, socialist and communist groups called for a general strike throughout Japan.

In light of these internal and external security considerations, alignment with the United States was the best course to allow focused pursuit of economic security goals. Help from the Allies was unthinkable at the time, as they and regional states favored harsh war reparations and tighter industrial restrictions against Japan. Stalin's desire to partition Japan into zones of occupation contrasted with the American aim of preventing a multilateral allied occupation of Japan. As a result, alliance with a militarily dominant, economically permissive state minimized uncertainties associated with rebuilding the national economy, thereby preserving some measure of economic independence (*keizai jiritsu*). To accomplish this, a Peace Treaty would first have to be obtained. On this issue, Japanese socialists, conservatives and revisionists were in basic agreement. The Ikeda Proposal followed, intent on securing this first step of national sovereignty.

May 1950: The Ikeda Proposal

The Japanese Government desires to conclude a peace treaty at the earliest possible opportunity. Even after such a treaty is made, however, it will probably be necessary to allow U.S. forces to remain stationed in Japan in order to guarantee the future security of Japan and the Asian region. If it is difficult for this desire to be tendered from the American side, the Japanese Government is willing to study the matter in which it might be offered from the Japanese side. Concerning this point, we are consulting the studies of various constitutional scholars, and these scholars indicate that there would be few constitutional problems if an article pertaining to the stationing of American forces were included within the peace treaty itself. Even if the Japanese side tenders a request for the stationing of troops in another form, however, that also will not violate the Japanese constitution.

Finance Minister Ikeda's[46] offer during a meeting with U.S. Special Ambassador Joseph Dodge to provide bases in Japan for U.S. forces was designed to obtain an explicit guarantee of U.S. military protection against external attack. Despite the presence of over 200,000 American troops in Japan, many Japanese doubted U.S. resolve to protect Japan itself, suspecting more self-interested American aims.[47] The need for a domestic political order and economic reconstruction was paramount. Until a peace treaty could be negotiated to end the state of war and reduce uncertainty about reparations policy, prewar obligations and postwar commercial relations, investment incentives would be repressed. From the Japanese perspective, the invitation to have foreign troops on one's soil was a dear price to pay to obtain an early Peace Treaty needed for national sovereignty and economic independence. Under the circumstances, early admission into the international political-economic system presented the best prospect for national welfare and security. One month after the Ikeda Proposal was tendered, however, Dulles rejected it as insufficient.

June 1950: The Korean War and The Dulles-Yoshida Dialogues

Three days before the North Korean surprise attack on South Korea, Dulles visited Tokyo to urge that Japan rearm for its own defense. Yoshida stiffly countered this on economic grounds, arguing for an early Peace Treaty and a bilateral security arrangement with the United States instead. By this time, both negotiators were deadlocked by the positions of key domestic groups attempting to define security issues.

Yoshida was constrained by leftists and rightists on the main issues — revision of the no-war Constitution, alignment with the United States in the form of a bilateral security pact, rearmament, and how comprehensive the Peace Treaty should be[48]:

Table 3.1—Key Issues and Stances (Japan)

Issue/Group	Socialists	Yoshida	Revisionists
No-war Constitution	Yes	Yes	No
Bilateral Security Treaty	No	Yes	Yes
Rearmament	No	Not yet	Yes
Comprehensive Security Treaty	Include China, Soviet Union	Exclude Soviet Union	Include China, Soviet Union

On the issues of Constitutional revision and rearmament, Yoshida balanced the socialists against revisionists. On rearmament, Yoshida's position of waiting until Japan's economy was on solid ground steered a middle course between both domestic groups. There was socialist-conservative-revisionist consensus on the national priority of obtaining a peace treaty, needed to regain sovereignty and control over the national economy. However, on this fundamental point, it was the U.S. administration that was deadlocked.

Table 3.2—Key Issues and Stances (U.S.)

Issue/Group	State	Dulles	Defense
No-war Constitution	Yes	No	No
Timing of Bilateral Security Treaty	Delay	Early	Delay
Rearmament	Eventual	Yes	Yes
Timing of Peace Treaty	Delay	Early	Delay

Dulles confronted both State and Defense on the peace treaty and security treaty issues. Kennan's State Department Policy Planning Staff and the Joint Chiefs of Staff had recommended against pressing for a peace treaty, largely due to uncertainty about Soviet intentions.[49] On the other issues, Dulles found himself trying to reconcile opposed positions.

The outbreak of the Korean War suddenly altered each domestic array in separate ways. The U.S. side realigned, favoring an early Peace Treaty after top decision makers read the attack as a Soviet-inspired communist threat. Dulles warned that if the Soviets controlled both Korea and Sakhalin, "Japan would be between the upper and lower jaws of the Russian Bear."[50] The State Department now favored an early peace treaty to permit a degree of Japanese remilitarization against this potential threat. This stance allowed Dulles to prevail over objections by the Joint Chiefs of Staff, and provided Yoshida an opportunity to achieve a peace treaty.

The domestic alignment in Japan, however, remained intact, as socialists and revisionists hardened their positions. So although the Korean conflict led to Dulles agreeing to the Ikeda Proposal and Yoshida promising to rearm, the ability of the latter to deliver was quite unsteady for two main reasons. First, there remained the problem of what the promise exactly was. Dulles had repeatedly pressed for force levels adequate to defend against a Soviet threat, and a sharing of the burden of defending not only Japan, but also South Korea, Taiwan, and the Western Pacific. Yoshida had never assented to such a high degree of military capability. Second, the relative security priorities of each side remained unchanged, with U.S. policy makers caught up in the immediacy of the military threat, and Japanese conservatives more concerned with the conflict's long term impact on economic revival and internal political stability. The following year, the San Francisco Peace Treaty and U.S.–Japan Security Treaty formalized the disparity in American and Japanese security priorities.

September 1951: The San Francisco Peace Treaty and the U.S.–Japan Security Treaty

The Peace and Security treaties coexisted as one diplomatic package to satisfy competing security priorities and interests. The Peace Treaty, which Japan desperately needed for admission into the world economy and the ending of the Occupation, could not have gained Allied and regional support unless Japan were disarmed. Yet, the Security Treaty clearly contained an American expectation of Japanese rearmament. In the end, the Security Treaty with the United States was the price Japan had to pay to obtain a Peace Treaty palatable to key Allies, yet acceptable to American security policy makers.

Articles in each treaty highlight the importance of economic security to Japanese conservatives and the significance of military security to the U.S. policy makers. Peace Treaty Article 12, the only Japanese declaration in the treaty, a statement of Japanese intent to engage in trade and commerce as soon as possible. Article 14 indicates the priority of Japanese economic reconstruction over the payment of wartime reparations, including a proviso "not to throw any foreign exchange burden upon Japan."

On the other hand, Articles 3, 5, and 6 contain military priorities of national security, while Article 3 refers to Okinawa, the Bonin Islands and others that the Joint Chiefs of Staff considered strategically important to provide military security against communist aggression. The demilitarized status of Japan meant that U.S. forces, not a rearmed Japan, would retain garrisons in strategic locations. Thus, Japan was afforded the rather ambiguous status of 'residual sovereignty" over the islands. Articles 5 and 6 legally allowed for subsequent agreement of a bilateral security treaty with the United States.

The bilateral exchange of relative economic and military security priorities occurs with the addition of the Security Treaty to the Peace Treaty. The notion of military threat formally justifies the existence of the bilateral security pact, referred to as Japan's desire for "a provisional arrangement for its defense ... to deter an armed attack on Japan."

In order to adhere the U.S. military guarantee to Japan, Yoshida's promise to rearm was codified in the treaty:

> The United States of America, in the interest of peace and security, is presently willing to maintain certain of its armed forces in and about Japan, in the expectation, however, that Japan will itself increasingly assume responsibility for its own defense against direct and indirect aggression, always avoiding any armament which could be an offensive threat or serve other than to promote peace and security in accordance with the purposes and principles of the United Nations Charter.

The American military guarantee served at least two pragmatic purposes for Japanese security. Of course, it deterred an external attack. Dependence on the U.S. military capability reduced the probability of an attack by raising the stakes to a major war.[51] Japanese leaders had chosen alliance with the United States in part due to U.S.–USSR conflict, Soviet seizure of Japan's northern islands at the end of the war, and the unreliability of a United Nations military guarantee. But the treaty's broader importance was to provide a politically acceptable military framework that would allow for postwar economic growth. Domestic opposition and regional resistance to Japanese rearmament militated against pursuing both commercial expansion and rearmament.[52] The cost of even four Japanese divisions, publicly presented as a minimum level needed to complicate a Soviet invasion, could be financed only with external assistance.[53] Moreover, basic needs such as raw materials, food and fuel comprised over 80 percent of Japanese imports. Japan had to accommodate major trading partners, as the ability of Japan to import constituted the chief limit to economic growth.

Due to these constraints, political stability and economic growth were at a premium. As a result, the Security Treaty's immediate military value was one-sided. Japan secured tangible U.S. military protection, and the United States received a tenuous promise of eventual Japanese rearmament. Taken together, both the Security Treaty and the Peace Treaty formalized a quid pro quo of different national military and economic security priorities.

February 1952: The Security Treaty's Administrative Agreement

Article 3 of the Security Treaty referred its implementation to an administrative agreement that would negotiate details of cooperation. Areas subsumed under the lengthy accord include matters of criminal jurisdiction, facilities and areas, rights and claims, and defense measures.

Sensitivities expressed by the Japanese side during negotiations included objections to continued facilities procurements by United States Forces Japan (USFJ), utilities rates for USFJ comparable to those accorded the Japanese National Police, import exemptions to contractors buying goods for USFJ, and personal withholding tax exemptions for USFJ personnel. Japanese demands included the notification of commercial cargo and passengers on aircraft and ships used for official U.S. government purposes, denial of contractors that filled orders for USFJ the same privileges given to civilians, and Ministry of Finance "over-all supervision" of American banks handling military payments.

The strongest objections were in the area of defense measures, Article 24. The American proposal gave the USFJ commander the right to take whatever actions necessary to ensure the security of U.S. forces in the event of hostilities or threat of hostilities. Pressure on the Yoshida government from opposition parties and the press on this issue, reminiscent of extraterritoriality, was high. The final version of Article 24 directed that the governments would "consult together with a view to taking necessary joint measures for the defense of that area...." Generally, the agreement was criticized by the press as an unequal arrangement.

In spite of this domestic pressure, the Administrative Agreement obtained for Japan, in the absence of a credible Japanese military force, deterrence and defense against external threats. For the United States, the use of an avowedly temporary overseas staging base for military containment of communism was obtained. Yoshida's promise of Japanese rearmament was not institutionalized in the agreement. Instead, cost sharing was instituted (Article 25), whereby Japan would subsidize the American military guarantee by providing transportation and services support.

February 1952: The Dodge-Suto Exchange

The same month the Administrative Agreement settled details of the Security Treaty, higher level officials exchanged the first formal long-range visions of bilateral economic cooperation since Japan regained national sovereignty with the Peace Treaty. The result was an exchange that displayed substantial differences regarding the primary threat to national security. In a memorandum to Japanese economic authorities, Presidential economic advisor Joseph Dodge indicated that the U.S. would rely on Japan to make contributions against the common communist threat. Dodge urged Japan to provide[54]:

    a. Production of goods and services important to the United States and economic stability of non–Communist Asia.
    b. Cooperation with the United States in the development of the raw material resources of Asia.
    c. Production of low cost military material in volume for use in Japan and non–Communist Asia.
    d. Development of Japan's appropriate military forces as a defensive shield and to permit the redeployment of United States forces.

The response of Suto Hideo, head of the *Keizai Antei Honbu* (Economic Stability Headquarters), made it clear that economic cooperation would be forthcoming, but only in accordance with a long list of Japanese economic security priorities[55]:

1. Japan shall establish a viable economy as quickly as possible by:
    a. Increasing production by utilizing her work force and unutilized industrial capacity
    b. Promoting and tightening her economic cooperation with the United States, South East Asian countries and other democratic countries in order to contribute to their defense production and economic development
    c. Assuring at the same time the volume of imports necessary for Japan
    d. Raising the standard of living
    e. Strengthening progressively her self-defense power

2. Japan will vigorously implement the following measures along the lines mentioned above:
    a. Japan will contribute to the rearmament plan of the United States, supplying military goods and strategic materials by repairing and establishing defense industries with the technical and financial assistance from the United States, and thereby assure and increase a stable dollar receipt
    b. Japan will cooperate more actively with the economic development of South East Asian countries and thereby increase the imports of goods and materials from this area and thereby improve the balance of sterling trade
    c. Japan will promptly increase the electric power supply, the shortage of which is proving to be the biggest bottleneck of the production increase necessary for such economic cooperation, with financial assistance from the United States.

The main difference in these two perspectives on economic cooperation lay in the purposes of economic growth. From the American perspective, Japanese economic growth and military procurement were to be directed against the undemocratic, communist threat. At least since January 1950, U.S. policy had been to combine economic and military aid to the Far East in order to counter communism and promote Japanese economic development. A chief problem had been that Japan's postwar exports had shifted away from traditional prewar markets. Although Asian markets had received over 70 percent of Japanese exports in 1938, less than half of Japan's exports in 1950 involved Asian outlets.[56]

By managing a regional military assistance and economic aid program that provided aid to non-communist Asian countries, the U.S. plan was to revive Japan's economy through export expansion. This in turn would increase regional trade, because the chief obstacle to balanced Japanese economic growth was assumed to be the inability of Asian markets to purchase Japanese manufactured goods. NSC 48/2 noted the miniscule trade between communist Asia and Japan, asserting that "Japan's economic recovery depends upon keeping Communism out of Southeast Asia, promoting economic recovery there and in further developing those countries, together with Indonesia, the Philippines, Southern Korea and India as the principal trading partners for Japan."[57]

From the dominant Japanese perspective, military procurement was needed only in the short term, until reliable markets were developed. Although such contracts served to better adhere the U.S. military guarantee to Japan, their material benefits had been particularly compelling since the outbreak of the Korean War. Since then, Japanese economic expansion had become dependent on military procurement by USFJ, rather than on developing markets of East and Southeast Asia. The dollar income from *tokuju* (special procurement) in the first three years alone ($590 million in 1949 and 1950; $894 million in 1951) amounted to 70 percent of Japanese exports.[58] This gain provided a tangible incentive for continued bilateral security relations during a time Japan desperately needed substantial foreign markets.

November 1952: The Charter Party Agreement

The Charter Party Agreement attempted to implement Yoshida's rearmament promise made under the Security Treaty. Anxious to enforce the stipulation that "Japan will itself increasingly assume responsibility for its own defense," American security officials worked toward joint defense planning by focusing on Japanese force goals and defense production. The Charter Agreement took an initial step in developing Japanese self-defense capability by leasing 7 patrol frigates to Japan's National Safety Force.[59] This provided the loan authority for 61 more vessels over the next 10 years, 80 percent of which would be extended on a five-year basis.[60] Both sides preferred the relatively quiet leasing of military hardware to formal agreements, as opposition party pressure against rearmament haunted the viability of the Yoshida government. But beyond the loaning of Coast Guard–type vessels to Japan, implementing details of rearmament in ground and forces, as well as military planning, proved quite difficult.

Regarding ground forces, American planners urged Japan rearm to a 10-division army (325,000 troops), which implied a substantial reduction and eventual elimination of U.S. basing in Japan. The Diet had authorized a much smaller force of 110,000 based on political concerns. Equipping Japan's ground forces was financed with U.S. Army appropriations ($528 million in fiscal year 1953), as the Department of Defense had not yet obtained congressional approval for a bilateral mutual security program. The prospects for a credible air force self-defense capability appeared still dimmer, as the nucleus of even a purely defensive air force had not yet been established. Despite the view of General Clark, Commander-in-Chief, Far East, that in 1953 the greatest threat to Japan's security was air attack, political and economic arguments against developing air combat capability remained strong. Finally, a Joint Military Planning Board was established, but no institution existed to deal with the political and economic considerations of rearmament. The smart politician and secure bureaucrat kept a low profile with respect to the issue of rearmament. Avoiding public attention on Yoshida's rearmament promise crippled attempts to achieve an independent self-defense capability.

October 1953: Ikeda-Robertson Communiqué

National differences among security priorities became more evident in negotiations between Finance Minister Ikeda Hayato and the Assistant Secretary of State for Far Eastern Affairs Walter S. Robertson.

During the negotiations, Ikeda persistently pressed for economic and military assistance, even offering to increase the 180,000 ground force level to obtain it. But American negotiators demurred on providing further economic assistance, citing Japan's now positive balance of payments. The U.S. relented, agreeing to extend military assistance under the Mutual Security Program, but only if Japan would increase defense expenditures by 50 percent over a two-year period.

In the joint statement upon the conclusion of the talks, the issue of military assistance was deferred "to the near future … with a view to reaching a definite understanding"[61] Furthermore, "the necessity of increasing Japan's self-defense forces in order to protect her from possible aggression, … under present circumstances there are constitutional, economic, budgetary and other limitations which will not allow the immediate building of Japan's self-defense forces to a point sufficient for self defense." Following this logic, $50 million in commodities would be given to Japan under the Mutual Security Act "to help develop the defense production and the industrial potential of Japan through offshore procurement and investment." This would later broaden into credits, trade and military assistance, all justified in terms of a common communist threat.

Overall, the Ikeda-Robertson talks had produced an agreement that recognized the insufficiency of Japanese rearmament efforts due to various constraints, while simultaneously providing aid for reindustrialization. In the expectation of eventual rearmament against the common threat, U.S. security policy makers now tolerated Japanese economic security priorities embedded in a domestic structure the Occupation helped create.

March 1954: The Mutual Defense Assistance Agreement and Defense Laws

The Mutual Defense Assistance Agreement (MDAA) and the Defense Laws passed by the Diet in the same month completed the institutionalization of the postwar security framework. These agreements laid the foundation for the sustained rearming and retraining of the Self-Defense Force. They reflect the full complement of different national security priorities.

In the 1950s, U.S. security policy makers sought to contain a perceived communist threat by constructing military alliances and promoting the national economies of American competitors. In this context, three important pieces of legislation overcame domestic pressures for protectionism. The Mutual Defense Assistance Act of 1949, Defense Production Act of 1950, and Mutual Security Act of 1951 reversed the "Buy American" Act of 1933, allowing military procurement officers and government contractors to purchase goods more efficiently to maintain an accelerated defense production program. Overseas production was sought to find more cost-efficient alternatives to U.S. production.[62] U.S. officials extended military assistance and defense support to the government of Japan under Article I of the Mutual Security Program (MSP). MSP and Japanese food requirements were incorporated into the MDAA Joint Communique (8 March 1954) which allowed a $50 million of surplus agricultural produce (largely wheat) to be "sold" to Japan. 20 percent of the surplus would be in the form of yen grants to assist Japan's defense industry, and 80 percent would be used by the United States to purchase goods and services in Japan as part of the Military Assistance Program.[63]

The legislation allowed the MDAA to further institutionalize the exchange of different military and economic security priorities. At its core was the provision of greater levels of U.S. military assistance and procurement contracts without obtaining a similarly tangible and significant Japanese commitment to external defense, such as increasing the National Safety Forces or amending of the Constitution. The MDAA's stated purpose to "provide for the furnishing of defense assistance by the United States of America," but it also explicitly tolerated Japan's special economic priorities:

> Recognizing that, in the planning of a defense assistance program for Japan, economic stability will be an essential element for consideration in the development of its defense capacities, and that Japan can contribute only to the extent permitted by its general economic condition and capacities.

While the MDAA tightened the bilateral quid pro quo of unlike contributions, the Defense Agency Law and Self-Defense Force (SDF) laws also made the first steps toward military alliance. Passed by the Diet almost simultaneously with the MDAA, these laws reorganized Japan's military force, creating the Japan Defense Agency (subordinate to Cabinet-level ministries) and a separate air self-defense force. With military reorganization came a steady expansion of the SDF, whose authorized strength rose from 152,110 at the time of the SDF Law to 230,935 by 1960 (actual manned strengths were 146,285 in 1954 and 206,001 in 1960).

The primarily internal security role of the self-defense forces remained unchanged, far from the real self-defense capability or regional role envisioned by Dulles. But from the U.S. administration's perspective, the Defense Agency and SDF laws provided a framework for defense rearmament which, together with the MDAA, were directed against the external communist threat. Japan was seen as the vital link in the American Pacific defense perimeter around Chinese and Soviet ideological hostility. Throughout the 1950s, MDAAs provided over $1 billion annually in a Far East network of military assistance and defense support to 10 nations.[64]

Contentious Quid Pro Quo

The Occupation's sequence of forcing the Peace Constitution on Japan's postwar authorities, then unleashing democratic competition against conservative rule, resulted in widespread Japanese opposition to rearmament. Precarious conservative coalitions were highly susceptible to criticism of this core quid pro quo of the security bargain. On the left, any rearmament was criticized as a return to prewar militarism. How could Japan simultaneously rearm while abiding by the Peace Constitution, which forbade war potential "forever?" On the right, vocal militarists drove moderates away from defense rearmament as well. As a result, the economic imperative prevailed over military considerations of security. The Mutual Security Act was not portrayed as rearmament, but as American aid needed for "domestic security." Even the external defense mission of the Self-Defense Forces, considered by American security policy makers to be a minimal requirement of military capability, was sought to gain full MSA status for Japan[65]:

> Something needed to be done to bring Japan into line with the law's requirements if my country was to be granted full MSA status, and as the situation also, both in Japan and abroad, required such steps to be taken, it was decided to include among the duties of the new Security Forces that of repelling foreign invasion, and to frame a new law for that purpose.

Yoshida's determination to obtain MSA status and delay rearmament balanced the differences between the political left and right on the issue of rearmament. Leftist opposition parties, while severely divided, managed to keep the public aware that "the big string which the United States will attach to the MSA is a request for increase of Japan's defense forces."[66] On the right, the Reform and Liberal parties, who together accounted for one-fourth of the Diet seats, had been calling for dramatic increases in defense spending. By gaining MSA status and its defense-related business opportunities, all parties could be materially compensated. At the same time, MSA funds could be used to launch development of a Japanese military capability with minimal economic impact on the populace. From 1951 to 1954, the Ground, Maritime and Air Self-Defense Forces received over 175 trillion yen of material assistance for new equipment, weapons systems, ammunition and supplies. By 1957, this Mutual Assistance Program funding total soared to over 345 trillion yen, providing the foundation for a modern, re-equipped Japanese military.[67] Crucial to gaining MSA status was timing; submission of a defense assistance agreement prior to budget deliberations in the Diet could generate funding leverage central to domestic political outcomes. Foreign Ministry negotiators obtained American consent to sign the agreement one day before Diet budgetary talks were scheduled.

The domestic political success of adopting the demands of both opposition groups turned on the ability to visibly dilute American demands for rearmament and gain material benefits for Japan. Dulles' demand for a Japanese force commitment of 10 divisions had been blunted with reminders to the American negotiators about the tenuous condition of Yoshida's conservative coalition. Procurement contracts flowing from mutual security programs, however, were welcomed. Of the 10 nations in the Far East receiving military assistance obligations, Japan placed highest in unliquidated obligations in 1957.[68]

Yoshida's success in resisting rearmament and gaining MSA status did not extend to the issue of export controls, where the American anti-communist position prevailed over Japanese preferences to relax controls on trade with China. Advocates of expanded trade with China included MITI Minister Okano, who pressured Yoshida to exempt non-strategic trade from export controls. The Chinese market had absorbed 42 percent of Japan's Asian exports in 1938, yet accounted for only 5 percent in 1950.[69] American pressure to restrict Japan-China trade put Japan in a difficult situation, with the only feasible alternative being reliance on the American economic and military security system. By impressing U.S. negotiators with the need to minimize unpopular military expenditures lest the Yoshida government fall, Japan's negotiators were able to avoid making good on the promise of rearmament. The strident U.S. interest in containing communism, an ideology that ran directly counter to American political and economic liberalism, proved to be the pressure point of "unconditional surrender." Just the lure of eventual Japanese rearmament seemed enough to secure the U.S. military guarantee to Japan. This promise, and the more tangible provision of bases for U.S. forces in Japan, provided the controversial core of a broad-based postwar security bargain that exchanged economic security for military security.

4

Security Treaty Revision

The 1960 Treaty of Mutual Security and Cooperation remains the only comprehensive mutual adjustment to the institutionalized security priorities established during and immediately after the American Occupation of Japan. Since this revision, both American and Japanese leaders have been loath to scrap, replace, amend or even reinterpret the Treaty, preferring instead its compromising accommodation of unlike national security priorities. In contrast to the U.S. network of defense-related commitments in the region, which today includes Australia, the Philippines, South Korea, Taiwan, Thailand, and Singapore,[1] Japan's only formal defense relationship remains this one. Although the revised treaty and the Constitution do not expressly prohibit other security relationships or collective defense, Japanese policy makers have continued to avoid formal security ties with anyone but the United States and collective defense altogether.

Looking back on the issue of whether or how to revise the original 1951 security treaty with the United States, one might reasonably question why Japanese leaders did not seize the opportunity to make a significant change in foreign policy, perhaps toward neutrality or another security partner. Japan seemed to be at a crossroads, with emotions running high against treaty revision and remilitarization. The American Occupation was benign by any historical benchmark of "unconditional surrender," and it was over. On the left of Japan's domestic political spectrum, the two atomic scars of Hiroshima and Nagasaki animated a genuine peace movement that advocated neutrality, fueled by fears of being drawn into another regional conflict. On the right, territorial losses (Okinawa, Pacific territories, Northern Territories, Korea, and Manchuria) and the specter of permanent dependence on U.S. foreign policy reactivated prewar visions of autonomy. In the end, the revised security treaty split the difference between Japan's strategic options, broadly redefining the Occupation's U.S.–Japan security bargain across its political, economic and military dimensions.

Historical Development

Efforts toward revising the original security treaty began as a Japanese initiative in August 1955, when Liberal Party Prime Minister Hatoyama sent a delegation featuring Progressive Party Foreign Minister Shigemitsu and Democratic Party head Kishi to confer with Secretary of State Dulles. Kishi Nobusuke would soon become a key figure in Japanese politics. He had entered the political scene after having been incarcerated for three years in Sugamo Prison by SCAP authorities as a "Class A" war criminal. This was the category of criminals who faced the possibility of execution, such as wartime Prime Minister Tojo. Kishi had been Prime Minister Tojo's Minister of Commerce and Industry, so many saw him as personally responsible for Japan's brutal exploitation of Manchuria. Although Occupation authorities purged Kishi and barred him from public service, he was released from prison in 1948. The purge was rescinded in 1952 as Japan regained independence. Benefiting from the Occupation's change in security priorities from demilitarization and democratization to rebuilding Japan's economy and defense forces, Kishi filled the vacuum left by the resignation of Yoshida to become Secretary General of the Liberal Democratic Party.[2]

The issue of whether to revise the treaty quickly became connected to several controversial issues, the first one being the core question of rearmament. In the face of Dulles' demand to double ground force troop strength to 300,000 troops by 1960, Shigemitsu offered a plan that would expand GSDF troop strength by 10,000 each year, reaching 210,000 by 1960.[3] This gap between expansive American and limited Japanese rearmament proposals reflected widely held frustration over differences in security priorities and the realities of Soviet military power in the region. U.S. post–Korean war policy involved a similar allied effort to build up the South Korean military, reduce the U.S. ground presence, and maintain offensive U.S. air and naval forces for deterrence and defense. In contract to the policy of the Truman administration which had fought the Korean war, President Eisenhower's support of the "hot pursuit"[4] of hostile North Korean, Soviet or Chinese forces into China in the event that fighting in Korea were resumed, was exactly the kind of policy Japanese leaders feared.

From a Japanese perspective, an expansion in JSDF capabilities could only provide more opportunities for U.S. leaders to pressure Japan into supporting such an unfortunate turn of events. The continued strict interpretation of the constitutional restriction on using force only for self-defense seemed to protect Japan from the effects of unwanted external crises. Despite the UN Charter's allowance for collective defense,[5] this door was better left shut. Paradoxically, Japan's Basic Policy for National Defense (1957) was to "deal with external aggression on the basis of the Japan–U.S. security arrangements, pending the effective functioning of the United Nations in the future in deterring and repelling such aggression." Yet, collective defense in support of an ally was not deemed to be a proper extension of realistic self-defense.

This logic made no sense to those who blamed regime type — imperial, militaristic Japan — for the Pacific War and advocated political-economic-military reform as the solution for responsible, trusted autonomous defense. But the logic was quite compatible with those who held to the perspective of an insular, passive Japan. Rightist "passivists" argued that Imperial Japan had no choice but to save Korea, then China, from foreign domination by seizing their markets for Japan and Greater East Asia's development to catch up with the predatory western powers. Leftist passivists renounced Japan's past imperial expansion, the current American security embrace, and any future military capability that would go beyond minimal self-defense. Across the domestic political spectrum, Japan as an object of external circumstance was an image rooted in the still popular phrase, *shigata ga nai* (there is nothing one can do). Japan the victim, now bound by an Occupation Peace Treaty and Security Treaty, was to stave off external aggression under the protection and hubris of the United States until no less than the United Nations would guarantee the defense of Japan.

Tensions between China and Taiwan, and the war across closer straits in Korea, stoked fears in Japan's domestic political cauldron that unpurged militarists might somehow rekindle their prewar security agenda, or that the U.S. might drag Japan into a Cold War. So, the Basic Policy interpreted self-defense narrowly but allowed military action to be taken before aggression actually took place if it met three conditions:

Three Conditions Allowing Self-Defense

(1) There is an imminent and legitimate act of aggression against Japan
(2) No other appropriate means to deal with the aggression exists
(3) The use of armed strength is done at the minimum level necessary[6]

The question of minimum level of force was not meant to prevent a decisive defense, but rather to be consistent other policies that proscribed a reactive, non-threatening defense posture:

Other Basic Policies

(1) An exclusively defense-oriented, passive defense strategy
(2) Not becoming a military power that might pose a threat to others
(3) Not possessing nuclear weapons, not producing them and not permitting their introduction into Japan[7]

Despite such idealism, the practical problem of how to translate broad policy aims into an actual defense against potential threats remained. Countering Soviet forces required interdicting supply routes, destroying munitions depots, communications networks and troop concentration points, controlling naval choke points outside Japanese territorial waters, and eliminating offensive air forces before they reached Japan. To defend Japan's basic needs such as access to raw materials, safe sea lanes and a secure industrial base, concrete military missions would have to be developed. The hard facts were that Japan Self-Defense Force (JSDF) capabilities fell far short of these tasks with a Ground Self-Defense Force capable of minor defensive operations, a Maritime Self-Defense Force able to execute limited escorts of coastal convoys, and an Air Self-Defense Force with heavily restricted tactical capabilities.

Despite the need for a credible defense, Japan's self-perpetuated policy restrictions seemed to consign Japan's contribution to security to that of bases and cost-sharing for U.S. forces in Japan. Going beyond Japan's territorial waters or airspace to defend the home islands against armed attack was judged to be an unconstitutional capability because it might constitute "war potential." The Constitution did not prevent Japanese forces from playing a role in defending against potential military attack. However, without American military support, success against the most likely adversary, the Soviet Union, seemed remote. Although Japanese planning assumptions about Soviet intent were officially limited to the threat of small-scale invasion, Soviet capabilities were in fact not so small. Soviet assault capability was estimated as an initial landing of three 12,000-man divisions and 9,500 airborne troops. If this assault succeeded, 6 more divisions could be docked immediately thereafter. The Soviet Far Eastern Fleet could easily muster an attack with 40 major combatant ships, and a 2000-plus air force capable of generating 1000 sorties a day. Japanese defenses against this potential threat consisted of only a 6-division Ground Self-Defense Force, the 9 major combatant ships in the Maritime Self-Defense Force, and a 14-squadron Air Self-Defense Force. Politically, the level of Japanese forces needed for autonomous defense was unthinkable as long as such capability was construed as war potential. Modest yet positive Japanese force improvements within the context of U.S.-Japan security ties provided the only realistic alternative to the offensive ban interpretation of the Constitution.

While relying on U.S. forces to repel a major attack, Japan's expanding economic ties with United States enjoyed a windfall of U.S. military procurements since the Korean War, increasing ten-fold since 1950–1951. The special dollar income (*tokuju*) in 1956 actually converted what would have been a deficit of goods and services into a $205 million surplus. During the same period, Japanese exports to the United States doubled. By 1959, Japan's exports to the United States increased by 50 percent over the previous year. The U.S. market absorbed 30 percent of all Japanese exports.[8] Relatively low equity capital ratios of Japanese firms were one-half that of prewar levels, indicating a high demand for funds at a time when American Mutual Security Program aid was rapidly expanding. From 1950 to 1958, the Mutual Security Program disbursed over $663 million to Japan.[9] The combination of these benefits and the restrictions on defense capabilities left Japanese leaders no better alternative than to increase non-military contributions to the alliance to retain the external military guarantee from the United States.

Japan's economic benefits were not lost on the American side, where the treaty revision question was one of how broad and vigorous rearmament should be. During the talks, Dulles sought to expand the JSDF regional role to the Far East and Western Pacific (including Guam) based on an assumed linkage between regional military threats and the narrower defense of Japan.[10] Japanese negotiators viewed this as a move to postpone revising the Security Treaty in favor of revising the Constitution, pending the results of the next Japanese elections.[11] Indeed, any overt linkage of Japan's defense to assuming military responsibilities in a greater East-Asian sphere was doomed to domestic defeat. But the Eisenhower administration desires for constitutional revision, considered to be a likely catalyst for a more normal Japanese rearmament, turned on the prospect that a stable Japanese conservative coalition would be elected. The U.S. National Security Council's recommendation to delay Security Treaty revision until Liberal Democratic Party predominance seemed intact explains why Dulles, despite later having to accept a GSDF force level of 200,000, rejected Shigemitsu's initial proposal of 260,000 troops.[12]

In addition to the question of rearmament, the issue of Japan's territorial integrity and in particular with respect to the Ryukyuu Islands (Okinawa), the Bonin Islands (Chi Chi Jima) and Volcano Islands (Iwo Jima) was closely connected to the potential terms of treaty revision. Occupation-era decisions over what to do with territories modern Japan had gained from others had already made American bases throughout these islands accomplished facts, well outside Japanese sovereignty. The Joint Chiefs of Staff continued to favor retention of critical island groups for bases but most strongly in Okinawa due to its proximity to Soviet bases in the Far East. Officially the JCS defended retention of Okinawa as a long-range strategic bomber and naval base, Chi Chi Jima as a submarine and destroyer base, and Iwo Jima as a standby airbase with weather and navigation facilities.[13] The vulnerability of Okinawa to a serious Soviet attack required the other two islands be ready for operations as auxiliary bases.[14] Privately the JCS intended to use Pacific bases to disperse nuclear weapons throughout the region.[15] The State Department was more sensitive to political issues such as Okinawa communist party influence and Bonin Islanders (evacuated by wartime Japan) wishing to return home. While State and Defense agreed on the importance of retaining Japan as an ally against communist threats, State tended to downplay the military bases as marginally important to U.S. interests.

Arguments among nationalists and leftists in Japan that U.S. retention of Japanese territories as prizes of war was no different than Imperial Japan's acquisitions or the Soviet seizure of the Northern Territories were met by American ambivalence. U.S. goals for the Peace Treaty had included exclusive strategic control of the Ryukyuus, recognized as the most strategic of the island groups, but intimated even their eventual return by acknowledging Japan's "residual sovereignty." President Eisenhower's 1954 campaign promise to "maintain indefinitely our bases in Okinawa" was challenged by a court case the same year that established Okinawans as Japanese citizens. In 1956, the free election of communist party candidate Senaga Kamejiro as mayor of Naha presented a dual challenge to U.S. support of Japanese democracy and U.S. anticommunist containment strategy. Consequently in 1958, the State Department downplayed the military importance even of Okinawa and recommended its return to Japan, but used it to compel the Soviet Union to return Japan's Northern Territories (the Kurile Islands).[16] The combination of the ensuing Soviet rejection, persistent JCS concern over the strategic importance of Okinawa and the Bonins, and U.S.–Japan policy makers' fears of a communist local government in Okinawa, made the military bases a higher priority than either island democracy or Japanese territorial integrity. When it came to treaty revision and American bases, Secretary of State Dulles was prepared to re-offer Foreign Minister Fujiyama the original security bargain.

Shigemitsu and Kishi argued for immediate treaty revision, citing rising anti–Americanism and communist influence in Japan and hoping early revision would bolster Japanese conservatives' election hopes. Kishi had been waging a two-year campaign to forge unity among conservatives divided over how to respond to labor movements spawned by food and energy shortages, inflation and unemployment from 1945 to 1949. Early in the 1953 electoral campaign, Kishi stressed the need for political stability and economic security priorities[17]:

> Japan cannot be reconstructed as long as it is flooded with small parties eternally struggling for power. Indispensable for a truly democratic government is a two-party system.... However, judging from the present political state in Japan, it appears that the conservative parties alone, when unified and regulated, can stabilize the political system and improve the life of the people.
> Independent Japan can be defended only through close cooperation with the defense plans of the other free nations. However, we cannot rush into a defense

build-up. Our defensive strength can only be increased gradually as our economy is reconstructed.

Dulles considered Shigemitsu's rearmament promise to be unreliable, doubting that revising the Security Treaty would help the conservatives unite prior to the elections.[18] Meanwhile, opposition in Japan grew over infringements on Japanese sovereignty, which were seen to be a result of certain unequal terms in the original treaty[19]:

1. Absence of an explicit American commitment to defend Japan, in spite of the granting of military bases to USFJ.
2. Lack of an American requirement to consult with Japanese officials in force and weapons deployment decisions, particularly the dispatch of U.S. combat troops to foreign areas and the apparent storage of nuclear weapons in Japan.
3. Loss of Japanese sovereignty over the Ryukyu and Bonin Islands.
4. Visible failure of Japanese authorities to exert some degree of control over American troops in Japan
5. Omission of any reference to the United Nations (Japan was not a UN member in 1951).
6. The prerogative of USFJ to be used in an internal security role.

Major opposition parties in Japan labeled the U.S.–Japan security relationship as illegitimate due to its birth during foreign military occupation, when Japan was arguably not sovereign. As the Japan Socialist Party and Japan Communist Party pursued this line of attack against the Kishi government, two foreign policy issues related to American security goals surfaced to become the new focus of domestic debate — nuclear weapons, and trade with China.

Since 1955, when the Japan Socialist Party unified left and right wing socialists, increases in public discontent about American nuclear tests and the possibility of nuclear weapons in and around Japan exerted domestic political pressure on the newly established conservative coalition. How could Japan sustain economic development and limit itself to self-defense if its guarantor of military security continued to occupy Japan and risk nuclear conflict? As Japan's conservatives walked the political line on the home front between economic growth and military rearmament, nuclear weapons were becoming more important to U.S. global security concerns. Facing budget constraints and rising responsibilities in the face of a hostile communist ideology, U.S. defense strategy turned to technology to do more with less. Nuclear weapons became an indispensable part of the Eisenhower administration's lean "New Look" security policy that would fill America's Cold War commitments with a mix of conventional and nuclear forces, reducing manpower through technology.²⁰ Unfortunately for treaty revisionists seeking the comfort of ambiguity, General McArthur's requests in 1950 to strike China with nuclear weapons to prevent American defeat in Korea, and Secretary of State Dulles' 1954 declaration of a nuclear deterrent based on "massive retaliatory power," seemed to clarify U.S. nuclear policy intent all too well.

In the expanse of East Asia, operationally this meant having strategic bomber airfields and weapons storage facilities in a system of bases throughout the Pacific, with or without a U.S. military presence in Japan. After war in Korea left a robust U.S. presence there, the prospect that a network of bases might be more important than bases in Japan proper added more pressure to Japanese conservatives' concerns. One JCS concept even assumed the eventual withdrawal of U.S. forces from Japan, and favored using the Bonin Islands for the following military purposes²¹:

> 1. As missile bases, including the necessary control apparatus and radars. The Joint Chiefs of Staff feel strongly as to the necessity of dispersal of our retaliatory forces with particular emphasis on locating a proportion of such forces outside the continental United States, thereby making the Soviet problem of surprise attack a harder one to solve, and also decreasing relatively the attractiveness of the continental United States as a target.
> 2. As a supporting base for NSA and CIA operations.
> 3. As an advanced submarine base.
> 4. As an advanced storage site for limited number of nuclear weapons.

Given the evident importance of strategic basing arrangements to U.S. security, it was clear that serious opposition to American nuclear capability put the U.S.–Japan security relationship at risk.²² U.S. nuclear strategy and its associated testing in the Pacific reinforced fears that the American military guarantee imperiled rather than protected Japan's security. In January 1955, a bilateral agreement compensated Japanese fishermen for damages resulting from the Bikini Islands nuclear weapons tests. The following year, the Ministry of Foreign Affairs asked the State Department to take precautionary safety steps during the planned Eniwetok nuclear test. The Diet passed a resolution calling for an American nuclear test ban. In July 1955, a Department of Defense official revealed the U.S. Army's intention of deploying atomic weapons launchers in Okinawa and nuclear-capable Honest John missiles in mainland Japan, prompting periodic anti–Security Treaty rallies in Tokyo for the next two years. The issues of territorial integrity and nuclear weapons became fused in 1957 when the negligent homicide of a Japanese civilian by a U.S. serviceman reinforced the specter of an uncontrolled long-term U.S. military presence in Japan. The anti-nuclear banner of state sovereignty proved to be an effective temporary unifier of leftist socialists and rightist nationalists.²³

U.S. trade policy toward China generated more divisive contention with respect to treaty revision. U.S. Mutual Security Program funds had been made contingent upon Japan's participation in the U.S. and North Atlantic embargo of strategic goods to Communist-bloc countries. A panoply of private groups, socialists, communists and government officials in Japan favored lifting sanctions and expanding trade with this prewar export market and source of raw materials. Private Japan-China groups such as the Association for the Promotion of International Trade, and the Japan-China Importers and Exporters Association actively sought any opening in the China market. The Japan Communist Party and Japan Socialist Party established dedicated committees for Sino-Japanese trade. In 1949, JSP General-Secretary Asanuma Inejiro[24] boldly led a delegation to Peking that issued a joint declaration naming the United States as the common enemy of the Chinese and Japanese people. The "Sino-Japanese Trade-Promoting Diet Members Union" comprised fully 50 percent of the Diet Members in 1958. Trade with China from 1955 (the year trade relations were reopened) to 1960 represented only 2 percent of Japanese foreign trade, but the potential for needed foodstuffs and raw materials (especially chemicals) from China and the export of some Japanese capital goods drew business interest.

Several factors favored increasing Japan's trade with China: geographical advantage, Japan's imbalanced dependence on American special procurement contracts, increased export competition from the European Economic Community, and a general desire to find stable export outlets to finance industrialization. MITI's 1956 White Paper on Japan's Trade called for improving the international trade environment by dropping the government ban on official trade with China[25]:

> Another major problem for Japan is the restriction on exports to Communist countries. Relaxation of restrictions is desired particularly in the case of Communist China, in view of the complementary nature of the industrial structures of the two countries.

But the Kishi government also faced certain economic realities. Compared to the potential of increased U.S.–Japan trade flows and economic ties, the Japan-China trade outlook was bleak. Given the central role U.S. dollars played in the global economy and the status of the U.S. as the dominant international creditor, Japan–U.S. trade was a much more attractive prospect. In addition, other national governments were also lobbying for favorable U.S. diversion of scarce dollar reserves. In 1959, Japan was relatively deprived of world monetary reserves, but rapidly increasing its share in the competition for U.S. dollars:

Table 4.1—Monetary Reserves ($ hundred million)

State	1957	1959	% increase
France	7.75	16.34	110
West Germany	46.34	55.29	19
Italy	15.32	28.29	85
Netherlands	9.24	17.10	85
Great Britain	23.74	31.86	34
Japan	5.24	12.90	146

The conservative government coalition hoped that the economic growth benefits of increased U.S.–Japan economic relations would dilute political opposition to the Sino-Japanese trade ban. Special tax credits for export-related products were provided (lasting until 1963) and excessive competition (*kato kyoso*) among Japanese commercial firms was discouraged. While capital reindustrialization imported food and raw materials, export-driven trade expansion would earn the dollars needed to purchase imports and develop key home industries. Increased trade with the United States still offered the best road to rapid expansion.

Kishi's 1957 election as Prime Minister of the faction-ridden Liberal Democratic Party, a merger of the Liberal and Democratic parties, was followed by the second major step toward treaty revision. In June, bilateral talks produced a lengthy joint communiqué containing the usual pledges to prevent aggression and preserve freedom and justice. Specific agreements were: the withdrawal of all U.S. ground combat forces and reducing the total number of U.S. forces; maintaining a high level of trade and economic relations; and forming an inter-governmental committee to discuss problem areas.[26] The major differences in the communiqué were: Eisenhower's stress on controlling exports of strategic materials to communist countries versus Kishi's emphasis on Japan's trade needs; and U.S. continued residual (administrative) sovereignty over Okinawa and the Bonin Islands versus Japan's desire for their return.

These points of contention reflected different security priorities. U.S. definers of national security viewed revision as an opportunity to achieve two somewhat opposed goals: (1) solidify the U.S.–Japan security relationship and (2) obtain a more equitable formula for military burden sharing. The first aim coincided with Kishi's desire to achieve domestic legitimacy of the U.S.–Japan security relationship. Without this embrace, the conservative coalition could not offer a realistic security policy that avoided looking like prewar autonomy. Kishi himself was extremely vulnerable to opposition groups (labor, peace activists, teachers, students) on this point due to his wartime and war criminal past. Department of State and Defense officials would work to remove certain irritants in bilateral relations, but stopped short of Japanese demands that did not recognize military realities in the Far East.[27] At a minimum, top State and Defense Department officials desired Japan to serve as a "defense industrial base" for the Far East. If this role could not be preserved, alternative areas would be sought (Dulles suggested Australia). Japan's strategic location, industrial capacity and military potential meant that Japan should be protected from Soviet or Chinese influence, regardless of Japan's level of military contribution to security. American business interests were less anxious than security policy makers to commit resources to Japan. This resulted in Japanese inducements designed to attract American loans, such as the establishment of the Asian Development Bank and the issue of dollar-denominated bonds. As these attempts were shrugged off by American businesses seeking more politically stable investment opportunities, Japanese anxiety over the reliability of the American security commitment increased.

The second American aim of improved military burden sharing was sought by linking substantial Japanese rearmament to the prospect of treaty revision. The communiqué explicitly tied the withdrawal of combat U.S. Forces Japan to increases in the Japan Self-Defense Force. Aware of the emerging dominance of Japanese conservatives interested in a long-range strategic partnership, Dulles considered this an auspicious time to achieve both aims. Although rearmament was desired, it was even more important to ensure the continuation of the U.S.–Japan security embrace, which Dulles hoped would sway other free Asian nations to align against Communism.[28]

Japanese negotiators officially recognized no such link between rearmament and treaty revision. To do so would provide the amorphous domestic opposition an opportunity to congeal based on public fears of the apparent remilitarization of Japan. Instead, officials made distinctions between increases in Japanese defense expenditures and the treaty issue of alliance burden sharing.[29] Treaty revision had to be clearly disassociated from the prospect of militarism, despite persistent American pressure to rearm. In this regard, the Kishi Cabinet policy goals for treaty revision were not directed solely at securing a military guarantee from the United States, but also allayed opposition concerns about rearmament. Japanese officials attempted to lessen fears of irresponsible rearmament by placing the treaty within the context of the United Nations Charter, stressing constitutional constraints on Japanese defensive forces, agreeing on prior consultation, and deleting the American internal security role:

Treaty Revision Policy Goals of the Kishi Cabinet[30]

(1) Clearly state the connection between the new Treaty and the UN Charter
(2) Clearly state an American duty to defend Japan and a Japanese duty to stay within constitutional constraints
(3) Obtain Japanese consultation before U.S. troops on bases in Japan are used for other than the defense of Japan
(4) Rid the treaty of an internal security role for American troops
(5) Obtain a limited Treaty term

In spite of the joint communiqué, the distance between American and Japanese negotiating positions did not narrow for another year. By the summer of 1958, Ambassador Douglas MacArthur II (nephew of General MacArthur) sensed severe domestic constraints on Japanese negotiators, and he appealed to Dulles to soften U.S. demands. In June, MacArthur advised Dulles that Japanese domestic opposition to the 1951 Security Treaty was so acute that failure to allow its revision jeopardized Japan's alignment with the United States.[31] Whether the outcome was going to be neutrality, autonomy or outright alignment with another prevailing power, was difficult to say due to the stirred up domestic situation. MacArthur urged that unless Dulles scaled down expectations of Japan's responsibility for mutual defense to include only the home islands (the four main islands, the Ryukyuus and the Bonins), the Japanese would likely interpret the U.S. position as lack of interest in revising the treaty. The apparent strengthening of Kishi's hand in the LDP electoral victory of May 1958, the first general election since the Liberal and Democratic parties had merged, offered an opportunity to support a moderate revision of the treaty. It seemed that only Japanese nationalists and the Eisenhower administration wanted a rearmed, sovereign Japan.

Three months later, Foreign Minister Fujiyama met Secretary of State Dulles with Ambassador MacArthur in Washington, reaffirming the importance of increased bilateral trade, the Communist threat to peace, and setting the schedule for treaty revision negotiations in Tokyo.[32] During the negotiations, which continued for the rest of the year and throughout 1959, U.S. negotiators considered U.S.–Japanese security policy within the broader U.S. foreign policy context, the central problem being how to create Asian bulwarks against communism. For their part, Japanese conservatives were constrained by the substantial opposition minority won in the 1958 election. Radical labor was energized by a communist ideology whose wartime adherents' resistance to Imperial expansion enjoyed a certain amount of credibility relative to many LDP conservatives.[33] The Japan Socialist Party alone controlled 166 of the 467 Diet seats, enough to block constitutional revision needed for rapid rearmament, yet U.S. negotiators demanded rearmament as a precondition to Treaty revision. Moreover, domestic turbulence in 1958–1959 pressured the Japanese negotiating position, virtually prohibiting an increased defense role.

Diffuse Japanese opposition to assuming a military role in the security relationship ended up massing for a time in a series of events, imparting a sense of domestic instability to the negotiating process. In October 1958, Kishi attempted revision of the National Police Bill in order to prevent labor unrest deemed threatening to reindustrialization. This provoked demonstrations the following month — Kishi was accused of marching down the road to militarism. Although Kishi ultimately backed down, his attempt to railroad the bill through the Diet left him vulnerable to opposition critics. Support for treaty revision from rightists, who in July had held the largest convention since the war to oppose the JSP position, was counterproductive. Groups interested in preventing a tilt to the right associated any resurgence of Japanese military power as militarist, hindering realistic discussion of actual Japanese military security needs. Although Ministry of Foreign Affairs officials held numerous public sessions throughout 1959 to argue against the foolishness of neutrality in a bipolar world, Japan's domestic climate continued to favor non-defense priorities.

This was particularly true during October–December, the period of intense bilateral negotiations in Tokyo. In November, for instance, a leading newspaper reported Japan's Air Self-Defense Force and Maritime Self-Defense Force as already being Asia's first and second largest.[34] In December, a large steel strike at Miike mines focused public attention on the vulnerable economy. In the same month, the Supreme Court afforded some relief to negotiators in a ruling on the "Sunakawa Incident," which sanctioned the pursuit of self-defense including "a common defensive system with a specified country."[35]

U.S. treaty negotiators were confronted with these domestic constraints in the form of Japan's "special characteristics" (*tokusei*) of security. In the face of such Japanese domestic unrest, achievement of both DoD and State goals of rapid rearmament and a domestically stable security treaty seemed impossible. The Eisenhower administration's fear of Japanese neutrality and perceived need for Japan to be an anti-communist fortress in the U.S. global chain of containment favored domestic stability over rearmament. A U.S.-aligned Japan, with a future possibility of rearmament, was preferable to risking a strong anti–American neutrality movement associated with premature rearmament.

A New Bargain

The revised Security Treaty's outcome was a modification of the original military-economic quid pro quo, and one that met all five of Kishi's Treaty Revision Policy Goals.[36] Two new characteristics of the 1960 treaty stand out. First, political-military matters were separated from economic affairs (*seikei bunri* [politics-economics separation]), allowing Japan's special military relationship with the United States to be protected from economic disputes. By sanctioning Japanese constitutional constraints on the military and calling for harmony in economic relations, the continuity of each government's different military and economic security priorities was preserved.

The Preamble to the treaty allowed Japan the right to collective self-defense:

> Recognizing that they have the inherent right of individual or collective self-defense as affirmed in the Charter of the United Nations.

Article III formalized Japan's constitutional constraints on developing a capability to resist external attack—

> The Parties, individually and in cooperation with each other, by means of continuous and effective self-help and mutual aid will maintain and develop, subject to their constitutional provisions, their capacities to resist armed attack.

—while Article II reemphasized the need for economic collaboration and conflict reduction, in accordance with the 1953 Treaty of Friendship, Commerce and Navigation that called for reciprocal and open economic relations:

> The Parties will contribute toward the further development of peaceful and friendly relations by strengthening their free institutions, by bringing about a better understanding of the principles upon which these institutions are founded, and by promoting conditions of stability and well being. They will seek to eliminate conflict in their international economic policies and will encourage economic collaboration between them.

The "prior consultation" clause and the Status of Forces Agreement mollified important political issues arising from the American military presence, but left the fundamental question of whether Japan's constitutional constraints applied to USFJ intact. The prior consultation clause in the First Exchange of Notes (19 January 1960) of the treaty gave some assurance that the United States would not entrap Japan in an unwanted military conflict. The broad scope of the clause included U.S. force deployments and changes in equipment:

> Major changes in the deployment into Japan of United States armed forces, major changes in their equipment, and the use of facilities and areas in Japan as bases for military combat operations to be undertaken from Japan other than those under Article V of the said Treaty, shall be subjects of prior consultation with the Government of Japan.

The Status of Forces Agreement (negotiated under Article 6 of the Treaty) settled the question of criminal jurisdiction regarding U.S. servicemen stationed in Japan, put in the limelight by the Girard case.

The second major aspect of the new treaty was incremental movement toward Japanese rearmament, without an explicit promise to rearm. Constitutional constraints on Japanese military capability were emphasized, replacing the more restrictive limitation of "no offensive" weapons capability. In addition, the U.S. internal security role in Japan was deleted. This role now properly fell to the National Police Force, established by a 1950 MacArthur directive as a proto-military force after North Korea's invasion of South Korea. While temporarily conceding American administration of islands over which Japan possessed residual sovereignty (principally Okinawa and the Bonin Islands), Japan gained participation in their joint defense. Now a United Nations member, Japan embraced the American external military guarantee and a Japanese self-defense role within the context of UN principles. As before, Japan promised constitutional rearmament and basing for U.S. forces capable of regional defense in exchange for U.S. external defense (and presumably, nuclear deterrence) for Japan. In the joint communiqué that followed, it was apparent that the American price for treaty revision was a more credible Japanese rearmament plan against the common political-military-economic threat of communism[37]:

> It was agreed that efforts should be made, whenever practicable on a cooperative basis, to establish conditions such that Japan could, as rapidly as possible, assume primary responsibility for the defense of its homeland and be able to contribute to the preservation of international peace and security in the Western Pacific. It was also agreed that when such conditions were brought about it would be appropriate to replace the present security treaty with one of greater mutuality.

A less noticed feature of the revised treaty, but one which was to provide a forum and sub-forums to resolve issues as they came up, was the establishment of bilateral security structure. The Security Consultative Committee (SSC) was established to ensure Ministry of Foreign Affairs and Defense Agency interaction to the U.S. ambassador and the four-star military commander of Pacific Command, usually an admiral. This was not designed as a peer partnership, as would have been the case if the American consultants comprised the Secretary of State and Secretary of Defense. It was also unequal in another way. While MoFA received little more than what it already had — routine access to the U.S. foreign policy line, JDA stood to gain access to a level above that of the in-country commander of U.S. Forces Japan. A subordinate structure to the SSC was also created, the Security Sub-committee, where issues could be defined and discussed in more detail. If military issues could be developed more than political issues, would this activate JDA more than MoFA? This was a subtle imbalance in the treaty's formalized expectation of mutual cooperation and consultation.

The new treaty sharpened the military-economic exchange of security priorities with an explicit American commitment to provide military security against external threats (under Article V). Kishi could present this explicit military security guarantee and the much-touted withdrawal of U.S. combat troops from Japan as proof of an American concession. The United States received continued basing arrangements for U.S. Forces Japan not only for the narrow defense of Japan, but to provide regional military security (under Article VI). Indeed from the U.S. point of view, countering regional threats deterred attack on Japan, and enhanced the capability to defend Japan if needed. Article VI also contained the agreement of burden sharing costs, incorporated in the Status of Forces Agreement (SOFA) where Japan agreed to continue furnishing base facilities and areas.[38] Articles V and VI formed the core bargain: Japan would receive physical security from external attack, and the United States would receive overseas bases:

> Article V. Each Party recognizes that an armed attack against either Party in the territories under the administration of Japan would be dangerous to its own peace and safety and declares that it would act to meet the common danger in accordance with its constitutional provisions and processes.
> Article VI. For the purpose of contributing to the security of Japan and the maintenance of international peace and security in the Far East, the United States of America is granted the use by its land, air, and naval forces of facilities and areas in Japan.

From the dominant Japanese government perspective, domestic economic and political priorities were more important than the American objective of rearmament against communism. Derived from a constitutional power structure written by American occupation authorities, Japanese security policy making occurred within a relatively small group of non-military officials. Among these, the civilian Director General of the Defense Agency ranked decidedly last. Limited to planning budgets and weapons systems within a self-defense role, the institutions that traditionally articulated military priorities of security were subordinated to those dominated by diplomats and economic ministers. The ministries of Foreign Affairs, Finance, and International Trade & Industry dominated security policy making, ensuring economic priorities received precedence over military considerations of security. Prime Minister Kishi had served as wartime Minister of Commerce and Industry in the Tojo cabinet. Foreign Minister Fujiyama was a dominant figure in financial and business circles, having served as President of the Japan and Tokyo Chambers of Commerce and Industry. Finance Minister Sato Eisaku, Kishi's younger brother, had served for 24 years in the railway and transportation ministries before the war. Ishii Mitsujiro, senior factional chief in the LDP and member of the 1960 Treaty signing delegation, served as Minister of Commerce and Industry, and Minister of Transportation.

In the National Defense Council (NDC), the official forum for security policy making, these cabinet ministers stifled rapid military rearmament.

Created in 1956, the NDC was given the role of advising the Cabinet. Its members were the Prime Minister, Deputy Prime Minister, Foreign Minister, Finance Minister, Director of the Economic Planning Agency, and Director General of the Defense Agency.[39] Within this circle of economically minded officials, Defense Agency planners had to present their budgets and propose weapons procurement.

Politically, treaty revision in Japan was driven less by desires to change military burden sharing arrangements than by the need to preserve domestic stability. At least for the conservative Kishi coalition, revision was deemed most important to ease frictions between USFJ and Japanese citizens.[40] Constitutionally, Japan was still in a position of requiring external defense yet constrained in its military force contributions. Since national security priorities were identified as rapid economic growth and the achievement of international competitiveness, requiring protection of certain domestic industries (particularly heavy and chemical industries), the idea that Japan would be a liberal bulwark against communism was rather alien.[41] For the time being at least, the provision of bases in Japan secured an explicit American military commitment, one which could provide a legitimate framework for modest increases in Japanese military power that would not derail economic security priorities.

In the top American forums of national security policy, however, matters of national security continued the traditional state pursuit of military advantage over state activism in economic security. In Cabinet and National Security Council meetings during the Truman administration, strategic export controls against communist states aimed to foster development of allied economies. Rather than deliberately strengthen a future economic competitor, American security policy makers meant to assist Japan's defense capabilities. At the time, U.S. economic predominance seemed natural and unchallenged: American exports accounted for one-fifth of the world total, the balance of international payments was still positive, and real GNP was more than six times greater than the next highest competitor, West Germany.[42] In addition, market competition had dispersed power throughout the U.S. economy, leaving a relatively decentralized structure that frustrated attempts to implement an industrial policy even if one were desired.[43] While Japan and America's European allies resisted U.S. export controls, the need for American credit and economic assistance proved to be too compelling. The Departments of Commerce and Agriculture, representing interests favoring a freer export policy, went along with Defense and State intelligence reports that promoted the need for export controls against the communist threat.

As a result, the development of an active state-led industrial policy aimed at achieving international economic advantage was consistently rejected.[44] Instead, economic controls were justified in terms of developing military forces against illiberal, communist adversaries. The National Stockpile Administration pressed for repeal of the "Buy American" Act of 1933 because it impeded acceleration of defense weapons production by eliminating foreign producers from consideration. The National Security Resources Board recommended a national rubber policy as part of an industrial mobilization policy for wartime. Similar initiatives include the Atomic Energy Commission, Economic Cooperation Program, and shipbuilding expansion. Under Eisenhower in particular, military alliance against a common threat clearly received priority over considerations of national economic advantage. As a result, treaty revision would bring no immediate change to the U.S. policy of containment, whose implementation required U.S. military plans to counter Soviet and Chinese military power, unassisted by Japanese military strength. Given the dim prospect of substantial Japanese rearmament under a revised treaty, there was no military reason to press for treaty revision. Indeed, the Joint Chiefs of Staff preferred the generous terms of the 1951 Security Treaty. Notably, in the 30 recorded NSC meetings that occurred between 4 April 1958 and 13 May 1960 — the period of U.S.–Japan Treaty revision negotiations — the Commerce Department was excluded from attendance in 21. In the 9 meetings where Commerce representatives' comments have been recorded, the Departments of State and Defense consistently rejected U.S. trade interests over military-strategic considerations.[45]

Given these stark national differences in political economic institutions, both sides could reasonably assume they had reached a workable exchange of interests for future security cooperation. Japan's negotiators had finally achieved codification of the economic security goals contained in the 1947 Ashida memoranda and 1950 Japanese draft treaty.[46] American security policy makers felt they had achieved progress toward a military alliance based on a common threat.

Aftermath

As Shigemitsu and Kishi returned to Tokyo to prepare for ratification of the treaty, they encountered a broad front of Japanese officials and politicians who evidently overcame presumed cultural passivity with respect to emoting in public. Shock was expressed at Japan's apparent commitment to greater military force levels and broadened geographic responsibility. Vigorous debate ensued over whether the definition of "Far East" included China and Taiwan or just the northern Philippines and Japan's surrounding waters. As opposition to the joint communiqué mounted, Ministry of Foreign Affairs officials began to move away from the definition used by U.S. authorities.[47] The Director-General of the Defense Agency eventually rejected any Western

Pacific role for the Self-Defense Forces, citing a prohibition against overseas operations in the Defense Agency Law. Socialists, Liberals and Democrats alike accused the Hatoyama cabinet of negotiating an illegal and unconstitutional agreement.[48]

The revised treaty and notes were signed in January of 1960 and ratified by the U.S. Senate and Japanese Diet in April. In Japan, violent anti-treaty demonstrations arose as the Diet deliberated on whether to approve the treaty. The LDP constituted the majority technically needed for passage, and forced the measure through the Diet in a hastily declared session to defeat the opposition. Kishi ordered hundreds of police to forcibly remove Socialist Party members who sat in the Diet's aisles to physically prevent others from voting. During the acrimony, Prime Minister Kishi ended up interpreting the Constitution to renounce Japan's right of collective self-defense mentioned in the treaty. Mass demonstrations against the treaty and Kishi's strong-arm tactics continued to swell.[49] President Eisenhower's planned trip to Tokyo in June was cancelled after his press secretary, in Tokyo as part of the advance party, was surrounded by thousands of protestors. Six million people went out on strike in June. One student was crushed to death and hundreds of students and police injured when protesters stormed the Diet grounds. A right-wing fanatic murdered the head of the Socialist Party, while another rightist injured Kishi in a stabbing attack at his home. The Prime Minister resigned in July.

Japanese negotiators had sought revision for domestic stability, political equality with the United States, and national economic growth, while American security policy makers had focused on rearmament against the communist threat. U.S. fears that Japanese opposition groups on both the left and the right might topple conservative rule, and the conservative coalition's willingness to push treaty revision through the legislature over violent objections by opposition groups, had produced a new treaty that permitted the pursuit of different Japanese and American relative security priorities.

Despite the short-term tumult, the 1960 modification of the original security framework subsequently preserved the complementary exchange of U.S. military security and Japanese economic security, allowing each partner to reap a different mix of political, economic and military benefits from security alliance. The income doubling plan of Prime Minister Ikeda, Kishii's immediate successor, led to a 15-year meteoric rise with an average annual economic growth rate of 10 percent. The security bargain survived American intervention in Vietnam, quiet Japanese profits from it, and strident anti-war protests in both nations. In 1965, as American troops began to pour into Vietnam, Japan recorded its first trade surplus with the United States and the Military Assistance Program ended, replaced by U.S. arms sales to Japan. The security bargain survived the Vietnam conflict, Japan's profits from it, and anti-war protests in both countries. In 1969, President Nixon and Prime Minister Sato bargained over the return of Okinawa. Nixon agreed to return the island to Japanese sovereignty in 1972, and gained Japan's agreement to continue the Security Treaty at its ten-year renewal point in 1970. Sato made an unfulfilled promise to reduce textile exports to the United States. As Japan's trade surplus rose, other trade disputes over automobiles, shipbuilding, steel, and electronics threatened but ultimately failed to derail steady increases in Japan's defense efforts.

In 1970, the Japan Defense Agency began publishing the *Boeihakusho* (White Paper), a smooth annual talker about the practical need for the Japan Self-Defense Forces. Under the strong leadership of Director-General Nakasone Yasuhiro, JDA established five defense industrial objectives, justified by the Mutual Security Treaty's charter for Japan to take primary responsibility for homeland defense and contribute to regional security: (1) maintain a defense industrial base for national security; (2) acquire defense equipment from domestic research and development efforts; (3) enlist civilian industries in armament production; (4) set long-term goals for defense research, development, and production; (5) create competition among domestic defense producers.[50] Nakasone boosted what had been modest increases in defense capability since 1960, doubling defense spending in the first half of the 1970's. Even the apparently insensitive "Nixon Shocks"[51] of 1971 did not destroy the security bargain's resilience. U.S. bases in Japan stayed, Japan's defense spending increased, and Japan's officially economic security priorities appeared to be quite intact. This status set the stage for a major act concerning the meanings of "alliance."

5

Division of Military Roles

As the first formal, tangible mutual military adjustment since the 1960 Security Treaty, the 1981 Reagan-Suzuki communiqué referred to the U.S.-Japan security relationship as an "alliance" (*domei*) based on a practical division of military roles. This news struck most Americans as a rather routine, if not trivial, announcement. After all, the United States and United Nations forces had fought a bitter war in Korea, historically "the dagger pointed at the heart of Japan." U.S. defense contracts with Japanese companies during that conflict had jump-started Japan's devastated economy. The ensuing Mutual Defense Assistance Agreement had steadily expanded Japan Defense Agency and U.S. government ties and improved Japan Self Defense Force interoperability with U.S. forces. Japan's prime ministers through the 1970's had even adopted a domestically risky policy that allowed U.S. warships into Japanese ports without revealing whether or not the vessels possessed nuclear weapons.[1] And there was the fact of 45,000 U.S. forces still serving in Japan under the auspices of the Security Treaty. However, following the release of the communiqué in the Japanese press, the response in Japan could scarcely have been more different. A domestic furor quickly arose over the military connotations of the term *domei*. The joint communiqué which attracted so little interest in the United States triggered the Japanese Foreign Minister's resignation and ultimately toppled the Prime Minister himself. It was as if diplomatic vagueness were necessary to indulge informal differences in security priorities, yet also formally declare bilateral agreement. After the dual resignations, Japan's domestic crisis subsided and security ties deepened with many of the basic attributes of bilateralism: policy discussions, defense planning, military exercises, intelligence sharing, and burden sharing. This chapter first explains the roots of this historic deepening of the military aspect of the security relationship by exploring U.S.–Japan defense policy since the Security Treaty revision, then considers incentives for alliance-building among policy makers.

Historical Development

The shift from Japan's total military dependence in 1960 to a formal division of military roles followed a pattern of persistent U.S. pressure for rearmament and incremental Japanese responses. Over this twenty-year period, U.S. security strategy consistently sought to contain regional communism and enlist Japan in that effort. Eisenhower's new look of massive retaliation gave way to John F. Kennedy's "flexible response,"[2] an upgrade of U.S. conventional forces designed to reduce the reliance on nuclear weapons and help deter limited war. Subsequent U.S. policies to the 1980's were essentially variations on flexible response, and perhaps as well the outcomes of seeking security with an offensive mix of nuclear and non-nuclear technologies.[3] During this time of intense U.S.–Soviet nuclear competition, important events in Japan's defense strategy and force structure laid the foundation for a basic division of military roles. Notably, when the U.S. military guarantee in the sixties and seventies lost credibility, Japanese force levels registered substantial increases. This is evident when one looks at Japanese defense strategy across five phases that correspond to the four defense plans (1956–1959, 1960–1964, 1965–1967, 1970–1975) and the period from 1976 to 1981, when the Defense Agency adopted an annual "rolling budget" approach.

SUMMARY OF JAPANESE DEFENSE STRATEGY

First Defense Plan, 1956–1959

Strategy
- Acquire minimum defensive capability in case of U.S. withdrawal
- Basic Program for National Defense urged gradual increases in defense capability according to national resources
- Importance of ground forces as replacements for withdrawing U.S. troops
- Traditional Imperial Army concept of land warfare stressed
- Ashida Memoranda implemented Japan internal role and U.S. external role

Force Structure
- Ground Self-Defense Force expanded from 50,000 police reserves to 180,000 troops

- Air Self-Defense Force and Maritime Self-Defense Force created; increasing total JSDF authorized from 197,000 to 231,000 members

International Events
- USFJ troop reduction from 200,000 to 90,000
- War in Korea
- China shells Quemoy and Matsu Islands

Second Defense Plan, 1960–1964

Strategy
- Bilateral Security Treaty with U.S. announced as "strategically defensive in nature"
- Reliance on U.S. forces for offensive capabilities
- JSDF role announced for first time as "coping with aggression using conventional weapons on a scale smaller than localized warfare"
- Possibility of delay in support from U.S. forces first publicly acknowledged

Force Structure
- Acquisition of missile capability
- Acquistion of air defense capability
- Domestic production of top-of-the-line McDonnell-Douglas F-4 fighter
- JSDF authorization increased to 246,000 members

International Events
- North Korea treaties with China and Soviet Union
- Bilateral Security Treaty with U.S. is revised
- Soviet Union launches first intercontinental ballistic missile and Sputnik spacecraft

Third Defense Plan, 1965–1969

Strategy
- Deterrence is added to defense as a JSDF role
- "Self-reliance" within the U.S. security guarantee is announced
- Joint Defense Council begins studies on how to conduct an "autonomous defense"

Force Structure
- Qualitative improvements of submarine and air defenses
- All essential military training programs become "self-contained" (JSDF-run)
- JSDF authorization increased to 258,000 members

International Events
- Soviet Union military buildup accelerates in the Far East
- Public criticism of Japan free-riding on U.S. military guarantee by members of Congress
- China tests first nuclear bomb and missile

Fourth Defense Plan, 1970–1975

Strategy
- "Autonomous posture" with U.S. guarantee is announced
- U.S. role announced as supporting JSDF external security role
- Defense funding explicitly tied to the state of the national economy

Force Structure
- Updated main battle tanks and aircraft
- JSDF authorization increased to 263,000 members

International Events
- U.S. withdraws troops from Vietnam
- Nixon Doctrine
- Regional tensions arise from North Korean shootdown of U.S. reconnaissance aircraft (EC-121) and seizure of *USS Pueblo*

1976–1981: Annualized Defense Planning

Strategy
- 1976 National Defense Program Outline (NDPO) identifies long-term force structure goals and moves to annual budgeting of defense resources
- Five assumptions that refer to a stable international environment are identified as premises for NDPO force structure
- Soviet Union military capabilities acknowledged for the first time in the Defense Agency's White Paper as a "potential threat"
- 1980 *Report on National Security* (directed by Prime Minister Ohira) seeks Japan's economic security, energy security, food security, and stability as a strategic goal
- 1981 agreement with the U.S. establishes Japan's responsibility to defend sea lanes of communication out to 1000 miles from Japan's shores

Force Structure
- Japan's 36 destroyers and 18 frigates compare favorably with U.S. Pacific Command Seventh Fleet's 29 destroyers and 47 frigates (responsible for both Pacific and Indian Oceans) and the Soviet Union Pacific Fleet's 13 destroyers and 22 frigates.

- U.S.–made over-the-horizon radar and AEGIS-equipped cruisers expand Japan's defensive perimeter
- JSDF authorization increased to 268,000 members

International Events
- Soviet defector pilot lands his MiG-25 at Hakodate Airfield
- President Carter announces intention to withdraw all ground troops from South Korea
- Soviet Union military construction and buildup in the Northern Territories
- Soviet Union tactical aircraft increase to 2,210 as U.S. aircraft are reduced by 400

Observing official strategy between these time periods, increases in stated objectives occurred after events that put the U.S. security guarantee into question. Increases in Japan's announced strategy are: acquiring a basic level for internal security // minimum defensive capability // conventional localized warfare // self-reliant defense // autonomous defense posture // comprehensive security. Events which one would expect to either have softened the U.S. security guarantee or threatened Japan's security during this trend of expanding strategic goals are: the Korean War // the U.S. partial withdrawal from Japan // the USSR buildup in Asia // the PRC's acquisition of nuclear capability // the U.S. withdrawal from Viet Nam // the Nixon Doctrine // President Carter's announced troop withdrawal from Korea // U.S. pressures to rearm. The primary territorial threat identified by Japanese defense officials at the time, whether due to estimates of enemy air, naval, ground and amphibious capabilities, or because of the continued seizure of Japan's Northern Territories since the end of the Pacific War, was the Soviet Union.

Changes in force structure basically involved incremental increases in JSDF capability. The ground forces' case for budget increases was the least controversial arm of the Self-Defense Force services to justify, even though it was predicated on the least likely threat of a small-scale Soviet invasion. Soviet capabilities and its occupation of the Northern Territories seemed to require a robust Japanese infantry and armor force in northern Japan. If Japan's northernmost main island were not defensible during a crisis, JMSDF and JASDF operations would be hampered at the onset of hostilities. A strong ground presence was not only needed for in-place defense, but also to deter other Soviet actions or policy intimidation. A solid base of ground operations in Hokkaido would increase the potential freedom of action for joint ground, maritime, and air operations. In 1960, however, the maritime force fielded only nine major combatant ships, and had been entirely dependent on U.S. naval power for external defense against a serious competitor. By 1980, MSDF surface forces comprised 32 Naruna class 4700-ton destroyers, 32 Nachikaze class 3850-ton destroyers, and 25 Chikugo class 1870-ton escort ships (1870-ton). In addition, 20 1850-ton submarines, 14 mine-sweepers, and 14 military transport ships were dramatic increases in naval capability which could work with U.S. naval forces in an external defense role. Japan's naval forces had, through incremental acquisitions and force improvements over the years, acquired an offensive capability required for credible defense. An offensive capability could be construed as the kind of "war potential of any kind" expressly prohibited by the Constitution of Japan. For political and constitutional reasons therefore, the capability to inflict damage was explained and defended by the Japan Defense Agency as one of tactical employment within a strategically defensive posture. That is, the intent of having offensive capability was to execute it only after an attack on Japan. In the event of an all out attack on Japan, however, the MSDF could and would attack enemy forces outside Japan's national boundaries to defend itself.[4] However, trusting the JSDF to refrain from using its capability for ultimately offensive purposes was evidently too idealistic for many constitutional theorists.

Practically speaking, the gap between Japan's strategic rhetoric and self-defense force reality was substantial. Even assuming that mid-term defense plans were completely attained, one study estimated the JSDF shortfall to carry out its self-defense mission as: 300 F-15s, 8–10 AWACS, 10–14 KC-10s, 60 assorted fighter aircraft, 3–7 surface-to-air missile groups, 10–12 attack submarines, 20 destroyers and 130 P-3Cs.[5] Other deficiencies included inadequate training, low ammunition stores, lack of a credible naval anti-aircraft capability (only 5 of 36 destroyers possessed AA missile systems), and persistent difficulties in meeting recruitment goals.[6]

Against this historical backdrop, a number of domestic and bilateral concerns faced Japanese and American policy makers interested in rearming Japan for self-defense. Given the continued sensitivity of exceeding the Occupation Constitution's vows, support had been building within the Suzuki administration for increasing official development aid (ODA) as a way to contribute non-militarily to the alliance. Since 1960, ODA as percentage of GNP had remained relatively constant[7]:

TABLE 5.1—JAPAN'S NET OFFICIAL DEVELOPMENT ASSISTANCE

1960	1965	1970	1975	1980	1985
.24	.28	.23	.23	.26	.29

However, Japan's ODA was part of a growing foreign aid program that had been under sharp American and European criticism for being a Japan Export-Import Bank-directed export promotion campaign. By 1980, Japan's foreign aid had increased exponentially from $246 million in 1960 to $1.6 billion (later rising to $4.7 billion in 1987). While much of Japanese foreign aid remained tied or limited tied aid,[8] aid extended to debt-ridden, pro–Western "conflict border" countries did provide a way to contribute non-militarily to global and regional stability.

In the 1970s, spurred by strong leadership from Prime Minister Sato (1964–72) and Director-General Nakasone (1970–72), Defense Agency officials recognized that technological breakthroughs could enable Japan to defend more than just territorial and coastal areas.[9] Defense of the littorals was inadequate to the task of securing freedom of transit along Japan's vital sea lanes of communication (SLOCs). Advantages in military technology were instrumental in securing and defending SLOCs from a quantitatively superior opponent such as the Soviet Union. Carrying out the primary mission of the Maritime Self-Defense Force, which was to secure the safety of sea lanes in the waters surrounding Japan,[10] meant at least having the capability during conflict to prevent Soviet naval forces from passing through the only three openings from the Sea of Japan to the Pacific Ocean. Two of the three Soviet Pacific Fleet naval bases, Vladivostok (the headquarters of the Far Eastern Fleet) and Sovetskaya Gavan, are located in the Sea of Japan at the end of the Trans-Siberian and Baikal Amur Mainline railroads respectively, both over 5000 miles to the far east from Moscow. The third, Petropavlosk, on the southeast tip of Kamchatka Peninsula, is even more isolated due to the absence of a railroad connecting it to the Eurasian landmass. Maritime access, therefore, is critical to the operation of these remote power projection hubs. However, Vladivostok is the only warm water Pacific port. The only way to conduct maritime operations in and out of Vladivostok is through one of Japan's three straits: the Soya Strait between Hokkaido and Sakhalin, the Tsugaru Strait between Honshu and Hokkaido, and the Tsushima Strait between South Korea and Japan. Japan's straits are the gates which could enclose the Soviet Far Eastern Fleet.

Prior to the advent of sophisticated detection devices, guided cruise and air-surface missiles, the isolation and containment of Soviet naval forces in the Sea of Japan required the stationing around Japan of a substantial force of submarines, mining and patrolling ships, and aircraft. But the increased range and lethality of naval weapons systems presented a challenge to distance-based definitions of "defense." Unless the JMSDF could counter enemy surface combatants who had the capability to threaten hostile action at increasing ranges, even an initial defense of Japan (prior to promised American assistance) was not possible. Advances in military technology provided a way to preserve an ability to defend the home islands. Systems such as the SOSUS (Sonar Ocean Surveillance Underwater System), OTH-backscatter radar, Mitsubishi ASM-1, Harpoon surface-surface missile, and the Tomahawk submarine-launched cruise missile made it possible to control ocean transit through the Sea of Japan. Moreover, if a technological edge could be maintained over the Soviet Pacific Fleet, Japan's defense could be accomplished with markedly reduced numbers of surface combatants. This freed existing Maritime Self-Defense Force assets for use in the SLOC mission, a zone of operations containing the sea routes upon which Japan depends for energy sources. Economic security for *shimaguni* (island nation) Japan was just as critical in 1980 as in was prior to the Pacific War. In the early 1980s, imports comprised 98 percent of oil and natural gas (mainly from Persian Gulf states, Indonesia), 90 percent of minerals (Australia, South Africa, Southeast Asia, Brazil), and 77 percent of coal resources (Australia, North America, India).[11]

Once military technological advances had extended the area of secure operations required for credible defense, dividing the roles of maintaining SLOC security between U.S. naval forces and the JMSDF became more operationally compelling. The larger the required zone of security became, the more sense it made to divide it. The tipping point occurred in 1978. By then, sea lane defense out to 1000 miles was being quietly planned for (publicly "studied") in the Maritime Self Defense Force, and joint, over-the-horizon naval practice maneuvers were being conducted.[12] The planning for an increase in defense responsibilities involved adjustments in the related details of how to operate in an increased area. The larger geographic area of operations demanded more coordination and control of the many individual choices and decision points available to the participants. This dictated more sharing of information through intelligence collection and processing, and actually practicing the process with joint training and exercises. This in turn required a higher level of interoperability among U.S. and Japanese weapon systems. From an allied strategic perspective, a credible Self-Defense Force capability to help defend the SLOC zone within 1000 miles of Japan could allow some U.S. naval assets to be diverted to the Indian Ocean. There, Japan's interest in maintaining an oil lifeline from the Persian Gulf coincided with longstanding U.S. policy in maintaining open access to it.

Notwithstanding these military strategic considerations, political incentives for expanding JSDF military capabilities depended on continued absolute growth of the Japanese economy. Japan's shift in the mid–60s from international debtor to creditor status did not produce relative increases in Japanese defense outlays, despite earlier Occupation era promises to rearm "as soon as economic conditions permit." The relative importance of economic over military security priorities held firm even as Japanese fiscal policies loosened. While the national debt rose from 3.5 percent of government outlays in 1970 to 12.5 percent in 1980, defense expenditures as a percentage of government outlays actually decreased from 7.2 percent to 5.2 percent in the same period.[13] Despite this restraint, overall economic growth supported absolute increases in defense expenditures, the 1975 defense budget being a prime example. Although it was at .84 percent of GNP one of the lowest defense allocations in relative terms, it was an absolute increase over the previous year by the largest margin in the postwar period — 21.4 percent. Although Japan's 1 percent of GNP defense spending average was substantially less than the 1980 U.S. 6 percent figure or NATO average of 3.3 percent, the overall growth of the Japanese economy consistently sustained annual increases greater than 5 percent.[14] By 1980, Japan's defense incrementalism yielded defense spending levels that had driven it to the eighth highest in the world.

Operating within this economic context of sustained growth were several political incentives embedded throughout the Japanese government that supported the SLOC mission. Clearly, a new security role for Japan's Self-Defense Force could help elevate the JSDF position in Japan's weapons acquisition process. A military service branch typically begins the formal acquisition process by identifying an operational deficiency or operational requirement needed to perform a role or mission. From this point on, Defense Agency officials from the Technical Research and Development Institute, and Finance and Equipment Bureaus engage more powerful representatives of military-industrial contractors, MITI, and the National Defense Council (*Anpo Kaigi*). Within the Defense Council, Ministry of Finance officials play their controlling role in exacting fiscal discipline. The JSDF's new SLOC role would provide the maritime and air force (and to a lesser extent, the ground force) a common legitimate mission area in which to identify new operational needs and shortfalls. This was an important consideration given the progressively tight defense budgetary environment which saw defense expenditures erode from 10 percent of government outlays in 1960 to 7.2 percent in 1970, then to 5.2 percent in 1980. In such a competitive funding arena, deep-rooted intraservice rivalries were intensified, which for the moment undercut the development of integrated, joint planning among the three main self-defense forces. However, at least the staking out of a politically acceptable mission area could help justify the acquisition of qualitatively improved weapons systems across a spectrum of interdependent military functions. Jointness could come later.

In addition to this bureaucratic push for a SLOC mission, two institutional changes helped Defense Agency officials increase expenditures during this period of fragmented opposition to LDP rule: the 1976 National Defense Program Outline, and the 1978 Guidelines for Japan–U.S. Defense Cooperation.[15] The 1976 NDPO (*Taiko*) ended the succession of defense buildup plans and instead outlined for the foreseeable future the desired size and composition of the Self-

Defense Force. By providing a concrete ceiling for defense capability, the NDPO politically enabled those forces to be programmed. The chief constraint now was how long it would take to do so (the defense buildup under the NDPO was fully achieved in Japan Fiscal Year 1991). A political laxative to facilitate the ensuing defense buildup was added in November 1976, when the government announced that annual defense-related expenditures would be limited to .1 percent of the GNP. This shrewd policy constraint softened the concerns of both antimilitarist skeptics on the left and economic security stakeholders on the right. In addition, a Self-Defense Force option for future expansion was put in place by explicitly linking force levels to "conditions in the international environment," which through the 1970s comprised annual Soviet defense spending increases of 5 percent in real terms. By 1976, Soviet Far East ground forces had grown to 31 divisions (300,000 troops), 2,030 combat aircraft and 755 naval vessels (1.25 million tons). Two years later, Defense Agency and U.S. officials expressed mutual concern over a continual, comprehensive Soviet buildup that included increases in the number of theater intermediate-range nuclear missiles (SS-20s), deployment of third-generation fighters (MIG-23, MIG-27 and SU-24), replacement of conventional with nuclear submarines, development of long-range bombers with improved capabilities to penetrate air defenses (TU-22M Backfire), and the stationing of a division of ground forces on the disputed islands of Etorofu, Kunashiri, and Shikotan. New Soviet Pacific Fleet surface combatants included 2 aircraft carriers, 14 missile cruisers and 13 destroyers which replaced conventionally equipped cruisers and destroyers.

Facing this strategic environment was the Defense Cooperation Committee of the U.S.–Japan Security Consultative Committee, an institution created by an exchange of notes attached to the 1960 Treaty of Mutual Cooperation and Security. This group's charter was to reinforce the previously stated goal of increased U.S.–Japan defense cooperation in case of an attack on Japan, which it did by drafting the 1978 Guidelines for Japan–U.S. Defense Cooperation. This agreement explicitly encouraged expanded joint planning and operations, exchanges of intelligence data, coordination of logistical support activities, and the planning of an emergency coordination center. The Guidelines also afforded the Defense Agency stronger legal grounds upon which to conduct joint "studies," the equivalent of American war plans. Japanese studies and American operations plans grew into joint planning projects that revised old concepts of operations and generated new contingency plans. Several Defense Agency officials have asserted that the establishment of the Guidelines in 1978 was the key event that enabled the actual sharing of roles and missions, later formalized in the 1981 joint communiqué.[16]

On the U.S. side, the apparent Japanese commitment to assume an external military role and increase financial compensation to USFJ was lauded as tangible proof of an allied approach to countering a Soviet threat. Sharing the military and economic burdens of the defense of Japan was certainly more realistic than the constitutionally-encouraged Japanese assumption that JSDF capability alone could defend against even a limited invasion. Since the original Japanese rearmament promise in the 1954 security treaty (*Japan will increasingly assume responsibility for its own defense ... always avoiding any armament which could be an offensive threat*) followed by a re-promise in the revised treaty of 1960 (*The Parties ... will maintain and develop, subject to their constitutional provisions, their capacities to resist armed attack*), American security policy makers sought ways to empower Japan to contribute to military alliance activities in light of increased Japanese economic ability, despite persistent domestic political constraints on Self-Defense Force activities. Economically, the decade since Treaty Revision was the period of Japan's historically unprecedented high economic growth.[17] In 1960, Japan's GNP totaled less than one-tenth that of the United States, two-way trade amounted to little more than $2 billion, and the U.S. enjoyed both trade and federal budget surpluses. The chief constraint to Japanese economic growth had been its negative international balance of payments, with Japan in 1960 still recompensing some $600 million in GARIOA (Government Appropriation for Relief in Occupied Areas) to the United States.

By 1980, Japanese GNP had grown to nearly 40 percent of U.S. GNP. By then too, U.S. military technology transfer procedures had been loosened to the level accorded NATO allies — partners who in contrast to Japan are bound by a reciprocal defense commitment toward the United States. Rather than serving as a common source of military commitment, reciprocity of another type was a cause of concern among U.S. and Japanese defense officials. A chief common fear was that trade disputes might derail positive military developments in the security relationship. Recent textiles and other light industrial exports to the United States had triggered protectionist trade policies in both countries. In contrast to deep and chronic American trade and budget deficits, Japanese export increases had registered surpluses for 13 consecutive years. Japan's $11.6 billion bilateral trade surplus and $28.3 billion current account surplus constituted record levels on the way to new highs. At the same time, economic ties with the United States multiplied in terms of trade, mutual direct investment, international lending, and capital flows, reinforcing the need for close security relations.

U.S. leaders also came to believe that the United States had neglected adequate levels of military spending while Soviet defense expenditures had risen quite rapidly. The Nixon Doctrine, political and economic effects of the Vietnam War, and the announced Carter troop withdrawal from South Korea seemed to define an American response of foreign policy retrenchment. Eager to reverse this trend, Secretary of Defense Weinberger was anxious to find a better way to prevent free-riding by America's allies against the common threat. The art of political judgment with regard to allied domestic constraints mattered. His predecessor's public ridicule of low Japanese defense expenditures had soured relations near the end of the Carter administration. So, the Reagan administration shifted tactics from demanding specific percentages of GNP to one of establishing a division of roles and missions. By emphasizing qualitative rather than quantitative improvement in military capability to perform agreed upon roles and missions, DoD officials hoped that increased Japanese defense expenditures would be more forthcoming.[18]

The decision to press the Japanese to increase financial support for U.S. forces in Japan contrasted with American reluctance during the 1960 agreement, which had deleted even the minimal Japanese compensation extended to the United States under the administrative agreement of the 1951 Security Treaty. By 1978, after a declining dollar dramatically increased yen-based U.S. labor costs in Japan, the Japanese government had begun to assume the costs of several categories of allowances for Japanese workers on USFJ bases. This totaled $31 million, even though Article 24 of the SOFA assigns these costs as an American responsibility.[19]

In 1980, Prime Minister Ohira Masayoshi died of a heart attack during a reelection campaign prompted by a vote of no-confidence. His protégé, Suzuki Zenko, was quickly chosen as the LDP replacement candidate and won handily in a sympathy vote-aided landslide under the consensus-building banner, "the politics of harmony." Suzuki was a loyal founding member of the LDP and recurrent chairman of its executive council. A diplomatic moderate well connected to the fisheries industry, Suzuki was largely unfamiliar with foreign policy issues and particularly so with respect to defense matters. His stances on security were passive, shaped by the countervailing pressures of the military-economic security bargain. Realistic Japanese self-defense, even under an American strategic umbrella, required increasing JSDF capability to meet or stay ahead of the improvements in Soviet military forces. Due to Japan's self-defense constraints, increased economic contributions were natural offsets for the American military guarantee, an umbrella which based on offensive capabilities. Japanese economic burden sharing was the path of least resistance during a time of high Japanese economic growth. After all, the Occupation Constitution clearly prohibited war potential of any kind. Thus, quite logically on the eve of departing for Washington in May 1981, Suzuki publicly rejected the idea of an anti–Soviet military buildup and threatened trade retaliation should the U.S. Congress pass protectionist legislation.[20]

A New Bargain

In general terms, the lengthy May 8th communiqué declared broad agreement between President Reagan and Prime Minister Suzuki:

5. Division of Military Roles 103

... pledged that they would work closely together in pursuit of world peace and prosperity ... recognizing that the alliance between the United States and Japan is built on their shared values of democracy and liberty....

... reaffirmed their position that the Soviet intervention in Afghanistan cannot be condoned ... the problems of Poland should be resolved by the Polish people themselves....

... agreed to continue respectively to expand cooperative ties with the People's Republic of China;

- to promote the maintenance of peace on the Korean peninsula as important for peace and security in East Asia, including Japan;

- to continue their cooperation in support of the solidarity of ASEAN [Association of Southeast Asian Nations] and its quest for greater resilience and development of its members.

... agreed that an early and comprehensive political settlement of the Kampuchea problem, including the withdrawal of foreign forces ... affirmed that the maintenance of peace and security in the Middle East, *particularly* in the Gulf region, is highly important ... the determined efforts of the United States in the face of fragile security conditions in the region contribute to restoring stability, and that many countries, including Japan, are benefiting from them.

... recognized the role that international efforts toward genuine arms control and disarmament should play in advancing world peace and stability....

... that all Western industrialized democracies need to make greater efforts in the area of defense, world economic improvement, economic cooperation with the third world, and mutually supportive diplomatic initiatives.

... reaffirmed their belief that the U.S.–Japan Treaty of Mutual Cooperation and Security is the foundation of peace and stability in the Far East and the defense of Japan ... acknowledged the desirability of an appropriate division of roles ... recognized their common interest in contributing to the defense of Japan.

... agreed upon the importance of the relationship between the industrialized countries and the developing countries ... affirmed that political, economic, and social stability of developing countries is indispensable for the maintenance of peace and stability of the world.

... expressed their concern about the rising pressure toward protectionism ... determined to continue their efforts to maintain and strengthen free and open trade.

... expressed satisfaction with the close bilateral economic relationship ... contribute to the long term development of the United States–Japan economic relations.

... reaffirmed the need for the two countries to make further efforts, together with other industrialized countries, in such fields as increase of energy production, promotion of development and use of alternative energy sources, and conservation of energy.

reaffirmed the need to promote international efforts ... preventing the spread of nuclear weapons ... cooperate further in promoting the peaceful uses of nuclear energy.

In addition to these pleasant sounding formal areas of agreement, Prime Minister Suzuki expressed the problematic desire to contribute to global security within Japan's Constitutional constraints by attempting to increase Self-Defense Force capabilities and financial compensation for USFJ expenses:

> stated his view that it is important for the industrialized democracies to have a shared recognition of the various political, military and economic problems of the world and to cope with them in a consistent manner in order comprehensively to provide for the security of the West as a whole.

> stated that Japan, on its own initiative and in accordance with its Constitution and basic defense policy, will seek to make even greater for improving its defense capabilities in Japanese territories and in its surrounding seas and airspace, and for further alleviating the financial burden of U.S. forces in Japan.

In some ways, the 1981 agreement appeared to leave the 1960 security framework intact. The American external security guarantee remained credible through Japanese military basing arrangements. There still existed no reciprocal allied obligation on the part of Japan to support the United States in case of attack. No explicit Japanese commitment to rearm against a common military threat was stated or evidently forthcoming. Also unaltered by the 1981 agreement were the relative military and economic security priorities codified in the 1960 Treaty. These differences were reinforced by references to the Basic Policy for National Defense (1957) and Constitution, as well as through the continued policy of separating military affairs from economic issues. Finally, Japanese military force levels remained constrained by constitutional interpretation, albeit in the form of new policy guidelines such as Prime Minister Miki administration's 1 percent of GNP cap on military expenditures "for the interim,"[21] and the problematic "no offensive weapons" limitation.

Despite these continuities, the 1981 security framework contained important changes. For the first time, state officials publicly announced an expansion of military relations, referring to the U.S.–Japan security relationship as an "alliance" based on a division of roles. The United States military no longer was the sole provider of Japan's external security, as the Self-Defense Forces committed to re-arming up to the level it would take to secure sea lanes of communication (SLOCs) 1000 miles out from Tokyo. The operational details of this commitment reveal its great extent. Bilateral military relations and Japanese military capability had expanded across a wide range of activities such as planning for a larger defensive zone; intensified coordination and control; joint intelligence collection; frequent joint training in command and operational exercises; and greater allied standardization[22] through modern weapons acquisition.

Employing Japanese forces to defend the sea lanes involved a significant expansion of the geographic area of responsibility, one that exceeded the 1960 division of labor. In addition to the greater distance from Japanese coastal waters to endpoints 1000 miles away, the sea lane area became formally defined (publicized in the 1983 Defense White Paper) as a zone extending from Tokyo to Guam to the Taiwan Straits and to Osaka.

Although the term "sea lanes" was used to describe the operational need to secure freedom of transit from Japan toward Guam, and from Japan toward the Philippines, the military usefulness of securing a narrow sea lane, in which planners are apparently supposed to assume an adversary will conveniently place his forces, is limited. At a minimum, highly traveled ocean routes are monitored and secured with the help of in-place intelligence and sensor systems. But for realistic defense, a commitment to secure sea lanes 1000 miles out from Japan requires that U.S. and Japanese naval forces closely coordinate and share several critical patrol, defense, detection and attack functions within a broad area of ocean. Anti-submarine warfare (ASW), mine-laying and minesweeping, naval blockading, and air defense missions must be coordinated closely. Typical ranges of potential adversary weapons systems easily encompass the JMSDF area of operations: Sovremenny-class destroyer — 14,000 miles, Tu-22 Backfire bomber — 2400-mile combat radius, and multiple classes of nuclear attack and ballistic missile submarines — unlimited range. Countering these types of threats requires a highly intelligence-driven environment where the need for close information-sharing by U.S. and Japanese forces increases as the number and capabilities of threats increase.[23]

The 1981 agreement changed the economic dimension of the 1960 security bargain in two major areas. First, Japanese ODA to countries deemed strategically important to both allies was expanded, part of an overall increase in foreign aid.[24] The significance of the change in Japanese ODA was more one of direction than amount. Although Prime Minister Suzuki pledged an ODA doubling program to Organization for Economic Cooperation and Development (OECD) members in January 1981, only incremental increases ensued. Second, host nation support payments and programs benefiting U.S. forces in Japan were to be increased. In 1981, the stationing costs of USFJ, which includes personnel, operations and maintenance, bulk petroleum, lubricants and military construction, totaled $3.16 billion, of which Japan assumed 28 percent. Both strategically-directed foreign aid and increased offset payments were intended to increase Japanese non-military contributions for the American military guarantee.

The political packaging of this exchange, however, involved the separation of political-military affairs from economic issues, or *sei iki* ("sacred area").[25] Both national leaders sought to create protected, sacred policy space for defense issues in order to prevent trade disputes from disrupting stable military cooperation. Prime Minister Suzuki obtained President Reagan's recognition of the need to be consulted on broad matters of vital interest, specifically including trade and political issues. This overall agreement, negotiators hoped, would guide U.S.–Japan security relations into the next century.

Aftermath

Soon after its signing, different American and Japanese government versions of what was meant by the term "alliance" generated public uncertainty over what the U.S.–Japan security cooperation was all about. On 13 May, Prime Minister Suzuki assured the Diet that the term "alliance" had no military meaning.[26] Instead, alliance was said to simply refer more broadly to friendly relations between two democracies, with Japan's security role being confined to political and economic activities. Suzuki immediately came under fire from both within the government and the opposition.[27] The Ministry of Foreign Affairs, which drafted the Japanese version of the communiqué, criticized Suzuki's denial that the alliance had any military meaning. Senior LDP members similarly maligned the notion that the agreement had no military context because LDP policy panels had consistently pronounced the 1960 Treaty of Mutual Cooperation and Security as the basis of U.S.–Japan relations. Socialist Party and Communist Party Diet members voiced alarm over the military implications of "alliance," charging that Suzuki had in fact made a commitment to greater defense cooperation. Two days later, Foreign Minister Ito attempted to clarify the government's position, elaborating that alliance meant "nothing more than the political, economic, and cultural relationship between our two nations being reinforced with the existing framework."[28] Subsequent explanations stressed "what the Prime Minister meant to say"—alliance included no *new* military meaning outside the existing context of U.S.–Japan security relations.

Within the week, Ito resigned. The State Department declared this an internal Japanese matter, with no impact on U.S.–Japan security relations. This prediction proved to be accurate. On May 19th, after former U.S. Ambassador to Japan Edwin Reischauer asserted that American nuclear weapons had transited Japanese territory in the 1950s and 1960s, the alliance's political process of increased burden sharing went on unabated.[29] On May 31st, the Japan–U.S. Working Level Meeting on Security met as scheduled in Honolulu, discussing how to improve combined planning and operations, as well as the coordination of bureaucratic processes to procure military hardware needed for SLOC defense. That October saw the first joint communications training and command post exercises held. Joint staff councils continued on an annual basis, involving 6000 Japanese and 7000 American participants in 1986.[30] Japanese participation in the largest exercise, the biannual RIMPAC

(Rim of the Pacific) exercise, began with 2 destroyers and 8 P-2J aircraft in 1980, expanded to include an entire escort flotilla of 9 surface combatants and at least 1 submarine. Major joint naval exercises around Japan, typically lasting one to two weeks each, have averaged 5 a year since 1981. In the same period, major USAF-ASDF exercises have averaged 13 a year.[31]

Japanese defense forces began to close the gap in the area of SLOC security with the acquisition of over-the-horizon radar, AEGIS-equipped cruisers, and other systems whose co-production under license had been first planned during the Defense Agency's short two Nakasone years. Some security experts criticized these acquisitions as going well beyond the National Defense Program Outline's policy of building a capability to "repel limited and small scale aggression."[32] But by the beginning of 1983, the Nakasone era of even closer U.S.–Japan military cooperation was well under way. The Prime Minister announced Japan as announced as part of the Western alliance, an "unsinkable aircraft carrier." This reference to an offensive power projection platform was an interesting analogy to a Churchillian image of Britain's role during World War II, but it was not appreciated by Japan's neighbors.

The bureaucratic means for sustaining Japan's newly acquired SLOC role had been established and set in motion. Sea lane defense requires countering threats from submarines, aircraft and surface combatants, thereby providing each service branch an opportunity to participate in the mission. Technological advances can be accelerated by co production arrangements that breed new missions and help justify modifications of weapon systems for those missions.[33] Indeed, the upgrading of an existing system to achieve a new capability tends to be a less controversial and lower profile than justifying a new weapon. As the effective range of enemy weapons systems and detection increases, so does the required defensive zone. For instance, in order to provide fleet defense against hostile aircraft with look down/shoot down radar and electro-optics weapons delivery capability (precision-guided munitions), the ship-based AEGIS phased array radar system detects, tracks and directs the destruction of aircraft hundreds of miles away. The Mitsubishi Heavy Industries SSM-1 cruise missile gives even the Ground Self-Defense Force a role in SLOC security. In the judgment of one naval officer, the combination of the SSM-1 and mining capability against submarines could "drastically alter the balance of power in the Far East."[34] Subsequent Defense White Papers have emphasized acquisition and co-production of numerous weapons systems for air defense and SLOC protection.[35]

Not unexpectedly, the growth rate of Japanese defense spending as a percentage of GNP experienced steady increases up to 1988, the starting point for the FS-X case analyzed in the next chapter[36]:

TABLE 5.3 — JAPAN DEFENSE SPENDING, 1980S

Year	81	82	83	84	85	86	87	88	89
Defense expenditures/ GDP	.91	.93	.98	.99	.997	.993	1.004	1.013	.997
Growth Rate	5.1	5.2	5.5	5.8	5.9	6.2	6.5	6.5	6.1

Since the 1981 agreement, Japan's compensation for U.S. Forces Japan in burden sharing arrangements has also increased. Although unsympathetic Japanese negotiators were able to reject American requests for increases in the labor cost sharing portion of the *omoiyari yosan* ("sympathy budget") in 1980, 1981, 1982, and 1984, by 1987 Japanese contributions had risen to 37 percent of a total $5.8 billion.[37] The re-engineered formula for cooperation appeared to work. In 1984, the Japan Defense Agency funded construction of facilities to house a USAF F-16 fighter wing (40–50 aircraft) at Misawa Air Base in Aomori Prefecture.[38] In 1986, Japan's Chief Cabinet Secretary announced the government's intention to participate in Strategic Defense Initiative research, and an agreement was concluded the following year. Later in 1990, agreement was reached on a 50 percent cost sharing plan — by far the most generous overseas cost sharing scheme of all U.S. allies.[39] At the time, U.S. officials considered this to be an approximate ceiling for host nation support, due to concern over the potential leverage Japanese politicians could gain if the 50 percent mark were surpassed. Despite this concern, in 1995 the Japanese government began paying all appropriate yen-based costs of the 47,000 U.S. troops in Japan ($4 billion), and 75 percent of U.S. stationing costs (excluding salaries of U.S. personnel). It became less expensive to run military operations out of Japan than from the United States.[40]

In addition to military burden sharing, Japan's ODA increased as a percentage of GNP to countries deemed strategically important as raw material/ energy sources or pro–Western regional stabilizers, such as Pakistan, Egypt, Turkey, and the Philippines. By 1986, Japan's ODA to those states compared favorably with American official disbursements, with the exception of Egypt (with Israel, the largest recipient of U.S. aid).[41] Other strategic areas include Kenya, Zimbabwe, Sudan, Jordan, Oman, and Jamaica — although for political reasons, this aid has not been characterized as strategic in intent.

Although the 1981 agreement overcame some political constraints to military cooperation and burden sharing arrangements, it also pried open new areas for disagreement. The expanded Japanese military role severely tested and stretched the "no war potential" interpretation of the Peace Constitution, while a tightened military-economic quid pro quo sought to reinforce and stabilize the old security framework. Together these pressures highlighted the uncertainty of the meaning of the security relationship. What was the basis for security cooperation? Was the relationship an alliance of cooperation directed against a common threat? Or was it a military-economic quid pro quo in which its partners contended over the appropriate mix of financial compensation and military guarantee?

Regardless of which of these perceptions was more accurate or legitimate, *sei iki* supported both versions. For their part, U.S. security policy makers consistently articulated a policy of traditional alliance against an ideologically hostile Soviet threat, while acknowledging the reality of unlike allied contributions to security. Japanese leaders seemed engaged in verbal contortions at home to reconcile the obvious fact of a growing military relationship with the avowed policy of non-military alliance. Politically resolving this inconsistency about the nature of the alliance was difficult because neither option — military alliance against a common threat, nor a patently unequal quid pro quo — was expected to enjoy enduring domestic support in Japan. Periodically, events focused Japanese public attention on this contradiction, forcing the conservative government to attempt to clarify the nature of the alliance. The result was often crisis, but a temporary one because opposition parties offered no realistic alternatives for Japan's security. As a result, the Liberal Democratic Party continued to dominate opposition parties throughout the decade of the eighties.

6

Co-Development of Military Technology

The FS-X (fighter support-experimental) aircraft was the U.S.–Japan security relationship's first joint design and manufacture of a major weapon system. Lauded at the time as an ambitious breakthrough in terms of jointly developing a product incorporating cutting edge technology, the unfortunate short-term result of the experience was excessive *miriteku masatsu*[1] (military technology friction). Heated debates ensued over differences in military goals and economic stakes, producing a prolonged period of bilateral bickering about the actual terms of cooperation. FS-X was more than just the first high tech weapon system co-development project. The issue forced together, in both a joint and combined forum, different definers of what properly constituted matters of national security. In contrast to the precedent of *sei-iki*, the separation of military affairs from economic concerns, this close collaboration on military technology required the deliberate and thorough integration of such matters.

In an alliance against a common threat, co-development is difficult enough. Competition tends to be keen, national economic interests create friction, and practical considerations of defense industrial autonomy often shape military procurement decisions. But at least the requirements of the project, particularly if it is a complex weapon system, tend to be tied to a common threat. If the product is a fighter aircraft, the central task of the joint enterprise is to design an integrated system whose combat performance in an "envelope" of altitudes, speeds, and maneuvers can successfully counter known or anticipated enemy threats. Even without an agreed focus on a set of common threats, different allied aims can be accommodated in the components of the weapon system if tactical tasks are clarified. Ultimately, the participants involved in the FS-X co-production arrangement produced a relatively underpowered and exorbitant ($120m per unit in 2006) F-2 aircraft for the Japan Air Self-Defense Force with guaranteed work shares for U.S. defense firm competitors. In so doing, FS-X revealed the potential instability of an asymmetric security bargain in a clash over changing economic and military security priorities.

Historical Development

Constrained Cooperation

Prior to FS-X, U.S.–Japan weapon system agreements were basically one-way American sales and transfers of technology to Japan that benefited U.S. defense industrial profits and sustained the development of Japan's domestic arms industry. Chasing what seemed to be the elusive postwar Japan's promise to "rearm as soon as conditions permit," immediate post–Occupation U.S. defense assistance expanded dramatically after a patent secrecy agreement allowed exchanges of classified information for defense purposes.[2] After the revised security treaty formalized the relationship's expectations of an expanded Japanese military contribution to mutual security, defense assistance broadened. Growing ties led to more involvement of the various policy and program agendas among Japan Defense Agency and Department of Defense bureaus and offices. Issues involving contracts, sales, budgets, export controls, research and development costs, and technological ownership joined operational discussions about training and exercises that flowed from military role-sharing. Burden sharing, particularly during a prosperous period of economic growth in Japan, came to encompass financial cost sharing. Database sharing led to cooperative research and engineering by identifying technical specifications and desired performance goals.

For many years, American policy makers regarded technological collaboration with Japan as a one-way flight to Tokyo due to a series of self-imposed Japanese defense policies which restricted arms exports and prohibited nuclear weapons. Japan's overriding diplomatic message to the world was to demonstrate commitment to peace despite security agreements that allowed American military basing in Japan. The persistent public affairs problem was the key role U.S. Forces Japan bases played in periodic regional interventions. During the Vietnam conflict, bases in Japan and Yokota AB (near Tokyo) in particular, had served as visible transportation nodes that produced U.S. military airlift missions and enabled air strikes on enemy targets. Despite Japan's Peace Constitution, the United States was waging war from Japan. Japan's leaders often did what they could to reduce the use of Japan as a platform for U.S. military operations. The Basic Policy for National Defense, for instance, was progressively stiffened by the addition of other "fundamental policies":

1. An exclusively defense-oriented policy with the minimum necessary level of defense forces
2. Not becoming a military power that might pose a threat to other countries
3. Adherence to the three non-nuclear principles
4. Civilian control of the military

In addition to these policies, Prime Minister Sato seemed to take the U.S. Cold War ideological position of prohibiting arms exports to communist states a step further to include any state targeted by a UN arms exports ban or involved in, or likely to become involved in, armed conflict. This jujitsu maneuver prohibited Japan's arms industry from supporting offensive U.S. military operations. The Diet formally renounced Japan's nuclear option by signing the nuclear Non-Proliferation Treaty after three years of debate, followed by the adoption of Sato's "three non-nuclear principles" policy into law: Japan will not possess, use or allow nuclear weapons to be introduced into Japan. Prime Minister Miki (Sato's successor) broadened Japan's conflict-related arms export limitation into a comprehensive ban on arms exports. As a result of these restrictions, Japan had become an ally with mainly bases to offer its partner.

Technology Leaks

While this history of cumulating domestic policy constraints prevented Japan's defense industry from exporting arms or developing nuclear weapons, these decisions did not prevent acquisition projects under Foreign Military Sales (FMS) agreements or the co-production of sophisticated systems. Transfers of technology from the United States provided Japanese defense industry a steady diet of leading edge equipment and manufacturing techniques. Major meals (paid for) include the North American F-86 interceptor, Lockheed F-104 interceptor, McDonnell-Douglas F-4 strike/air interceptor, McDonnell-Douglas F-15 air superiority and strike aircraft, and Lockheed P-3 anti-submarine and maritime patrol aircraft. The 1981 Reagan-Suzuki Communiqué encouraged further feeding by providing the JSDF new missions to fulfill a more credible defensive role.

But this time however, steady postwar American pressure to rearm Japan met rising Japanese economic confidence and capabilities in sectors with defense technology applications, such as steel, automobiles, integrated circuits, telecommunications, and aerospace. A mechanism to accommodate these new realities was forthcoming.

In 1983, a key document enabled genuine two-way flow of "military technologies."[3] The Exchange of Notes on Transfer of Japanese Military Technologies outlined transfer procedures and established the Joint Military Technology Commission.[4] The technology transfer procedures granted the United States the only exemption from MITI's 1976 ban on military technology exports. Still, the two sides of the alliance represented significantly different backgrounds and security priorities.

On the Japanese side of the JMTC were officials from the Ministry of International Trade and Industry (MITI), Ministry of Foreign Affairs (MOFA), and Japan Defense Agency (JDA). MoFA could be expected to balance MITI's focused priority on economic security concerns with acknowledgement of the importance of the U.S.–Japan relationship. Both supported JDA efforts as long as they advanced Japanese defense technology. Of these two ministries and one agency, generally only JDA officials possessed expertise (usually second-hand) with respect to military operations. The absence of a JSDF member who might articulate first-hand operational details of countering threats, particularly in an air-ground-maritime environment, was a significant blind spot. Although JSDF experts were distributed throughout the staff offices (Air Staff Office, Ground Staff Office, and Maritime Staff Office), and the JDA's Central Procurement Office and Technical Research and Development Institute (TRDI; *Gijutsu Kenkyu Honbu*), the linkages back to JDA were typically highly dependent upon personalities and social connections.

The American side of the JMTC sat without a counterpart functionally equivalent to MITI. Representatives consisted of State Department officials from the U.S. Embassy and DoD officials from the Mutual Defense Assistance Office. The long-term presence of MDAO in the U.S. Embassy and relatively unfettered military counsel through in-house attaches gave State Department representatives a well informed military perspective. For their part, MDAO officials had enough operational experience or sufficiently close connections to military experts to know and value the complex threat environment within which weapons systems and their operators work.

The JMTC performed its mission of reversing the one-way flow of U.S. military technology to Japan. With oversight from MITI and MoFA, The Japan Defense Agency was able to offer the Department of Defense to such technologies as Nissan ducted rockets, Toshiba/Mitsubishi millimeter wave infrared hybrid seekers, Oki Electric submarine magnetic degaussing, Asgal gas dynamic lasers for optical jamming, and Daikin anti-armor fin-stabilized disposable sabots. DoD requested access to advanced ceramics and ceramic fibers, dynamic random access memory chips, optoelectronics, ferro-electrics, and high temperature superconducting coatings.[5]

Mili-Tech Politicization

FS-X military technology became a political issue as JDA led a charge for *kokusanka* (national autonomous development) in defense-related high technology, an initiative promptly countered by DoD's promotion of American aerospace industrial interests. From 1981 until May 1986, JDA staunchly advocated domestic production of a new Japanese fighter, while DoD pressed for a foreign military sale or co-production of an existing U.S. fighter.[6] Japan's defense officials, economic bureaucrats, and industrial contractors were adamant on retaining the F-1 support fighter market. A domestically developed and produced FS-X seemed a natural extension of advances in defense manufacturing and design engineering, perhaps best illustrated by the rise of semiconductor firms whose microchip processors are elemental ingredients of sophisticated weaponry.[7] Japan's policy prohibitions against arms exports did not prevent the growth of Japan's domestic defense industry, which supplied 80 percent of Self-Defense Force weaponry, including: Toshiba's TA1–3AG ground-to-air missile, short-range Type 81 surface-to-air missile, and laser-guided anti-tank missiles; Mitsubishi Heavy Industries (MHI) Type 74 tank, SSM-1 cruise missile, OH-4 helicopter, and electronic countermeasures equipment; Mitsubishi Electronics Company (MELCO) Active Phased Array Antenna (APA) for target tracking; and Kawasaki Heavy Industries (KHI) XT-4 supersonic jet trainer aircraft.

Japan's special government accounts and corporations promoted investment in the emerging modern defense technology base, and funded national R&D laboratories, government-industry joint projects, and other programs to develop strategic technologies. MITI established the Japan Key Technology Development Center and the New Energy and Industrial Technology Development Organization which funneled various investment funds to the design and construction of aerospace materials, engines, and avionics. In 1988, MITI's Agency of Industrial Science and Technology developed a list of 40 high technology areas to guide basic research, R&D investment, international technological exchanges and construction of large-scale research facilities. By the mid–1980s, Japanese defense-related technologies could proudly claim excellence in key strategic areas such as communications satellites, superconductive materials, amorphous alloys, computer aided design and manufacturing (CAD/CAM), advanced composite materials, and armor ceramics.[8]

As a military operational requirement, FS-X began as a replacement for the obsolete Mitsubishi F-1 ground attack fighter, a converted trainer aircraft whose 20-year service life was set to expire in 1995.[9] The domestically built F-1 was first produced in 1975 and provided a basic close air support capability to counter a Soviet amphibious attack on Japan. The F-1 was not originally designed to counter this specific threat, but was a modified version of the Mitsubishi T-2 jet trainer aircraft which first flew in 1971. Outfitted with large anti-ship missiles for its primary mission of maritime defense, the F-1 would be used to attack warships ("ground attack"). Survivability, however, was problematic because air defense was a secondary mission. As an air-to-air interceptor, the F-1 relied on superior electronics — particularly its search and detection radar — rather than its aerodynamic qualities. The airframe's aerial maneuverability deficit compared to Soviet fighters was intended to be overcome by superior air-to-air missiles, intensive pilot training and disciplined tactics.

The lack of a joint operational mindset in the JSDF hampered optimal integration of training and tactics. While any military suffers to a degree from disproportionately deep service or even weapon-specific loyalties, the U.S. military had just undergone an ambitious reorganization in 1986 to strengthen cross-service, interdependent joint operations.[10] The authority of the individual service chiefs and secretaries was weakened while the roles of the Secretary of Defense and the Chairman of the Joint Chiefs of Staff were strengthened. Naturally reporting directly to the President, the Secretary of Defense was given direct operational control over combatant commanders, the four-star generals and admirals who command the U.S. military's regional and functional cross-service commands. That same year, Japan's Security Council was established, replacing the National Defense Council that had served as a defense advisory group to the Prime Minister since 1956. As was the typical case in the Defense Council, JDA's voice on the Security Council was dominated by other members, almost all of whom held cabinet minister rank.[11] In contrast to the U.S. reform, the newly organized Security Council did nothing to change the status of the Joint Staff Council (the equivalent of the Joint Chiefs of Staff), which remained equal in status to the Air Self-Defense Force, Ground Self-Defense Force, and Maritime Self-Defense Force. This meant that individual services had little incentive to reach joint agreement and tended to politick directly with the Director General.

Expectedly (*yappari*) then, JDA sought to preserve a balance of ground attack and interceptor aircraft in the Air Self-Defense Force, and planned to deploy 130 FS-X from 1997–2001 as the three F-1 squadrons retired. The new ASDF would comprise three FS-X (F-2) squadrons, 28 aircraft warning and control units, 4 F-15 and 6 F-4 air superiority/attack interceptor squadrons, 1 reconnaissance squadron, 3 tactical airlift squadrons, 1 early warning radar squadron, and 6 high-altitude surface-to-air units. Because of this balanced total force mix, the successor to the F-1 presented what appeared to be Japan's last chance to continue its tradition of developing and producing home-grown fighter aircraft. Of the three wartime producers of Japan's famed imperial air forces — Kawasaki, Nakajima, Mitsubishi — only the latter remained in the fighter aircraft business.

The JASDF air-to-air fighter mission had been filled in succession by American designed airframes and major components: the North American F-86 *Sabre* assembled from 1955–1961, the Lockheed F-104 *Starfighter* co-produced through 1967, the McDonnell-Douglas F-4 *Phantom* co-produced into the 1980's, and the McDonnell-Douglas F-15 *Eagle* co-produced beginning in 1981. In each case, Mitsubishi led as prime contractor, beginning with the acquisition of aircraft provided by a U.S. producer, then assembling aircraft from patterns and kits, then (for the F-104, F-4, F-15), and finally transitioning to complete licensed production in Japan. Range-based definitions of "self-defense" and selective indigenous components produced specially restrained models of America's front-line fighters: an exclusively interceptor version of the F-104 with radar limited to air-to-air modes; a multipurpose F-4 incapable of air refueling, and an F-15 with reduced radar and electro-countermeasures capabilities. The short-ranged F-86 was the notable exception to such technological straight jacketing. The *Sabre* was assembled in Japan in both the ground attack (F-86D) and air-to-air models (F-86F) from American kits urgently designed for wartime operations in Korea.[12]

By 1982, the intent to replace the F-1 with another Japanese aircraft had been discussed in a July National Defense Council meeting (*kokumu kaigi*). F-1 replacement was justified as part of a comprehensive force modernization program financed by annual defense spending increases of 5–6 percent. Japan's dependence on American defense technology was broad, but not total. The F-104 was being replaced by another U.S. aircraft, the F-15; the co-produced McDonnell Douglas F-4 aircraft's radar avionics was being upgraded by Mitsubishi Heavy Industries; Lockheed's E-2 early warning aircraft were being modernized; and Kawasaki C-1 transports were being replaced by Lockheed C-130 multi-mission transports and Sikorsky CH-47 helicopters.[13]

Mission Creep

As JDA discussed the FS-X as a concept, FS-X garnered more missions, consistent with domestic political incentives to modernize qualitatively rather than expand quantitatively. Assisted by the 1981 authorization of the SLOC mission, FS-X first collected the sea patrol mission. In 1983, new Prime Minister Nakasone provided advance top cover for a SLOC–related aircraft as he outlined operational objectives for the Self-Defense Force during a four-day trip to President Ronald Reagan's Washington[14]:

> ... the whole Japanese archipelago ... should be like an unsinkable aircraft carrier putting up a tremendous bulwark of defense against infiltration of the Backfire bomber. To prevent Backfires from penetrating through this wall should be our first goal.
> The second target objective should be to have complete and full control of four

straits that go through the Japanese islands so that there should be no passage of Soviet submarines and other naval activities.

The third objective is to secure and maintain the ocean lines of communication.

DoD-JDA channels of communication widened and strengthened under the comfortable relationship of "Ron-Yasu" diplomacy. By 1985, FS-X was incorporated into the 1986–1990 Mid-Term Defense Program (MTDP),[15] which filled requirements first established in the 1976 National Defense Program Outline (NDPO). Institutional incentives to find or develop capabilities in order to fill NDPO requirements were clear. The bureaucratic task was to ensure that all NDPO requirements were met by the finite number of weapons systems in the MTDP. If JDA could not offer options, then those hard-won requirements surely would be revisited by defense wary Diet members. The SLOC mission itself called for an aircraft with improved avionics for detecting surface ships at long ranges and penetrating their defenses, as well as heavier weapon payloads to sink large surface combatants.

By the spring of 1987, the JDA Bureau of Defense Policy had added the ASDF air defense mission as yet another FS-X function, and stressed the need to consider a broad range of missions when choosing among FS-X options. The three options raised for consideration in fulfilling the upcoming Mid-Term Defense Plan were: domestic development and production of a new aircraft, purchase of an existing foreign aircraft, or modification of the F-4 aircraft.[16]

JDA pushed for the domestic option through the Technical Research and Development Institute, which by September 1985 had completed a feasibility study of Japan's aerospace industry. The study concluded that all FS-X components except the engines could be domestically produced, and dismissed the option of modifying the F-4 aircraft on the basis of an inability to meet new threats.[17] With initial prodding and steadfast support from Japan's aerospace and ordnance industries, domestic development gained the upper hand within the Defense Agency, particularly among TRDI's technical experts, the Air Staff Office, and the Equipment Bureau. The goal of developing fighter technology in general was supported by the desire to build a more autonomous SDF rear support structure, the prestige of defending Japan with Japanese technology, reducing dependence on U.S. weaponry, and interests in retaining the F-1 market.[18] The Air Staff Office then established the FS-X Program Office, which began a study of the domestic option against the F-16, F-18 and Panavia Tornado. ASO considered the single-engine F-16 as an alternative, despite the fact that initial JDA operational requirements, unknown to the U.S. side at the time, called for a two-engine aircraft. The F-15E Strike Eagle, whose air-air C model was already being produced under license in Japan, was not initially studied in spite of its unmatched air-to-ground attack capabilities.

Negotiating Operational Requirements

In November of 1985, the Defense Agency sent surveys to DoD's Defense Security Assistance Agency (DSAA) to elicit F-16 and F-18 performance and cost data. As the key U.S. agency involved in Foreign Military Sales, DSAA saw an opportunity for another direct sale of an American fighter, and consulted with Air Force (F-16) and Navy (F-18) service officials, and U.S. industry representatives. DSAA primary interests were to ensure the U.S. fielded the best competitor against Japan's domestic option in terms of mission-relevant performance and cost, and to prevent a bidding war between General Dynamics and McDonnell Douglas that might undercut economic returns to U.S. industry as a whole. The main problem for DoD was ignorance of FS-X operational requirements. JDA's tactical denial of specific information frustrated a thorough mission area analysis and reliable estimate of prospective economic returns to U.S. industry. U.S. officials were at a bargaining disadvantage. Operationally grounded arguments about the importance of military requirements to the aircraft selection process seemed to have no effect on JDA officials tied to mili-tech priorities. Consequently, when Defense Security Assistance Agency officials returned the completed JDA questionnaires, they included their own list of questions designed to elicit information to benefit General Dynamics and McDonnell Douglas design proposals.

At this point, the question of what operational requirement FS-X would fulfill remained rather ambiguous to the American side of the alliance. This particular information evidently was a tightly held secret within the Air Staff Office. Consequently, the precise range of capabilities that FS-X was supposed to perform was not focused on a current or anticipated threat. In this manner, the U.S. competitors to Japan's indigenous development would not know the criteria by which their proposals would be judged. The effect of this kabuki dance was not limited to enhancing Japan's domestic option during the structured competition. From a military standpoint, a military aircraft's envelope of performance ought to be defined by its operational requirements. Without a clear specification of what those requirements were, FS-X appeared to be collecting more missions than it could optimally operate against. And the performance envelope looked to be much smaller than the missions should have required. It was a formula for "satisficing" multiple requirements rather than achieving focused superiority.

One month before the source selection deadline, JDA did release specific FS-X operational requirements to DoD and U.S. industry, which rushed General Dynamics and McDonnell Douglas to develop blueprints of its major modifications to F-16 and F-18 aircraft. Meanwhile, JDA rejected two DoD requests — one for a joint comprehensive feasibility study to evaluate the most suitable aircraft, and the other for a government-to-government memorandum of understanding prior to source selection. Next, ASO and TRDI presented three operational requirements that seemed to eliminate the F-16 option[19]:

1. An increased combat radius (F-16C's is 600 miles)
2. Larger wings to support a weapons payload of 22,000 lbs (F-16C's maximum external payload is 20,450 lbs)
3. A narrow flight profile and anti-ship mission scenario

DoD officials pointed out that the designed combat radius for the FS-X was slightly over 500 miles — less than F-16 variants, and the F-16C were capable of carrying four anti-ship missiles — the military reason for the FS-X's larger wings. Furthermore, although FS-X had picked up various missions during its planning phase in the Defense Agency, the ASO Study Team defined FS-X mission requirements quite narrowly, as if to exclude U.S. fighter aircraft from consideration. The FS-X anti-ship flight profile, for instance, was portrayed as based on one threat only. Missions such as offensive and defensive counter-air,[20] minimal tactical requirements needed for flexibility during combat operations, were dismissed by the Defense Agency as not fitting FS-X's particular needs. "Force multipliers" such as employing a joint allied strike force of different aircraft with separate weapons and radar capability and performance, were also rejected. In addition, the FS-X anti-ship mission was assumed to be flown from a fixed operating base, rather than considering the effect of multiple base loading.[21]

Defense Agency officials countered U.S. complaints over the selection process by citing high cost as the reason for eliminating the F-15, an aircraft that met or exceeded all FS-X operational requirements. ASO/TRDI cost effectiveness studies estimated FS-X domestic development costs as one-third to one-half that of comparable U.S. fighters, a figure widely doubted on the American side.[22] When JDA claimed that the F-18 failed to meet payload considerations, American officials suspected the real reason was the likelihood that the F-18's closely guarded technical data would not be released to Japan anyway.[23]

According to Air Self-Defense Force assessments, FS-X mission requirements included coastal defense and protection of the three key Japanese straits, but excluded protection of SLOCs 1000 miles out.[24] The three FS-X procurement options of domestic development, modification of the F-15 and modification of the F-16 were then ranked according to how each met two mission capabilities — countering an invasion and air defense — as well as according to cost effectiveness[25]:

landing invasion	air defense	cost effectiveness*
1. F-15	1. F-15	1. domestic
2. domestic	2. F-16	2. F-16
3. F-16	3. domestic	3. F-15

*development costs estimates: domestic ¥130 billion;
F-16 ¥165 billion; F-15 ¥200 billion

As DoD attempted to obtain an early MoU to lock in U.S. interests, Japanese contractors and government agencies appeared to work just as hard to lock them out. Both sides claimed to be ahead in key areas as low visibility stealth material, active phased array radar, control-configured vehicles, co-cured wing processes, and electronic warfare systems. McDonnell Douglas had applied composite structures to wings and fuselages in the F-15, F-18 and AV-8 aircraft. American firms active in the development of the next generation Advanced Tactical Fighter (ATF), such as Northrop, Lockheed, Westinghouse, and Texas Instruments, had experience in all key technologies proposed as Japanese improvements to the F-16C. Japanese aerospace contractors had made their own technological advances: composite structural materials for the wing (Fuji Heavy Industries), radar absorbent stealth material (Mitsubishi Heavy Industries), active phased array radar (Mitsubishi Electric Corporation), control configured vehicles (Mitsubishi Heavy Industries), integrated electronic warfare system (Mitsubishi Electric Corporation and Tokyo Keiki Co.), improved radar housing and internal fuel capacity (Kawasaki Heavy Industries and Fuji Heavy Industries), and high-thrust engines (Ishikawajima-Harima Heavy Industries).[26]

In June of 1986, American proposals arrived in the Defense Agency, effectively stalling a JDA budgetary decision to proceed with domestic development. Following failed TRDI and ASO bids to gain FS-X funding in August, the Defense Agency invited General Dynamics and McDonnell-Douglas to present their proposals the following month. When they arrived in Tokyo, American officials and industry representatives were furnished a specific list of operational requirements for the first time, which included the need for two engines. In view of this late revelation, both American firms requested and received six more months to resubmit their proposals. While General Dynamics quickly worked on plans for a twin-engine variant of the F-16 and McDonnell-Douglas reworked its proposals, TRDI's Director General visited Department of Defense in December to gauge U.S. support of the domestic option, which DoD officials continued to reject. Once again, TRDI refused a DoD counter-proposal that JDA and DoD form a Joint Executive Group to study all FS-X alternatives.

While the U.S. Air Force performed a cost-performance study of the F-15E and the Office of the Joint Chiefs of Staff prepared a regional threat analysis, the Defense Agency announced the establishment of the FS-X Joint Research Council, a consortium of the five leading Japanese aerospace firms supporting domestic development. In March and April of 1987, Assistant Deputy Undersecretary of Defense Gerald Sullivan led a team to the Defense Agency, which criticized the domestic option on grounds of excessive cost, failure to take into account multiple threat scenarios, and inadequate consideration of combined U.S. and Japanese military capabilities. During the meetings, the consortium also submitted a report, recommending autonomous development of an aircraft capable of carrying four air-to-ship missiles produced by MHI, powered by twin engines produced under foreign license by IHI, and capable of Mach 2 flight. The cost was estimated to be ¥5–6 billion per plane, compared to ¥2 billion for the F-16, ¥3 billion for the F-18, and ¥5 billion for the F-15. The higher domestic cost was defended as "necessary for strengthening the ability for technology development for domestic production and also for strengthening the rear-support set-up of the SDF."[27]

Resolution

On the heels of this deadlock came the 1987 Toshiba shock — an announcement that Toshiba Machine Company had sold highly sensitive submarine propeller-milling technology to the Soviet Union. The failure of MITI's Security Export Control Office to prevent Toshiba from circumventing the COCOM (Coordinating Committee for export control) ban against the transfer triggered rising Congressional pressure for sanctions against Toshiba, and calls for a better sharing of the alliance's military and economic burdens.[28] From this perspective, a substantial investment in submarine technology used to defend Japan against Soviet intrusions and provide regional security had just been neutralized by the Toshiba betrayal. Moreover, Japan's military contributions to the alliance were viewed as still minimal in spite of decades of U.S. rearmament programs. In the absence of a common military commitment to security, Japan's growing defense technology was seen as military-related economic competition against an "ally." The rise of Japan's semiconductor firms since the military role-sharing agreement of 1981, and attempt in 1986 to buy Fairchild Semiconductor Industries, a leading U.S. defense contractor, raised concerns about Japan's strategic intent. In this context, it seemed reasonable to hold the Japanese government accountable for damaging the alliance's submarine detection capabilities.

In Japan, the Toshiba incident was regarded as an inappropriate intrusion of trade concerns that stemmed from the American failure to compete against Japanese firms, especially in the semiconductor industry. JDA and the defense industry tended to view America's rearmament of Japan as simply a way to generate sales revenue for U.S. defense contractors. Limited by the constitutional prohibition against war potential and by policy proscriptions against military exports, advocates of domestic development could not publicly make a convincing case for autonomy. Instead, Diet members derided U.S. pressure tactics in light of Japan's broad contributions to mutual security. Indeed, economic aid to promote the stability of strategically important Jordan and Oman had just been boosted by $500 million. Funds for labor cost-sharing on U.S. bases in Japan had been increased as a way to compensate U.S. naval escort of Kuwaiti tankers in the Persian Gulf, the starting point of Japan's energy lifeline. Facilities for an entire American F-16 wing had been constructed at Misawa Air Base, making it less expensive for to maintain the wing in Japan than in the United States. In addition, the Diet was currently debating purchases of expensive American defense hardware, such as the AEGIS missile cruiser and AWACS aircraft.[29]

Facing the mounting pressure to link FS-X to broader trade concerns, Japanese pro-autonomous development groups sought to preserve the domestic option. This was accomplished with skillful ambiguity in two meetings in May 1987. In a National Defense Joint Meeting consisting of three LDP departments concerned with national defense, Defense Agency Director General Kurihara won acceptance of three principles to guide FS-X selection: (1) selection from strictly a military technology standpoint (2) importance of Japan–U.S. interoperability (3) not being swayed by the defense industries.[30] Five days later in a Lower House Diet Security Special Committee meeting, the JDA Defense Bureau Chief announced a two-stage formula that would retain independent development as the core of the FS-X co-development project. Co-development would proceed, but the decision to mass-produce would be subject to change in seven or eight years.[31] With the two-stage formula in mind, JDA planned to accept the findings of the Sullivan report, offer co-production, and preserve the domestic option. In June 1987, Defense Policy Bureau Chief Nishihiro visited DoD, offering co-development of either the F-15, F-16, or F-18 to Assistant Secretary of Defense for International Security Affairs Armitage and Defense Security Assistance Agency Director Gast.

Following this announcement, the FS-X Joint Study Team visited General Dynamics and McDonnell Douglas to discuss aircraft selection and work share arrangements. Besides the work share issue, both sides haggled over the choice and timing of source selection. In July, Prime Minister Nakasone publicly added cost-effectiveness to JDA Director General Kurihara's three principles for FS-X selection, producing the possibility that the single-engine F-16 might prevail over the twin-engine F-15 and F-18. Some U.S. officials interpreted the confusion as JDA stalling source selection until U.S. ire over the Toshiba incident subsided. The U.S. side also considered the economic impact of FS-X selection on the U.S. aerospace industry terms of opening market access. This point appeared to favor General Dynamics over McDonnell Douglas, since GD was a relative newcomer to the Japanese market. In the fall of 1987, the U.S. FS-X Steering Group decided to press for a government-to-government MoU before source selection to lock in specific economic objectives such as a 40 percent minimum work share for U.S. industry in development and production phases, free and automatic flow back of FS-X derived technology, and reimbursement for non-recurring recoupment costs of each aircraft produced.

In the fall of 1988, before the end of Prime Minister Nakasone's term, Bureau Chief Nishihiro revealed to Assistant Secretary of State for International Security Affairs Armitage in Washington that Japan's options for joint development had been narrowed down to the F-15J or single-engine F-16. The next day, Defense Agency Chief Kurihara and Secretary of Defense Weinberger announced the decision to cooperate in co-development. On 23 October, the Japanese National Security Council approved the F-16 SX-3 plan, reportedly following JDA recommendations. As government-to-government MoU negotiations began in Washington, meetings between Mitsubishi and General Dynamics stalled on the free flow back issue.

Substantive negotiations were delayed by Japanese officials' inability to make commitments until the first year of FS-X funding had been passed in the Diet. Meanwhile, Japanese negotiators held fast to the 70 percent work share position and overall project leadership since Japan was funding the entire project. DoD expressed concern over leaks of classified technology in light of the Toshiba incident, and refused to budge from their 40 percent work share stance. At the core of the problem in resolving new issues of technology transfer was an asymmetry in government-owned military technology. In contrast to the DoD's R&D investments and ownership of defense technology, JDA did not own most of the desired FS-X technology, so legally could not force Japanese firms to hand it over to the United States.[32] Japanese firms wanted payment for providing any FS-X derived "flow back" technology to U.S. competitors. Thus, there was general agreement on the goal of supporting U.S.–Japan relations by strengthening defense ties. However, on the details of project leadership, work share percentages, flow back of FS-X technology, and patent rights, considerable disagreement prolonged the talks for a year.

A New Bargain

On 29 November 1988, the FS-X MoU was finally signed. Japan won acceptance of program leadership based on its assuming 100 percent of program costs, and a commitment to run a joint effort within a framework of mutual defense[33]:

1. The Government of Japan will bear all FS-X program costs, and will plan and implement FS-X development in cooperation with the United States.
2. Both Japanese industries and U.S. will participate in FS-X.
3. FS-X will adhere to MDAA guidelines and the 1956 Patent Secrecy Agreement.
4. Government of Japan financial obligations are subject to Japanese budget authorization procedures.

In January 1989, General Dynamics and Mitsubishi signed the License and Technical Assistance Agreement, and subsequent detailed negotiations over technology transfer issues began in the FS-X Joint Steering Committee. The first of six FS-X prototypes, XF-2, rolled out in March 1995 and began flight tests that October.[34] Production contracts for the 130 aircraft planned so far range from eight to eleven aircraft per year, with the first aircraft deploying to operational squadrons by 1999.

In the FS-X government-to-government MoU and in subsequent inter-governmental "clarifications," the Japanese government agreed to bear the entire cost of the FS-X program ($6.5 billion) and still provide a 40 percent work share for U.S. industry in development and production.[35] The U.S. won access to all Japanese technology brought to the program ("background knowledge"), and improvements based on U.S. technology flow back to the U.S. free of charge. Technologies solely developed by Japan during the FS-X project ("foreground knowledge") were available for purchase.[36]

The LTAA between General Dynamics and Mitsubishi allowed General Dynamics to receive $1 million per FS-X in recoupment costs for F-16 airframe R&D costs, and $500,000 per aircraft in additional royalties. A work share memorandum between General Dynamics and Mitsubishi Heavy Industries promised GD 30 percent of the overall FS-X budget. Quality of work share was assured by joint participation in all phases of FS-X development and production, whether conducted at MHI or GD. The question of the FS-X engine became a co-production project by Ishikawajima-Harima (IHI) and General Electric of the F110-GE-129 (29,000 lbs. thrust rating).[37]

Technological gains for the Self-Defense Force were dubious, with the notable exception of systems integration knowledge.[38] F-16 technical data flowing to Japan was screened by a DoD-State-Commerce interagency review process that updates the Military Critical Technologies List, a "classified listing of materials, processes, industrial technologies, components, subsystems, data, and end-items that are considered militarily sensitive."[39] Top DoD officials had made it clear "there will be absolutely no U.S. advanced tactical fighter technology involved in building the FS-X."[40] Instead, baseline F-16C technology transferred to Japan dated from the 1970s, and the 1989 worldwide F-16 inventory of 2100-plus aircraft involved 15 foreign military forces.[41] By avoiding the need to develop this level of F-16 technology on its own, Japan's aerospace industry saved an estimated $3 billion.[42]

Derived technologies for Japanese commercial uses, however, were more evident. Dual-use technology with military and commercial end-use possibilities was not subject to the government's "no export policy" restriction on military technology. Especially for FS-X prime contractor MHI, whose aerospace business accounted for only 15 percent of total sales, derived technologies provided valued gains.[43] Ishikawajima-Harima saw possibilities in the FS-X turbojet engine with high performance fan, since IHI had been studying air turbo ramjets for use in a "space plane" with Japan's Science and Technology Agency and National Aerospace Laboratory. TRDI had been funding jet engine research since 1985.[44]

To ease the implementation of FS-X's foreign terms, the Japanese government provided direct and indirect incentives to Japanese aerospace firms. Indirect compensation involved designating MHI as the import agent for F-16 modification, after a fierce competition with four other general trading companies (*sogo shosha*) — C. Itoh, Mitsui, Sumitomo, Marubeni, and Mitsubishi. Direct compensation involved JDA budget requests to disburse funds. In 1988, Mitsubishi received reimbursement for R&D co-development costs of the six prototypes amounting to ¥190 billion.[45] Initial JDA FS-X expenditure requests totaled ¥12 billion for basic design and technical assistance fees.[46] In 1989, the Defense Agency requested ¥25.8 billion for basic design work, and planned a five-year funding request in 1990 of ¥124 billion for detailed design and prototype construction.[47] The following year JDA made additional payments to Mitsubishi, settling a dispute with General Dynamics over the appropriateness of technology guidance fees.[48]

Overall, the FS-X security bargain tightened and aggravated the military-economic quid pro quo. The Defense Agency underwrote economic benefits flowing to U.S. aerospace industry, while U.S. armed forces continued providing military security to the world's second largest economic power. As a compromise between two extremes of autonomous Japanese domestic development and the purchase of an existing American fighter, FS-X attempted to institutionalize bilateral military-technological cooperation as a matter of national security. In the process, bitter differences about legitimate competition surfaced. U.S. officials rightly expected Japan to buy the best aircraft for the alliance's military mission in a transparent, head-to-head competition with America's large defense establishment. Japanese officials, constrained by the ban on military exports and empowered by a rising dual-use technology industry, rightly expected to retain their domestic fighter market as they built their self-defense capabilities. The issue of Japanese sovereignty lurked in the background, providing a nationalistic incentive to gain and sustain some degree of self-respecting military technological autonomy. The sense among the FS-X participants was that the alliance had chosen a project that was too large and too symbolic of both nations' strengths to be successful as the first co-development prototype.

Had the alliance gone too far in forcing co-production and sharing of dual-use technology? Perhaps change needed to be forced. Years of *sei iki* had made direct talks over each other's core military-economic concerns a sacred area indeed, one which was basically avoided. This gulf of separation created a no man's land where issues were not worked out, but where mutual misunderstanding could thrive. The FS-X security bargaining arena revealed another challenge — the presence of influential security experts who held fundamentally opposed views about threats to security. Despite the recent formality of announcing the U.S.–Japan security relationship as an alliance, actual agreement on tangible military threats to plan and train against was confined to military staff and operators familiar with relevant intelligence and possessing an adequate understanding of operational details. This policy-operations void contributed to the high-level political duel of different security priorities. FS-X effectively merged economic and military security issues without a process to work them out at an appropriate level. It was a frustrating sort of cooperation that was unstable at the time.

Aftermath

Disagreement about the FS-X agreement quickly arose out of its unequal terms. In early 1989, Mitsubishi demanded that General Dynamics pay "technology guidance fees" to reimburse MHI for certain background knowledge, claiming to be the originator of techniques that integrated plasticizing of compound materials, part of the FS-X co-cured wing process. MHI interpreted the 1983 technology transfer agreement as permitting such fees, since the exchange of notes did not explicitly prohibit it. General Dynamics acknowledged that the technology was unique, but refused payment based on the government-to-government agreement, which had determined background technology/knowledge as subject to free flow back. GD's interpretation of the 1983 agreement was that only the non-recurring recoupment fees mentioned in the exchange of notes were intended to be included. The Defense Agency and Department of Defense reflected the competitive positions of their nation's firms. The issue was finally resolved by forcing the Defense Agency to pay compensation. JDA had to bear the total cost of the fees as FS-X development costs in order to preserve the overall military-economic quid pro quo, a situation resented by a number Self-Defense Force and Defense Agency officials.

In July 1989, the American officials serving on the Defense Science Board

Task Force recommended that military and economic security be addressed together, drawing on lessons learned from the FS-X experience.[49] The same year, the Defense Authorization Bill specified that the Defense Department should include the Commerce Department in consultations on memoranda of understanding with foreign governments, just as MITI had accompanied JDA on the JMTC. As a result of this additional review, the final list of releasable U.S. technical data denied militarily sensitive information such as the software source codes for the Digital Flight Control System (DFCS). This was unacceptable to JDA officials, delayed production by several months, and led to Japan developing its own DFCS.

In March of 1990, the DoD Director of the Defense Advanced Research Projects Agency (DARPA) was dismissed after advocating Japan-style government financing of high technology to compete with Japan's fifth generation 64-megabit microprocessors. In Japan, the timing of Diet member Ishihara Shintaro's 1989 paper which quickly became a book, *The Japan That Can Say No*, reflected if not celebrated the rise of Japanese techno-nationalism. Although U.S. industrial technologies were discussed during the mandated interagency review process, they were considered matters of national security policy only when needed to maintain a superior military system.[50]

Some U.S. congressmen felt differently, delivering their aftershock to the FS-X agreement by way of hearings required under the Arms Export Control Act of 1976. Citing the Toshiba sellout of alliance know-how chronically unfair trade practices, Senator Dixon introduced a resolution that would have prohibited American involvement in FS-X. Although it was narrowly defeated (52–47), a subsequent motion led by Senator Byrd passed (72–27). The Byrd Amendment demanded a 40 percent American work share in the production phase, and prohibited the use of U.S.-supplied FS-X technology to Japan's civilian industry. President Bush preserved the FS-X bargain by vetoing the amendment, which prevented a formal reopening of the negotiations, but insisted on certain Japanese "clarifications" of the MoU: assurances of a 40 percent production phase work share, free flow back, and access to all Japanese technology brought to the FS-X program.

U.S.–Japan security relations continued to develop as an economics-for-military security bargain. Overseas development aid in 1988–1992 disbursed over twice the amount as in 1983–1987.[51] In 1990, total Japanese host nation support payments increased to 50 percent of total costs, including 100 percent of the costs of employing Japanese workers supporting U.S. forces. In 1991, the Japanese government passed a tax to subsidize its massive $12 billion financial commitment to Saudi Arabia and Kuwait in support of the UN resolution against Iraq's invasion of Kuwait.[52] The Cabinet approved, then was forced by political opposition to rescind, an ordinance that would have allowed Japan Air Self-Defense Force C-130 aircraft to transport Gulf War civilian refugees in the region. Overall, Japan's economic contributions to mutual security substantially increased, while its expanding military role was still small scale and confined to a non-combat scope.

Technology transfer issues spawned by FS-X complicated management of these different security priorities. Whether a technology was singularly military or dual-use mattered very much to Japanese security policy officials. If categorized as military rather than dual-use, then American foreign military sales procedures and Japanese export prohibitions applied, allowing U.S. access to the technology (other states were not allowed access). Because the "no export" ban does not apply to "dual use"[53] technologies, Japan's only incentive in bringing this singularly military technology to the bargaining table was to sell it to the United States, since Japan was prohibited from exporting it. In this case, the U.S. interest was to claim it already had the technology anyway, to obtain free "flow back."[54] When the technology was categorized as dual-use, complications arose over who owned the technology, and the problem of enforcing the 1956 patent secrecy agreement.[55]

By the mid–1990's, as the first F-2 prototype completed its successful first flight, new institutions helped channel these dueling incentives into other joint projects. The DoD Defense Technology Office (DTO), Systems and Technology Forum, and Industrial Forum for Security, generated technology steering groups, technical review groups, and joint working groups under the authority of the Joint Military Technology Commission.[56] However, JDA was limited in its ability to transfer leading technologies with military applications to the United States, due to most technologies' commercial potential. Japanese defense industrial firms suspected U.S. firms wanted to acquire commercial advantages rather than desire to produce a better weapon system.[57] Even in technologies with high military value, achieving reciprocity was difficult. Distinctions over "background knowledge" (technology derived from the joint program), and "foreground knowledge" (non-derived technology that each side brings to the project) became objects of dispute, since only foreground knowledge resulted in free "flow back" to the other side. Japanese officials favored short military technology lists because of the prohibition on military exports. U.S. government and industry officials viewed this as Japanese unwillingness to transfer technology, and considered it the number one obstacle to improved bilateral cooperation.[58] These issues complicated the drafting and execution of various MoU's and licensing agreements across all armed service branches:

U.S. Air Force	Advanced Hybrid Propulsion (air-to-air tactical missile)
	Aircraft Ejection Seat Modification (pilot survivability)
	Hybrid Rocket Engine (air-to-air missile)

U.S. Army	Ducted Rocket Engine (surface-to-air missile)
	Eye-Safe Laser (mapping, designating, targeting)
	Ammunition Propellants (30 mm gun)
	Ceramic Diesel Engine (reduced: thermal signature)
U.S. Navy	Advanced Steel Technology (ship and submarine hulls)
	Shallow Water Acoustics (anti-submarine)

The confusing mix of competition and cooperation over technology reflected the nature of the security bargain, and generated a sense of "alliance drift,"[59] particularly in Japan. Both sides were less optimistic about the ability to cooperate on large, complex projects that involved military and economic interests. But like the value of the overall relationship, the inequalities of the FS-X deal seemed to outweigh any military operational demerits. While Japan shouldered all of the development and production costs, the U.S. had no say in design decisions, and technology transfer continued to be mutually controlled. Japanese officials emphasized that in other joint aircraft development ventures, participation is generally proportional to the supply of funds brought to the enterprise.[60] If the Americans really wanted armaments cooperation instead of one-way foreign military sales, then they ought to be willing to acquire certain Japanese defense-related technology. But no interest was apparent, and the deal seemed to be a major concession to the U.S. aerospace industry. In such a situation, how could Japan find a way to build up its industrial capabilities for self-defense, separate from continued dependence on American military superiority? From an American point of view, however, the terms of FS-X were long overdue and unlikely to be easily replicated, given the postwar pattern of early American economic assistance and one-way technology flow to Japan. If Japan were taking its expanded military missions seriously, why build an exorbitant fighter of modest performance[61] unless "defense cooperation" was mostly about economic tech theft? Dissatisfaction among those involved in the FS-X process led to criticism and complaints about the unequal relationship. Clearly the participants wanted to avoid the negative lessons of FS-X, but no one seemed to have an executable alternative to muddling through the complexities of an unequal alliance.[62]

7

Allied Military Commitment

The negative lessons of the FS-X ordeal and the strategic uncertainties of the 1990's called for reassessments of security priorities. Post-FS-X armament programs proceeded steadily but cautiously, along the lines of armaments cooperation rather than one-way American assistance to allies. Ironically with respect to U.S. objections to Japan's indigenous fighter option in the previous chapter, the Clinton administration emphasized the importance of technological leadership and leveraging allied capabilities to rejuvenate the U.S. defense industrial base. Dependence on foreign technologies such as semiconductors, liquid crystal displays, microelectronics, ceramics, and shipbuilding were the subjects of several key studies that merged government and private interests in defense.[1] The Defense Technology Office was established in 1991 within the Mutual Defense Assistance Office[2] to transition from foreign military sales to two-way armaments cooperation. During this period, Gorbachev's historic reforms in the USSR, the fall of the Berlin Wall, and dissolution of the Soviet Union seemed to eliminate the traditional common threat assumed by many to be the basis for the military dimension of the U.S.–Japan security bargain. In response to these significant alterations in the strategic landscape, DoD reevaluated America's global security commitments, while JDA studied ways to update the bilateral context of its military role, the 1978 Guidelines for U.S.–Japan Defense Cooperation. Two specific crises sharpened the need to rethink specifics of the alliance — the Persian Gulf War of 1990–91, and the North Korea nuclear crisis of 1994. Both events exposed the security alliance as not militarily credible, and in danger of becoming irrelevant to the challenges of the next century.

Historical Development

War in the Persian Gulf

On August 2nd, 1990, eight divisions totaling 100,000 Iraqi troops, led by two elite Republic Guard divisions, sliced across the border toward Kuwait City. Within twelve hours, they had subdued the 16,000-member Kuwaiti Army and controlled all strategic nodes, doubling Iraq's share of global oil reserves to 20 percent.[3] A third Republican Guard division deployed against the Saudi Arabian border and threatened another one-quarter of the world's oil production capacity.

In the United States, the reaction to this surprise invasion was swift. President Bush convened the National Security Council, demanded an immediate Iraqi withdrawal, and led a unanimous United Nations resolution against the invasion. He then called for a global freeze of Iraqi financial assets and implementation of full economic sanctions. Secretary of Defense Perry boarded a flight to Saudi Arabia to discuss defense of the Kingdom with King Fahd.

In Japan on August 2nd, the reaction to this far flung aggression was muted. Prime Minister Kaifu convened a meeting of the Cabinet in a consensus-seeking discussion about Japan's response to this problem in a region that provided Japan 70 percent of its oil imports. Defense Agency inputs safely stressed intelligence reports of what was happening rather than suggest politically contentious military options. The Ministry of International Trade and Industry (MITI) opposed economic sanctions, fearing oil prices would rise and Iraq would default on its $40 billion debt to Japanese trading companies. The Ministry of Foreign Affairs (MoFA) urged support of the U.S. position and prevailed over MITI in an emergency session on August 5.[4] The next day, Japan joined the nearly unanimous UN embargo against Iraq. The U.S. Secretary of Defense reported he had received permission from King Fahd to deploy U.S. troops to Saudi Arabia.

The closest U.S. military forces were two aircraft carriers in the Mediterranean Sea and Indian Ocean, four heavy armored and mechanized divisions in Germany, and nine tactical fighter wings deployed throughout Europe. President Bush ordered F-15 aircraft from the 1st Fighter Wing and the 2,300 troops of the 82d Airborne Division's ready brigade to Saudi Arabia to deter a southward advance by the growing Iraqi army in Kuwait. As American military forces began streaming into Saudi Arabia, MoFA bureaucrats blocked Defense Agency suggestions that Japan dispatch a portion of its 43 minesweepers, arguably the world's best, to the Gulf to help enforce the economic sanctions. Even Japan's economic contribution seemed difficult. Foreign Minister Nakayama initially explained Japan could not provide financial support to any country that sent military forces to the Gulf. By the end of August, as Japan struggled to respond to the reality of 550,000 Iraqi troops in Kuwait, President Bush had ordered 200,000 troops to the Gulf in a steady buildup of forces.

Various U.S. officials urged their Japanese counterparts to contribute to the allied cause in various ways: (1) dispatch minesweepers, C-130 airlift, and SDF personnel; (2) provide cash to coalition forces; (3) provide aid to Middle East states losing oil revenue due to the crisis; (4) plan to purchase major U.S. weapons systems; and (5) increase host nation support of U.S. forces in Japan.[5] In response, Japan's first aid package announcement on August 29th pledged $1 billion, of which $10 million was a cash grant to Jordan.[6] Officials made general references to longer term support for Turkey and Egypt in the form of Japanese construction projects. Medical supplies, tents, and food had to be sent aboard commercial chartered aircraft, since JSDF aircraft naturally were forbidden to enter a war zone. Japan Air Lines and All Nippon Airways flights reluctantly agreed to a limited number of flights to the Gulf ... as long as they carried no explosive material, no weapons, no military personnel, and were guaranteed a safe journey.[7] Due to these self-imposed restrictions, the government of Japan decided to simply pay U.S. commercial flights to transport military equipment and personnel.

Congressional ire swelled at their supposed ally's inability to contribute meaningfully to the rising international military effort. In September, the House of Representatives passed an amendment to the defense authorization bill that would have begun a phased withdrawal of U.S. troops from Japan. A frustrated Japan Defense Minister taunted the U.S. to send its forces in Japan home.[8] The U.S. government responded by sending a team to Japan that requested a financial contribution, after which the Kaifu administration announced a second aid package of $3 billion more. Half of this contribution would flow to "non-lethal" military efforts and half would be economic aid. Following Bush—Kaifu talks in New York, the Prime Minister announced Japan would increase its host nation support of U.S. forces in Japan.

In October, as the international coalition waited for economic sanctions to work and worried about the prospect of heavy casualties in a military response to Iraqi aggression, LDP faction leader Ozawa Ichiro attempted to reverse Japan's 1980 policy against collective self-defense. Japan's Constitution prohibited the use of force in "international disputes," so Ozawa defined international disputes as interactions between two states rather than between the United Nations and a state. Ozawa argued the SDF could participate militarily in the Gulf since the UN-coalition made the situation was not strictly an international dispute. Faced by an opposition majority in the Upper House of the Diet, Prime Minister Kaifu would not support this verbal twist. His legal alternatives to dutifully abiding by existing political constraints on Japan's military were either to amend the Self-Defense Force (SDF) law so the SDF could be sent to an overseas combat zone, or introduce a new law.

The Prime Minister chose the latter course. He announced the UN Peace Cooperation Corps Bill, which would establish a Peace Cooperation Corps for United Nations duty. The Corps would consist of 1000–2000 individuals, including SDF individuals who would first lose their status as SDF members, then provide non-combat, rear support to the multinational coalition. During the intense debate in the Diet, government officials contradicted each other in tortuous attempts to contribute to a massive buildup of international military force without supporting the use of force. Prime Minister Kaifu finally testified that Japan's constitution permitted only unarmed SDF participation in the UN coalition. To dispatch an armed SDF overseas constituted the use of force and collective defense, which in 1981 had been deemed unconstitutional. The absurdity of sending unarmed self-defense forces to the Gulf with neither the intent nor the capability to use credible force finally became clear to LDP and major opposition parties. They tabled the bill in November. LDP and Komeito, the largest opposition party, agreed to propose a new bill during the next Diet session.[9]

The U.S. Congress narrowly passed a war resolution[10] in January, ending the debate on whether to continue economic sanctions or force Iraqi forces from Kuwait. The day the air war was launched, the Kaifu Cabinet established the Gulf Crisis Countermeasure Headquarters in a sputtering search for constitutionally acceptable ways to contribute to a common cause. Meanwhile, the month-long air war destroyed one-half of Iraqi forces, and a 100-hour ground war in February evicted the invaders in a successfully integrated air, naval and ground campaign. The 32 allied nations suffered 240 killed and 776 wounded. At one point, Prime Minister Kaifu suggested sending five C-130 aircraft to the Gulf to evacuate refugees as part of the UN coalition. However, opposition parties threatened to withdraw support of the economic aid already pledged, and the idea was pragmatically dropped. Instead, Japan pledged an additional $9 billion in economic aid, silencing most American criticism about the amount of Japan's financial commitment.[11] Approved by the Diet three days after the surrender of Iraqi forces, Japan's overall financial contribution of $13 billion had become the third largest behind Saudi Arabia and the United States. Outside Japan, however, this significant contribution to security was generally regarded as too late, low risk, and not nearly equivalent to any level of military commitment.

In April in accordance with constitutional restrictions, six JMSDF minesweepers departed for the Persian Gulf. The Prime Minister's Office established a Secretariat of the International Peace Cooperation Headquarters to negotiate among government ministries about the scope of Japan's participation in international peace efforts. The Lower House finally passed the

UN Peacekeeping Operations and Other Operations Bill in June. Cabinet members were still divided on the issue of collective action. Prime Minister Kaifu first supported, then rejected, distinctions made between collective defense and collective security.[12] The final agreement allowed Self-Defense Forces to be authorized, case by case, to participate in UN non-combat missions (peacekeeping and humanitarian operations) under five conditions[13]:

> Parties involved in conflict agree to a cease-fire
> Parties involved consent to the presence of the peacekeeping force and Japan's participation
> The peacekeeping force maintains impartiality
> Japan reserves the right to withdraw its participation if the above conditions are not followed
> Weapons are restricted to the minimum necessary for self-protection.

Most Diet members and cabinet ministers, however, did claim to generally authorize the Defense Agency to defend Japanese territory. From this narrower perspective, the Gulf war siphoned American troops away from Japan and Korea to participate in the geographically remote crisis. Officials agonized over how American forces could possibly handle two major regional contingencies,[14] as U.S. doctrine claimed, when it had to deploy 80 percent of the VII Corps from Europe to generate an offensive ground force in the Gulf. The American answer was to initiate a delaying action in one theater, presumably Korea, while quickly resolving the other theater conflict, then shifting forces. This was not particularly consoling to the few military security advocates in Japan, and to the many in vulnerable South Korea.

U.S. concerns about its supposed security partner ranged from bitter resignation to hopeful optimism. Some officials concluded that Japan's contributions would simply continue to be financial, so U.S. forces will have to carry on planning and executing military operations independently. Others were more hopeful that Japan would expand its ability to provide military contributions in times of crisis. As officials reflected on the performance of the security alliance during the Gulf crisis, they raised uncomfortable questions. If U.S. forces had suffered more casualties during the Gulf war, would Americans support the U.S.–Japan alliance? Private criticism tended to be more blunt. What was the value of Japan as an ally if it could not or would not contribute militarily to a clear act of aggression in a region of shared and vital national interests? Why did Americans disregard Japan's huge financial contribution made under constitutional constraints originally imposed by the Americans themselves?

Post-War Adjustments

Following the Gulf War, the United States and Russia resumed post Cold War strategic nuclear force reductions, including the removal of tactical nuclear weapons from the Koreas and from U.S. surface vessels. At the same time, growing unrest in Central Europe and Africa reinforced the view that the future held a dangerous potential for more regional conflicts. Although American national security policy was officially one of "engagement," the post–Cold War drawdown of military forces presaged disengagement. The pre and post–Gulf War East Asian Strategic Initiative reports in 1990 and 1992 announced a gradual withdrawal of U.S. forces from Asia, raising Defense Agency concerns of a potential power vacuum in the region. How could Japan's politically constrained self-defense forces deal with resurgent China, Russia in disarray, and the enduring military standoff on the Korean peninsula?

Events in 1992 only reinforced Japanese uncertainty about the regional security environment. In February, China passed the Territorial Waters Act, claiming Japan's Senkaku Islands as Chinese territory. Would the Americans publicly commit to defending the Senkakus against Chinese claims? In June, the U.S. and Russia agreed to massive reductions of strategic nuclear weapons. Would the American nuclear umbrella protect Japan against the rising power of China? In August, China and South Korea established diplomatic relations. Would an eventually reunified Korea lean toward China, away from Japan? In October, China's 14th National Party Congress emphasized the importance of military strength and the defense of territorial sovereignty. In December, China and Russia declared a strategic partnership after more or less resolving a longstanding border demarcation dispute. Russia still held the four strategically located northern islands and islets it seized in 1945: Kunashiri, Etorofu, Shikotan, and Habomai — referred to in Japan as the Northern Territories. In addition to these developments, the policies of the new Clinton administration seemed to signal a shift away from Japan toward China: the eleven-month vacancy of the ambassadorship to Japan; the influx of China experts in place of Japan experts in the State Department; and the emphasis of economic security issues rather than post–Cold War military roles. These events and concerns conspired to promote cautious support for a broader Japanese military role in world affairs, marketed rather ambiguously under the undefined rubric of "security."

The UN Peacekeeping Operations and Other Operations Law provided the legal means for more multilateralism. Each year since its enactment leading up to the Defense Guidelines, the Cabinet won Diet approval for and sent the SDF on UN peacekeeping or humanitarian missions.[15] In 1992, the Miyazawa Cabinet sent two successive 600-member engineer battalions and supply troops to support the year-long United Nations Transition Authority in Cambodia (UNTAC).[16] In 1993 and 1994, the Miyazawa and Hosokawa cabinets dispatched some 200 JSDF transportation and staff personnel to Mozambique, supporting the United Nations Operation in Mozambique (UNUMOZ) over a 20-month period. 1994–1995 saw even the socialist

Murayama Cabinet send medical, sanitation, transportation and airlift forces to Zaire, in support of the UN High Commissioner for Refugees' response to refugee outflows from Rwanda. In 1996, the Hashimoto cabinet sent 43 transportation and staff personnel troops to Syria and Israel as members of the UN Disengagement Observer Force (UNDOF).

While Japan tested its ability to participate in peacekeeping and humanitarian missions, U.S. participation in peace enforcement missions clarified the human costs and domestic political limits associated with multilateralism. In 1993, 18 American soldiers were killed in a shootout with armed gangs in Somalia. Under congressional pressure, President Clinton withdrew all U.S. forces from the United Nations Operation in Somalia (UNOSOM) by 1994. The next year, all other UNOSOM forces had withdrawn. In 1995, NATO's pinprick air strikes prompted Bosnian Serbs to seize 400 UN hostages from the ranks of the so-called UN Protection Force. No hostages were Americans, however, because the U.S. government had declined to provide ground troops to the militarily constrained 37,000-member force. NATO eventually responded by creating a more powerful and credible Implementation Force of 60,000 troops, which won U.S. participation.[17]

Japanese attempts to broaden its security role through closer defense ties to South Korea registered sudden gains. Through 1991–92, annual Republic of Korea (ROK) defense white papers accused Japan of planning to become a military superpower with an aggressive forward defense that would replace a receding U.S. presence. The 1992 White Paper, however, emphasized the importance of military personnel exchanges with Japan, encouraged Japan's enhanced defense relationship with the U.S., and acknowledged Japan's expanding regional security role. The ROK Ministry of National Defense organized a policy group to manage Japan issues as a bilateral security relationship. Defense Minister Rhee Byoung-tae visited Japan and proposed exchange visits and student exchanges, port calls, and air safety coordination. Even the October demand by Defense Minister Choi Sae-chang that the International Atomic Energy Agency (IAEA) upgrade its inspections of Japan's nuclear reactors in preparation for the 1995 review of the Non-Proliferation Treaty (NPT) did not halt increased security ties.

North Korean Crisis

On the surface, the collapse of the Soviet Union made the mercurial Korean peninsula appear relatively stable in 1992. Russia's cutoff of funds to North Korea led to a South-North agreement on non-aggression, exchanges, and de-nuclearization of the peninsula. North Korea agreed to put into permanent storage spent fuel rods that contained enough plutonium for several nuclear bombs. Even the negative developments in North Korea — GNP decline of 20 percent, $10 billion in foreign debt, shrinking trade, and massive starvation — were interpreted as signs of the north's weakness.[18] But the undercurrents of Cold War stability proved capable of instantly reversing sanguine predictions of North Korean pliability and peninsular peace. In March 1993, North Korea announced its withdrawal from the nuclear Non-Proliferation Treaty, simultaneously heightening regional fears of its nuclear potential, challenging the U.S. nuclear guarantee of its Asian allies, and stoking concerns about a broader Japanese military role.

The predicament dragged on for a year with successive delays, a UN resolution calling for inspections of suspected nuclear sites, and repeated North Korean control of those inspections limiting their effectiveness. The final agreement, the 1994 Agreed Framework, called on the U.S. to compensate North Korea with two light water reactors and oil supplies, in return for the sealing of three nuclear facilities, removal and storage of plutonium waste, and IAEA monitoring of the suspected nuclear sites.[19]

During the crisis, South Korean officials expressed ambivalence toward any nascent Japanese military role, while expanding ties with Japan's defense officials. Foreign Minister Han Sung-joo stated that Japan was unlikely to become a military superpower, while President Kim Young-sam openly worried that a North Korean nuclear capability might tempt Japan to follow suit. ROK Ministry of Defense and JDA officials exchanged views on organizational restructuring and weapons procurement policy. Annual exchanges started between the Defense Ministers, Chairmen of the Joint Staffs, and ROK War College and Japan's National Institute of Defense Studies. Korea Institute for National Unification officials made regular visits to Japan to discuss security cooperation. Annual defense talks began between the ROK Defense Counselor and Japan's Director of Policy and Plans, and among lower-level plans, intelligence and operations officers. The Maritime Self-Defense Force and the ROK Navy began mutual port calls.

In light of the new ROK-Japan ties and Japan's ongoing peacekeeping operations, DoD and JDA officials discussed the possibility of joint responses to North Korean scenarios. A North Korean missile capability outside the context of the Non-Proliferation Treaty was acknowledged as a common threat, but Japan's policy restrictions precluded SDF military action unless Japanese territory were attacked or clearly about to be attacked. The absence of emergency defense legislation posed a particular problem. If the SDF used force to resist even a limited incursion, it would lack legal authority and political cover against a certain barrage of opposition criticism. JDA officials expressed to their DoD counterparts a desire to support U.S. forces in worst case scenarios, but bemoaned the lack of a legal framework upon which to actually act.

Consequently, even in a clear case of North Korean aggression, U.S. military forces would act in coordination with South Korean forces, but could not expect to act with Japanese forces. Prudent military planners excluded Japanese participation based on the political unreliability of Tokyo's military commitment. Just as in the Gulf war, the U.S.–Japan alliance seemed incapable of producing a joint military response. In a debrief similar to that of the Gulf conflict, American and Japanese officials wondered how the alliance could survive Japan's non-participation in a shooting war on the nearby Korean peninsula. The failure of the relationship to stand up to an obvious regional threat to Japanese security clarified the need for change.

Post-Crisis Adjustments

Change had been in the works since February 1994, when Prime Minister Hosokawa appointed an advisory group chaired by Higuchi Hirotaro to recommend revising the 1976 National Defense Program Outline. Changes in the external environment alone called for such a revision: the Gulf coalition against regional aggression, the evaporation of Soviet hostility, the isolation of North Korea, and the prospect of a unified Korean peninsula unconstrained by constitutional proscriptions. Japan's domestic economy, in recession since 1990,[20] only reinforced Japan's strategic quandary. Absent the political will to change the Constitution, Japan's only realistic option was continued dependence on the U.S. military guarantee.

Drafted during the North Korean crisis, the Higuchi Report was completed in August under the brief tenure of Prime Minister Murayama.[21] The usual ambiguous references were made about the need for cooperative and comprehensive security, using the tools of diplomacy, economics, and "defense."[22] Collective defense was ruled out again, and all previous policy constraints were affirmed such as Japan's 1957 Basic Policy for Defense, the exclusively defense-oriented policy, not becoming a military power, and three non-nuclear principles. The Higuchi Report made more tangible recommendations regarding military forces. Increases in air mobility, satellite capability, and logistic support to U.S. forces, and improvements in U.S.–Japan planning, training, and consultations could arguably be accomplished with a smaller force that emphasized air and naval capabilities. GSDF divisions would be reduced by one-third and main battle tanks by one-fourth. Reductions allowed equipment upgrades and mobility for more joint and multilateral missions within budget constraints.[23] The report's overall thrust was to retain the U.S.–Japan relationship as the core security tie, but to reduce dependence by expanding Japan's freedom of action. This required initiating military ties with other states and increasing participation in PKO, arms control, and regional dialogues.[24]

Japan's multilateralist tilt attracted the attention of DoD policy makers interested in the principal, tangible military benefit of the security bargain —

bases. U.S. officials were particularly concerned about how to maintain an adequate combat edge in Japan due to growing local constraints on military training.[25] Assistant Secretary of Defense for International Security Affairs Joseph Nye initiated DoD-JDA meetings to promote better consultations, and in February 1995 released the United States Security Strategy for the East Asia-Pacific Region report. The DoD report pledged to continue the familiar formula of unlike contributions to security, citing Japan's ODA, host nation support, and humanitarian/peacekeeping operations as advancing mutual interests in regional and global stability. For its part, the U.S. would maintain 100,000 U.S. troops in East Asia, including the 45,000 presence on bases in Japan, to preserve the military capability to respond to regional crises.

With North Korean scenarios in mind, JDA convened meetings to discuss the impact of the new National Defense Program Outline recommendations on the 1978 Guidelines for Defense Cooperation. In July and August 1995, China conducted pre-announced live-fire naval exercises near Taiwan, presenting Tokyo and Washington with the externally sensitive and internally divisive question of how the alliance might respond to regional aggression. Discussion of this perennial problem was derailed the following month, however, when U.S. servicemen raped a schoolgirl in Okinawa. Just as in the Girard case of 1957,[26] public outrage over the brutal crime was inflamed by the fact that the offenders were U.S. military personnel based in Japan. As opinion polls registered a spike in public disapproval of the U.S. military presence in Japan, Prime Minister Hashimoto organized the Special Action Committee on Okinawa (SACO) in November to deal with the burden placed on Okinawa, where 75 percent of the land used by U.S. Forces Japan is located.

Joining in the public's rage against the U.S. military presence, Okinawa Governor Ota Masahide refused to renew land leases agreements that permitted U.S. military use. Prime Minister Hashimoto felt acute pressure to win the return of the 11 American facilities, training areas, airfields and seaport. The 1995 NDPO was approved in November, beginning the force restructuring recommended in the Higuchi Report with a succession of five-year Mid-Term Defense Plans. With Japan's incremental increase in defense capability programmed, months of intense bargaining ensued between DoD and JDA, the central government and Okinawa prefecture, and among Okinawa municipalities. As layers of officials chiseled out a tentative agreement on the partial or complete return of each of the sites, Chinese military actions tested the security alliance's resilience.[27]

In March 1996, China again announced live-fire naval exercises near Taiwan, neatly timed to influence Taiwan's first free presidential elections and drive a wedge into the U.S.–Japan discussion about defense guidelines. During SACO negotiations over the details of U.S. basing, Japan's need for the U.S. military guarantee overcame anxiety about being drawn into a Taiwan crisis. Intelligence assessments of involved Chinese military forces matched Beijing's verbal assurance that there was no intent to invade Taiwan. The U.S. deployed two carrier battle groups east of Taiwan (USS Independence and USS Nimitz), publicly supported by the Hashimoto Cabinet and materially made possible through basing arrangements at Yokosuka. Not divulged at the time was the Prime Minister's order to deploy an Air Self-Defense Force E-2C early warning aircraft near the Taiwan Straits. The surveillance aircraft patrolled and monitored the area, while the Maritime Self-Defense Force supplied oil to U.S. carrier group vessels.[28] Despite domestic concern over the U.S. presence, the security alliance produced a successful result consistent with its unequal contributions. What Chinese leaders saw was an American military countermove made possible through an alliance with Japan.

Negotiating Alliance Terms

The month following China's intimidation of Taiwan, Prime Minister Hashimoto met U.S. Ambassador Mondale to finalize the SACO recommendations, then hosted President Clinton in a summit that reaffirmed the security alliance to its multiple audiences. The Clinton-Hashimoto Joint Declaration on Security announced the general terms of the continued U.S.–Japan security bargain: the U.S. military presence and commitment to the defense of Japan, increased Japanese financial support, and enhanced Japanese military capability. In addition, the declaration proclaimed a regionally relevant alliance based on common values: freedom, democracy, and human rights. Finally, the declaration set forth joint objectives: cooperation with key neighboring powers China, Russia, and South Korea, and more multilateralism in UN peacekeeping operations, humanitarian missions, and crises in the Middle East and Balkans.

From April 1996 to September 1997, Defense Guidelines negotiators from JDA/MoFA, and DoD/the State Department wrangled over how to achieve these joint objectives and coordinate a credible JSDF role within existing constitutional and policy constraints.[29] The Acquisition and Cross-Servicing Agreement (ACSA), which would provide some Japanese support of USFJ training, joint exercises, and operations during emergency situations, was approved in the spring.[30] A routine procedure in other U.S. military relationships throughout the world, U.S.–Japan ACSA negotiations had labored on for two years. Finally the Cabinet National Security Office, working with U.S. negotiators to gain assurances of reimbursement for supplies, broke a deadlock between the Ministry of Foreign Affairs and Defense Agency. In August, the Defense Agency decided to study SDF participation in a Theater Missile Defense (TMD) system, prior to a government decision on joint development with the United States.[31] Although TMD was considered separately from the guidelines as a part of the technology cooperation process, DoD negotiators considered the project vital to protecting deployed U.S. forces.

The trickiest talks concerned military operations, which were eventually categorized into three groups. First, there were actions that clearly could be done within existing constraints, such as defensive counter-air or naval operations in Japanese territory. Second, there were steps that clearly could not be done, such as Japanese air or naval strikes against strategic targets outside Japan's territory. Third, there were gray areas where constitutional or political prohibitions were unclear. Scenarios such as Japanese defensive counter-air or naval operations against forces in hot pursuit of U.S. forces in international airspace or waters would fall in this category.[32]

Referring to the precedent of expanding regional cooperation in the 1978 Defense Guidelines[33] and the defense line (*boei sen*)[34] against potential attacks on Japanese territory and administrative areas,[35] negotiators now portrayed a more complicated threat environment. For the first time, negotiators were forced to shed ideological assumptions of the Cold War that a heavily armed Soviet Union constituted a common threat to the alliance. There were insufficient grounds to assume hostile intent from China, and the guidelines were not directed against China or any particular state. Indeed, whether China would threaten U.S. or Japan interests depended on Chinese actions. In the absence of an assumed common threat agent, threat conditions such as civil unrest causing regional instability, the spread of catastrophic weapons, or a cross-border external attack in the region, were to be evaluated and decided upon by each government quite separately. Policy positions arrived at independently would then be coordinated in an effort to achieve an exchange of interests under the general terms of the April 1996 Clinton-Hashimoto Joint Declaration on Security.

Despite the more sophisticated conceptualization of the threat environment, there remained the practical military necessity to plan and practice defense scenarios if the alliance were to be credible. U.S. policy makers viewed Japan's lack of political commitment to take military action against clear aggression that affected Japanese security as damaging alliance credibility. Some Japanese defense officials were frustrated at the lack of political will to counter any threat other than the remote chance of a direct attack on Japan. In the post Cold War setting where the main threat was more a condition of insecurity rather than the predatory intent of a specific state, relations with neighboring states seemed more important. However, there were different U.S. and Japan security priorities toward China, Russia, and South Korea. As a result, rather than possessing specific plans and policies against common threats, policy makers encountered limits to cooperation that allowed only incremental improvements in coordination.

First was the joint objective of cooperation with China. This crucial ingredient of regional stability was put at risk by any revision of the defense guidelines that increased Japan's military contribution to security, because China viewed any increases in Japanese military capability as a threat. U.S. priorities were to enlist Japan in regional defense, promote democratization and human rights in China, and encourage economic openness and free trade. Japanese priorities focused on retaining the U.S. military guarantee while playing a regional role, and promoting economic development without preaching to sensitive neighbors principles of liberal politics or economics. Additionally, due to domestic constraints and the need to accommodate China in the absence of an independent Japanese deterrent, Japan held to defense guidelines that narrowly defended Japan. As a result, Japan sought more cooperation with China than did the United States. Concomitantly, Japan viewed Chinese military actions in regional scenarios as less threatening.

Second, the normalization of Japan-Russia ties and return of the Northern Territories, the top security priority toward Russia for Japan, was thwarted by the U.S.-led NATO expansion to the east. Russian opposition to an enlarged NATO on to the west complicated resolution of the territorial dispute with Japan to the east. Japan's diplomats walked a tightrope between acknowledging Russian fears of strategic encirclement and ascribing expansionist motives to NATO that undercut the position of Japan's guarantor of military security, the United States. Consequently, Japan favored mollifying Russian anxieties toward NATO expansion in order to resolve the dispute over the Northern Territories. U.S. security interests in normalizing Japan-Russia relations, however, were secondary to the priority of expanding NATO among democratic, economically solvent states. U.S. security policy of supporting political and economic reforms in Russia (as in China) contained liberal assumptions about individual rights, economic competition without government intervention, and the legitimate use of military force that lacked support by Japan's ruling coalition.

Third, the joint objective of cooperation with South Korea contained differences fatal to joint operations. Japanese officials sought bilateral cooperation to a greater degree than South Korean officials due to residual South Korean public resentment against the Japanese occupation of Korea 1905–1945. The U.S., as a traditional military ally of South Korea, dealt with each state independently according to the institutional frameworks erected with each security partner. The presence of a joint command structure in the U.S.–South Korean military alliance, and its absence in the U.S.–Japan security bargain, meant that any trilateral mechanism would involve Japan in a coordinated rather than an integrated role. Domestic constraints on the military prevented Japan from making any military commitment to South Korea, while emotional South Korean opposition to military ties to Japan precluded any commitment to Japan's defense. Given these differences, U.S.–Japan cooperation with South Korea could not be a truly joint effort, but rather a coordination of separate activities.

Lack of a Liberal Democratic Party (LDP) majority in Japan's Lower House since October 1996,[36] and the LDP alliance with the Sakigake and the Social Democratic Party in the Upper House, meant there was little chance for domestically driven changes in Japan's relationships with China, Russia and South Korea. Main opposition party leaders Ichiro Ozawa of Shinshinto and Naoto Kan of the Democratic Party of Japan were keen to jump on any opportunity for a center-left alternative to the LDP's conservative coalition. In the United States, Republican control of both the Senate and the House similarly constrained any substantial policy changes considered by the Democratic Clinton administration. So in September 1997, when the Security Consultative Committee (Foreign Minister Obuchi and Minister of State for Defense Kyuma, and Secretary of State Albright and Secretary of Defense Cohen) unveiled the new Defense Guidelines, they announced only modest clarifications of military roles. Within the scope of the Security Treaty, the guidelines called for enhanced coordination within existing constitutional constraints.

A New Bargain

The September 1997 Defense Guidelines announced an outward orientation to promote regional peace, prosperity, and stability, and attempted to provide an inward clarification of what each side can actually deliver to the relationship. Instead of emphasizing cooperation during conflict as in the 1978 guidelines, the new guidelines outlined more effective and credible U.S. Japan cooperation during peacetime. U.S. contributions to security were unchanged. The U.S. would continue to provide nuclear deterrence, forward-deployed forces in the region, and other forces that can reinforce those forces. Japan's military contributions, however, were specified with respect to context and content. The guidelines established three general situations that proscribed broad parameters of defense cooperation — normal circumstances, during armed attack, and in areas surrounding Japan that will have an important impact on Japan's security.

During normal circumstances, cooperation would involve increased information and intelligence sharing, more policy consultations, promoting regional security dialogues, defense exchanges, international arms control and disarmament, and UN peacekeeping or humanitarian relief operations. The guidelines vaguely promised to look for more ways to provide mutual support, but gave specific authorization to prepare procedures to cooperate in the fields of transportation, medicine, information-sharing, education and training, emergency and disaster relief, and defense and mutual cooperation (operational) planning. By endorsing the need to coordinate details of military activities, the guidelines forced practical discussion of what could and should happen once the firing starts.

In the event of armed attack, arrangements would be nominally the same as before, with U.S. and Japanese forces conducting bilateral operations to defend Japan. Under the 1978 Guidelines, at least one "plan" (U.S. planners' term) or "draft study" (Japan planners' term) was developed for the defense of Japan against a Soviet threat. However, combined (bilateral) operations would have been hampered by politically mandated differences in assumptions about military threats. Even though Japan's defense line excluded the Soviet Far East and North Korea, for instance, it had to be assumed that the threat would originate from one of those two areas. This illogic prevented bilateral analysis of specific threats, hampering strategy and preparation. Moreover, Japan's policy prohibition against collective self-defense prevented a single command structure to effectively control the wide range of defense activities. Without actually planning and practicing the most likely scenarios, bilateral operations would have been at best coordinated unilateral operations, and at worst uncoordinated actions that reduced mutual effectiveness.

Under the new guidelines, a commander's concept of operations would be developed into a jointly constructed operational plan against specific threats. In the event of having to defend Japan against an attack or large-scale infiltration, combined and bilateral operations centers would be formed, manned by U.S. and Japanese forces. Due to the continued restrictions on collective self-defense, American and Japanese forces would work through coordinated national chains of command, a process which gobbles up precious time during a crisis. Alliance credibility is enhanced by spelling out national commitments: "the United States will introduce reinforcements in a timely manner, and Japan will establish and maintain the basis to facilitate these deployments." Japan would receive verbal reassurance that the U.S. will provide additional mobility, strike power, and reinforcements during hostilities.

Between normal circumstances and armed attack lay a panoply of scenarios — emergencies in areas surrounding Japan that have an important impact on Japan's security. In these cases, the guidelines laid out three types of functions the SDF might perform[37]:

> Cooperation in activities initiated by either Government, including relief activities and measures to deal with refugees, search and rescue, non-combatant evacuation operations and activities for ensuring the effectiveness of economic sanctions.
> Japan's support for U.S. Forces' activities such as use of facilities and rear area support (supply, transportation, maintenance, medical services, security, communications, and others).

Japan–U.S. operational cooperation, including surveillance, minesweeping and sea and airspace management.

In contrast to the previous guidelines which only generally referred to cooperation in regional situations, the new guidelines would institutionalize cooperation by establishing two mechanisms, complete with bilateral committees that coordinate policy, and plan and execute operations: the Bilateral Coordination Mechanism with its Bilateral Coordination Forum and Bilateral Coordination Center, and the Comprehensive Mechanism with its Bilateral Planning Committee.

The Comprehensive Mechanism and its Bilateral Planning Committee (BPC) of military planners would establish a three-layer process that generates joint concepts and plans: a joint management board consisting of the directors of plans, a joint coordination group consisting of the deputy directors of plans, and joint working panels consisting of those who plan the details of operations based on guidance from their respective national chains of command. They would meet regularly to create concept plans and more specific contingency plans[38] for regional scenarios.

The Bilateral Coordination Mechanism (BCM) was called for to coordinate bilateral operations, intelligence, and logistical support, and obtain necessary support from Japanese government agencies. The components of the BCM are the Bilateral Coordination Forum and the Bilateral Coordination Center. The U.S. side of the Bilateral Coordination Forum consists of military functional directors in U.S. Forces Japan and political military officers in the U.S. Embassy. On the Japan side of the Forum, directors from the Defense Agency, Ministry of Foreign Affairs, and Cabinet Security Affairs Office would attempt to coordinate U.S. requests for support, and task a dozen government agencies. The Bilateral Coordination Center is the bilateral military linkage consisting of USFJ and the JDA Joint Staff Office to manage operations, intelligence, and logistic support activities. This military Center is subordinate to the civilian-dominated Forum, with the former sending explicit requests for support to the latter for decisions. The coordination function would allow military planners to count on what merely had been assumed before: fuel supplies, airport and seaport access, holding areas for troops, repair and maintenance facilities, radio frequencies, medical supplies and treatment of casualties, and a host of other details that many of Japan's prefectural politicians oppose.

Aftermath

After the Guidelines were announced, military coordination paved the way for political implementation and ultimately, mutual commitment. The

Comprehensive Mechanism got off to an early start, producing a Memorandum of Understanding in January 1998. Planning guidance was issued, planning panels formed, and regular meetings began to agree on a common strategic concept. Over a period of several months, JDA's priority of defending Japan and DoD's priority of countering a broad range of threats in East Asia were written into a compatible plan. In contrast, the Bilateral Coordination Mechanism languished between the Ministry of Foreign Affairs and Defense Agency, where a turf battle simmered over how to broker the interagency process. No MoU could be produced until the Diet passed legislation arguably needed to implement the guidelines due to constitutional restrictions.

Because of fears that any change in the SDF mission would be subject to criticism both at home and abroad, a guarded approach to the guidelines ensued. That is, only minimal SDF action would be permitted without specific legal authorization. Control of SDF activity depending upon the situation, rather than flexibility and rapid response, was the overriding objective due to public scrutiny of any change in SDF missions.[39] The Defense Guidelines implementation laws contained three elements. First, a new guidelines law regarding "measures Japan may implement in response to situations in areas surrounding Japan" would allow the provision of rear area support to U.S. forces, authorize search and rescue (SAR) operations, and define cabinet coordination procedures. Second, amendment of current Self-Defense Force laws would add ships and helicopters to aircraft for non-combatant evacuation operations (NEO) transport, would permit the evacuation of non–Japanese citizens, and would give field commanders the authority to use weapons in self defense. Third, the Diet would approve the revised ACSA.

The ruling coalition's price to win Diet passage of these laws was set by a shifting scene of opposition parties[40] whose leaders generally favored more restrictions on the SDF. Endless rounds of negotiations included not only guidelines legislation, but also tax reform, governmental restructuring, and an economic stimulus package.[41] Members of Komeito (Clean Government Party), Japan Communist Party (JCP), and the Democratic Socialist Party (DSP) were eager to debate legalities of the guidelines, regarding even logistic support to U.S. forces as unconstitutional. JCP Policy Coordination Committee Chairman Fudesaka Hideyo charged the new guidelines were based on preemptive U.S. strikes against third parties, with Japan being drawn in through its support role. LDP spokesmen countered by clinging to key policy limits such as rear area support being separate from a combat zone, and allowing SDF participation strictly on a case by case basis.

In January 1998, the announcement by Prime Minister Obuchi and Secretary of Defense Cohen to jointly research a TMD system drew more criticism, based on a 1969 Diet resolution on the peaceful use of space and a 1976 government ban on weapons exports. In July, the Maritime Self-Defense Force declined to participate in Non-combatant Evacuation Operations maneuvers during the well-established Rim of the Pacific (RIMPAC) exercise,[42] citing lack of legal authority to practice rescuing Japanese citizens overseas. As the Diet deliberated over multifarious legal distinctions, the prospect of a divisive public debate chilled the ruling coalition. Fearful of potential paralyzing policy differences, LDP leaders postponed the submittal of guidelines legislation until after Upper House elections. The 11 July elections handed the LDP a convincing defeat, with the LDP losing 16 seats and opposition parties DPJ and JCP registering large gains. Prime Minister Hashimoto resigned. He was replaced by Obuchi after an LDP election on July 24th.

The Guidelines debate became more urgent in August by the stark reappearance of a North Korean threat. Without warning, Pyongyang test-fired a two-stage missile[43] over Japan, claiming it was just an attempt to launch a satellite. The first and second stages bracketed Japan, falling into the sea to the west and east. American and Japanese allies quickly disagreed on the purpose of the launch and laid blame on each other for military deficiency and political machination. U.S. officials said the launch was a failed attempt to put a satellite into orbit, and claimed to have warned Japanese officials that North Korea was about to launch a missile. Japanese officials regarded the launch as a Taepodong I, and interpreted Washington's satellite theory as a desire to not derail North Korean compliance with the 1994 Agreed Framework. Tokyo officials also blamed U.S. intelligence for withholding information on where the missile impacted. Still, the U.S. Pacific Command sent six B-2 and B-52 aircraft to Guam and put 36 F-16's at Misawa Air Base on alert, while the Defense Agency alerted the AEGIS missile cruiser Myoko in the Sea of Japan.

The alliance's immediate policy reaction was also at odds. Japan announced its unilateral withdrawal from the Korea Energy Development Organization (KEDO), leaving South Korea and the United States as the formerly multilateral organization's only members. This action, later reversed at the behest of U.S. officials, suspended food aid and assistance for light-water nuclear reactors, as well as talks to normalize diplomatic relations between Japan and North Korea.[44] As details of the post-launch crisis action became public, Japanese journalists criticized dependence on U.S. satellite intelligence, lack of coordination among internal governmental security agencies, and the evident inability to do anything about a surprise missile attack.

After the launch, four initiatives sowed the seeds of improving Japan's ability to respond to actual threats. First, the government decided Japan did indeed possess the right to attack missile sites in North Korea based on self-defense. However, as Defense Agency Director General Nukaga made clear during Diet hearings, aircraft with air refueling capability were needed to actually reach the offending launch sites. Second, there was broad recognition of the need to improve the emergency notification process among the Defense Agency, Foreign Ministry, key Diet members, and Prime Minister's office. New JDA Director-General Norota[45] proposed to lead a study of emergency legislation to deploy the SDF during security crises.[46] Third, support for an independent reconnaissance satellite capability grew, partly out of the disagreement over what the launch was and whether warning was adequate. Japanese accounts of the intelligence flow claimed U.S. intelligence was not forthcoming, therefore not reliable. U.S. officials insisted Japanese Foreign Ministry officials did not share the information that the U.S. amply provided.[47] Fourth, elements of the ruling coalition began the politically dangerous step of revising the Constitution itself. A group initially established in 1997, consisting of members from five parties, prepared to submit a bill that would create a Diet research panel to study constitutional amendments.[48]

As the LDP and Liberal Party maneuvered to form a coalition for an Upper House majority, Komeito merged with Shinto Heiwa (New Peace Party) in November to form the New Komeito, the second largest opposition party behind the DPJ who held 65 seats. In December, Okinawa Governor Ota was defeated by Keiichi Inamine, whose election promises included the construction of a joint-use (military-civilian) airport somewhere in Okinawa to replace the U.S. Marine Corps' Futenma Air Station. This breakthrough in the Tokyo-Okinawa deadlock immediately won economic aid to Okinawa. The 1999 budget deadline brought Inamine to Tokyo on his first day of office. Because of the need to achieve consensus with New Komeito, LDP-LP leaders needed to resolve the Okinawa issue before drafting sensitive guidelines legislation in the spring.

In April 1999, the Lower House approved the Defense Guidelines implementation legislation drafted by the special committee. The laws contained three revisions intended to reduce Prime Minister's implementation options. First, the law that originally was to provide for "measures Japan may implement in response to situations in areas surrounding Japan" was narrowed to "situations in which the peace and safety of Japan are gravely threatened." Second, the clause concerning inspections of ships was removed, delayed to a later Diet session. Ship inspections were to occur only with United Nations authorization, or in situations determined by Tokyo authorities. Third, a new clause was added to require Diet approval before SDF support operations in non-combat zones and search and rescue operations. In theory, Diet approval could follow SDF actions in high-level emergencies. The Diet ironically restricted its own SDF from seeking unfettered support of its actions, while allowing U.S. forces direct contact with Japanese private organizations, central or local governments. The stage was set for a crisis to trigger an American expectation of military support which, depending upon the Prime

Minister and domestic coalition at the time, might or might not be forthcoming.

In the year 2000, Prime Minister Koizumi Junichiro was elected Prime Minister, riding a populist promise of electoral reform. Enabled by the Defense Guidelines, Prime Minister Koizumi led Japan's strong reaction to the 9/11/01 terrorist attacks in the United States, support of subsequent U.S. operations in Afghanistan and Iraq, and JSDF deployments to Iraq. The level of Japan's participation was unprecedented as JSDF military commitments and actions expanded within the rhetoric of constitutional self defense constraints. Following a verbal crescendo of support by the Prime Minister immediately following the attacks,[49] the Diet passed the Anti-terrorism Special Measures Law the following month and began to support Operation Enduring Freedom in November with combat support (logistical, search and rescue, and refugee relief). In December 2001, the SDF fired its first shots in anger since the Pacific War, sinking a North Korean spy boat found in Japan's 200-mile exclusive economic zone.[50] Prime Minister Koizumi put it bluntly: This was justifiable defense ... the situation is deplorable that armed, suspicious boats are infesting waters around our country in this manner. We need to consider countermeasures.

In 2002, JMSDF minesweepers and destroyers escorted the USS Kitty Hawk out of Yokosuka port, and a flotilla of two destroyers and one supply ship was deployed on-station in the Indian Ocean to provide rear guard support of American and British combat operations. JASDF C-130's flew to Pakistan in support of Operation Enduring Freedom for refugee resupply.

In 2003, JASDF AWACS and F-15's accompanied USAF forces during Exercise Cope Thunder, demonstrating for the first time the cross–Pacific air refueling capability of Japan's premier air-to-air fighter aircraft. Chinese and Korean objections notwithstanding, the Diet approved deployment of 1000 SDF troops to Iraq to aid the reconstruction efforts, in the first-ever dispatch of GSDF to a combat zone. Koizumi acted, often without Japanese public support, to be as credible an ally as possible.

In 2004, the Diet extended the JSDF commitment in Iraq for another year despite vocal domestic opposition. South Korea dispatched a brigade to Iraq in the same year. In October, when Islamic extremists captured a wayward Japanese translator in Iraq and threatened to execute him unless Japan withdrew the SDF from Iraq, Tokyo stood as a firm ally of the United States as the youth was tragically beheaded. At about the same time, U.S. officials had announced a plan to realign its forces in East Asia as part of the Global Defense Posture Review, with some key implications for U.S. Forces Japan. The posture review in the Pacific region would consolidate bases in a system of power projection hubs and main operating bases. The power projection hubs consist of the continental U.S., Hawaii, and Guam), while the Pacific region main operating bases are Japan and the ROK. Overall U.S. goals are to transform its forces to become more globally mobile with increased lethality and flexibility across regions. The three main issues in Japan involve the transfer of Fifth Air Force headquarters from Tokyo to Guam, the transfer of an Army corps headquarters from the U.S. to Japan, and the relocation of some of the U.S. Marine Corps presence in Okinawa to northern Japan. Initially Japanese officials sought to limit U.S. Forces Japan "to maintain peace and security in the Far East," in accordance with Article 6 of the Security Treaty. Prime Minister Koizumi led a verbal intervention that closed the debate, stating that adjustments to USFJ force levels "should be discussed from the viewpoints of the security treaty and the Japan–U.S. alliance in the global context."[51]

In December, Prime Minister Koizumi's Council on Security and Defense Capabilities (named the Araki Commission for its chairman) released "The Vision for Future National Security Capabilities," which recommended strengthened ties with the U.S., exceptions to the 1976 arms export ban and a permanent law to enable overseas SDF deployments.[52] The report encourages Japan to increase the credibility of the U.S.–Japan alliance, implement an "integrated security strategy" across the government, and adopt a "multifunctional defense force concept" in the SDF to flexibly accommodate more missions.[53]

Of particular note is the National Defense Program Guidance (NDPG) for 2005–14, which contains a number of Araki Commission recommendations likely to expand Japan Self-Defense Force roles such as closer U.S.–Japan missile defense cooperation. The NDPG can be interpreted as an application of the U.S.–Japan Defense Guidelines as it invokes the need for strategic dialogue on role sharing, the U.S. military posture, intelligence, and ballistic missile defense. Recall the Defense Guidelines called on Japan to cooperate during emergencies (in between "normal circumstances" and "armed attack") during situations surrounding Japan in the three broad functions of relief activities and economic sanctions, rear area support, and operational cooperation (see footnote 35). By stating Japan's military commitment as program guidance, the NDPG maintains the momentum of the Defense Guidelines. The NDPG naturally goes beyond the Araki Commission in the key area threat assessment, citing North Korean missile proliferation and Chinese military modernization as security threats to Japan.

The aftermath of the Defense Guidelines has seen a series of "normal" changes which are unprecedented for Japan. The measured reactions and concerns about the 9/11 terrorist attack on the U.S., North Korean incursions into Japanese territory, U.S. operations against terrorism, North Korean nuclear ambitions and missile proliferation, and Chinese military modernization indicate an increasing willingness in postwar Japan to express national security interests and take appropriate action to achieve them. These expressions of JSDF commitments reflect the changing nature of the U.S.–Japan security bargain as the relationship continues to adjust to a dynamic security environment.

8

Past Patterns, Future Options

As stressed in the introduction, this book has sought to understand the historical origins and transformation of the U.S.–Japan security relationship. While the importance of this bilateral relationship is generally recognized, there continue to be periodic episodes of sharp disagreement over its nature and future direction. Complicating the debate is the idealistic assumption that security relations ought to consist of alliances primarily based on common conceptions of external threat. This maxim misses distinctive features of the U.S.–Japan relationship's origins and ignores formative realities of alliance dynamics.

The book's thrust, therefore, has been in how differences in relative security priorities affect actual alliance origins and subsequent changes in the basis for continued cooperation. My key working assumption has been that states pursue national security by seeking various mixes of military, economic and political advantage, depending on how they filter and perceive threats to national well-being. This hypothesis requires a more detailed view of alliances than elegant approaches singularly grounded in the assumption of a common threat. As an alternative to traditional models of alliance behavior such as balance of power or public goods (free-rider) theories, this comparative approach is more realistic in situations where states emphasize different economic and military security priorities. Such an approach better addresses the dynamics of alliances as complex security relationships, which is what they really are.

The idea that states seek to balance power remains very much a part of this framework. The stability of Japanese military force levels during a time of changing external military threat, for instance, does not mean that Japanese officials have declined to balance power. Relative power and influence can be pursued with respect to a variety of non-military national advantages — percentage of world trade, relative labor productivity, ability of national industries to adjust to external economic forces, internal political controls, religious or ideological authority, technological adaptation, and the like. In Japan's case, the defining domestic institutions of national security priorities have stressed economic threats to national well-being, and have depended upon assurances of an American military guarantee to deter military threats. This calculus of power and interests is not an objective one directly derived from self-evident international factors, but is also a domestic process in which institutional biases shape threat perceptions, power assessment, and interests. Both methods of analysis are needed, but it is at this level of interaction among state institutions that the nature of alliance and patterns of change can most accurately be examined.

Furthermore, if we consider the relevance of public goods theory to the U.S.–Japan security relationship, it is unclear whether Japan's reliance on the U.S. military guarantee has been a "free ride" enabled by "soft" American security policy makers who have valued the alliance more than Japanese leaders. Given the desperate postwar economic condition of Japanese industries and citizenry, and the great lengths that every Japanese administration has taken to cling to the U.S. military guarantee, it is unreasonable to say that U.S. leaders have appreciated the alliance more than their Japanese counterparts. Each side has regarded the alliance highly, but for different reasons. This asymmetric exchange of interests often results in both alliance partners looking at the relationship and self-righteously concluding that the other side has the better deal.

As a departure from conventional alliance theories and through historical comparison of differences in institutionalized security priorities, this study has presented U.S.–Japan cooperation and competition as a strategic security bargain. Alliance relations have been analyzed in terms of negotiated overall agreements consisting of political, economic and military components. Over time, the substance of each security bargain has transformed from one set of institutional arrangements to another in a response to fundamental forces of change acting on the relationship.

This concluding chapter first summarizes and reflects upon major past patterns evident in the U.S.–Japan security relationship. Given the influence of historical context on institutions during their formative periods, and the impact institutions have in defining matters of national security, these historical patterns merit emphasis here. Second, theoretical and policy implications of these findings are considered with a practical orientation toward identifying and anticipating future strategic options. My hope is that realistic planning of alternative paths for the security relationship will be based on an understanding and appreciation of how and why the actual basis for cooperation originated and transformed in the past.

Origins

Chapters 2 and 3 explained how the security bargain historically originated. The central argument is that the prevailing Japanese and American conceptions of national security historically differed due to contrasting priorities about military and economic threats to the state, and that these differences were institutionalized in security agreements during the postwar American Occupation of Japan. Allowing for differences in values and priorities, and recognizing resultant asymmetric exchanges of security interests are key to understanding the bargain that has served as the actual basis for alliance cooperation, as well as subsequent periods of bilateral discord.

From the beginning of U.S.–Japan security relations in the mid-nineteenth century, Japanese perceptions of external threat led to a state conception of national security that was comparatively broad; both economic and military means to achieving national advantage were considered well within the purview of state security policy. The sudden shattering of Japan's isolation by economically and militarily superior external powers and the resultant forced industrialization[1] of Japanese society account for this broad conception of national security. In contrast, the American self-concept was narrower in the sense that active state pursuit of relative national advantage was largely confined to military matters. To be sure, the American state supported and protected private prerogatives (typically claimed as "rights") in commerce, finance and industry. But state-led innovation focused on military, not economic security concerns. In the absence of external economic threats, a condition facilitated by adequate levels of American military technology, the prevailing American national security conception has been imbedded in liberal economic ideas of open trade and free access.

The prewar interaction of U.S.–Japan national security conceptions illustrates how ignoring such differences can allow for temporary cooperation, but eventually can lead to conflict. The competing definitions of security interests among key sub-national institutions (the Ministry of Foreign Affairs and the armed forces in Japan, and the Departments of State and War in the United States) account for the timing of the ensuing breakdown in cooperative security relations. From an American perspective, as long as a relatively narrow American definition of security tolerated Japan's broadly defined pursuit of military and economic security, conflict was avoided. From a Japanese perspective, military and economic security was an expansionist state imperative in order to compete against the proven fact of hostile western penetration in pre-industrial China, Korea, and Japan.

American tolerance and policy passivity were associated with two attitudes—a disregard for the importance of nuances in local conceptions of security, and an expectation that Japan would naturally come to accept the liberal separation of economic activities and military affairs. Self-righteous American administrations consistently refrained from applying effective economic sanctions during the early phases of Japan's prewar expansion. When the Pacific War did arrive, it was after the State and War Departments had defined Japan as a military threat, too late to halt Japanese imperial advances, and after years of selling Japan the means to wage war.

This economic-military connection may seem obvious in historical retrospect, but at the time, U.S. policy makers behaved as though Japanese bureaucrats' conceptions of national security were identical to their own. The realization that this was not the case was an unfolding process of increasing threat perceptions, beginning with the Japanese invasion and annexation of Korea in 1905 and the Imperial Army's subsequent march through China's open door in the 1920s. In 1934, President Roosevelt and Secretary of State Hull pressed for an arms embargo, but only after Japan signaled threatening military intent by the abrogation of the naval arms limitation treaty (an outcome of the Washington Naval Conference of 1921–22). Effective American economic sanctions (the freezing of assets and the oil embargo) were withheld until the summer of 1940. By this time, following three years of Japanese military brutality in China, U.S. security policy makers finally concluded that business as usual with a regime that embraced a broad concept of national security was simply feeding a military threat.

In Japan, there seemed to be more recognition of the fundamental differences in security concepts. However, the prevailing domestic consensus was that Japan's vulnerabilities were to be overcome by forcible empire rather than external norms of legitimate competition. Since the onset of bilateral security relations, Japanese policy makers sought to insulate Japan from the harmful reverberations of foreign economic forces. The annexation of Korea in 1910 was part of a process begun in 1882 in which Japanese officials sought commercial and trade advantages strikingly similar to those extracted by Western powers in the region. Soon thereafter, China became the Japanese state's ambition for stable markets and a secure supply of resources (oil, scrap iron, raw materials). Bureaucrats within the Japanese Foreign Ministry and armed forces increasingly found common cause in ensuring regional stability through economic and military means. Once territory had been seized and occupied, state centralization of the economic and military means to achieving comprehensive security proceeded apace. Despite efforts within the wartime Cabinet to seek a negotiated settlement after the war had turned against Japan, the key definers of national security remained in gridlock for the duration of the war.

In the aftermath of war, a truncated version of the "broad-narrow" formula of prewar U.S.–Japan security cooperation resurfaced in several important institutionalized agreements mostly negotiated during the Occupation.

Japanese conservative economic elites peddled and Truman-era American officials eagerly swallowed the "militarist conspiracy" as the basic cause of the war. Massive reforms aimed at Japan's demilitarization and democratization from 1945 to 1948, then shifted to re-industrialization from 1948 to 1951. This shift, often glibly referred to as the "reverse course," was not a thoughtless or simplistic reversal of priorities at the time. Rather, Occupation reformers managed a pragmatic sequence of phased changes to begin to transform Japan into a non-threatening, democratic, prosperous capitalist state. This required balanced judgment, difficult tradeoffs and the willingness to make decisions on tough questions: when was de-militarization sufficient? What constituted a decent start on a democratization process likely to be successful? How do we go about re-building a sustainable and growing Japanese economy relatively quickly? These were not easy questions to answer. By 1954, three years after Japan regained national sovereignty with the San Francisco Peace Treaty, a patchwork of ten agreements provided the basis for security cooperation. In total, this postwar security bargain exchanged a U.S. military guarantee for Japan's continued pursuit of economic development, provision of bases for U.S. forces, and a promise to rearm.

This original postwar formula for security cooperation did not seem puzzling at the time. To the contrary, seen from the perspective of state institutions that defined security policy, the framework was a natural outgrowth of national historical experiences. It is not that the United States did not recognize the importance of economic factors. Indeed, U.S. security policy makers rested their whole conception of the postwar world on liberal-principled beliefs that free trade would best provide prosperity and stable political relations among the industrial democracies, thus enhancing their ability to provide resources for the common defense. And it is not that Japanese policy makers were suddenly unconcerned about military security. Constitutional constraints, demilitarization, and internal reforms essentially had cut off the military policy component of comprehensive security. In its place, the United States provided an avowedly temporary external military guarantee that allowed Japan to concentrate on the immediate national priority of economic redevelopment.

Rather, the puzzle has been the resilience of the original security framework over time, which has survived contentious disputes over the pace and scope of Japan's rearmament promise and sharp accusations about each partner's strategic intent. As a result of such uncertainty and in spite of the alliance's success in providing mutual yet different benefits, there is chronic anxiety about the nature of the security relationship. Do we have alliance against a common threat or a device to achieve relative economic or military advantage over one another?

The strategic security bargain that emerged in 1954 and has basically endured since, has behaved not simply on the calculus of a common threat, but according to a broader set of negotiated military-economic-political agreements and expectations. The nature of alliance has been a dynamic combination of different relative security priorities and peculiar national means to achieve them. The security bargain, once set in motion, periodically adjusted to its political-economic-military environment. During this process, the structure of the original framework has largely been preserved, promoted by two internal factors: (a) Japanese domestic satisfaction with an arrangement that allowed for the popular pursuit of economic priorities while avoiding a painful public profile of military rearmament, and (b) American reluctance to push rearmament too quickly, fearing that might trigger instability in anticommunist (and now perhaps, antiterrorist) Japan. The outward appearance of a static alliance belied the existence of profound changes taking place in the security bargain's political, economic and military texture. The second portion of the study investigated the main cases of alliance transformation.

Transformation

In order to understand how and why the U.S.–Japan security bargain has transformed over time, chapters 4 through 7 explored the four cases of significant, mutually agreed upon alliance change: a new security treaty in 1960, the division of military roles in 1981, the agreement to co-develop an advanced weapons system in 1987, and the establishment of a framework for mutual military commitment in 1997. These cases of alliance change are significant because at the time, each was an overarching and deliberate "first-ever" or "only" change to the original bargain. Other policy changes such as Japan's Basic Policy for National Defense, Three Non-Nuclear Principles, the Self-Defense Forces laws, and successive self-defense budgets and national defense program outlines, have been publicly presented rather adamantly as additive in nature, serving merely to reinforce the original economic-for-military security formula.

Each chapter applied the security bargain approach in three basic steps. First, the historical context of the new bargain was related in terms of military considerations, economic context, and political factors. Rather than uncomplicated or ideological agreement regarding common threats to security, these were cases of asymmetric security involving mixed motives and competing national priorities. Second, the dimensions of the new security arrangement were identified. Although each agreement was primarily a diplomatic, military, or military-economic accord in its own right, each case also was part of a broader political-economic-military context that established its

TABLE 8.1-RESIDUAL ELEMENTS OF ORIGINAL BARGAIN

1954 Framework	1960	1981	1987	1994
Constitution				
Ashida Memoranda division of roles: U.S. external, Japan internal	USFJ internal role deleted	JSDF external role broadened		JSDF external role broadened
Ikeda Proposal Acceptance: bases for rearmament deal	Reaffirmed	Host nation support increased; steady rearmament	Host nation support increased; steady rearmament	JSDF rear area support strengthens bases; steady rearmament
Security Treaty / Administrative Agreement	Replaced with new Treaty and SOFA			
Peace Treaty				
Dodge–Suto Economic Accord (U.S. aid)		Overtaken by economic growth		
Charter Party Agreement (naval vessels) & Mutual Security Program (aid)		Overtaken by rearmament		
Mutual Defense Assistance Agreement and Defense Laws	Co-production agreements	Co-production agreements	Co-development agreements	

8. Past Patterns, Future Options   159

overall significance. Third, the historical aftermath of the bargain was analyzed as a prelude to the next change in the security relationship.

What happened to the original security framework in each of these key cases? As illustrated in the preceding diagram, the institutional remnants of the original bargain are three-fold: constitutional constraints on Japanese military forces, the bases-for-rearmament deal, and the Peace Treaty.

These three institutional survivors of environmental change remain at the core of bilateral security relations today. The Constitution remains untouched since its acceptance in 1947, despite its tainted Occupation origins. The image of the *Heiwa Kenpo* (Peace Constitution) in Japanese society is still largely one that highly regards the idea of placing constraints placed on its military. Japanese views of the Constitution still tend to equate peace with the absence of an offensively capable national military force. Offensive military capability tends to be associated with national imperialism, preemptive aggression, and war, rather than with defending legitimate values or interests. Post-Pacific War generations see the obvious contradiction between current realities of Self-Defense Force offensive capabilities (top-of-the line fighter, strike, tanker and early warning aircraft; main battle tanks, mobile rockets and artillery; missile cruisers), and the continued written prohibition against war potential of any kind. Domestic calls for constitutional revision continue to press for tangible results and now include a draft Constitution floated by the ever-ruling Liberal Democratic Party. As JSDF capabilities incrementally increase to remain a viable force that can perform contemporary missions with a reasonable expectation of success, the technical and geographic interpretations of "war potential" and "self-defense" are certain to generate more controversy in Japan.

The bases-for-rearmament deal, supposedly a temporary arrangement, also has persisted, and is directly related to the constitutional constraints on Japan's military means to pursuing security. At the time for Japan, concluding a peace treaty at the earliest possible opportunity and the impossibility of Japan's rearmament at that time led to Prime Minister Ikeda's explicit offer in May of 1950 to Ambassador Dodge to provide U.S. bases for a guarantee of Japan's security. Ikeda's desired economic effect — that of creating sustainable investment incentives for Japan — was achieved and then accelerated by Korean War business. But Japanese economic growth did not produce a better bargain taken. In the absence of constitutional revision to permit an autonomous military role, or a reduced threat environment, or neighbors that really trust a rearmed Japan, Japanese prime ministers and defense officials have, over a fifty-year period, regarded U.S. bases as essential to the security of Japan and the Asian region. Today, Department of Defense efforts to transform the U.S. military for more agile global engagement still regard Japan's basing arrangements as critical to U.S. security strategy. Short of a Japanese military capability to provide adequate protection of Japan's expanding global economic and political interests and perceived as non-threatening by its neighbors, this arrangement seems to provide the only pragmatic alternative for Japanese military security.[2] Without a Japanese military commitment to U.S. security then, what Japan offers the United States in terms of tangible security commitments are bases, and the associated economic compensation to retain U.S. forces at those bases. The bases-for-rearmament deal still reflects the core of what each ally has to offer to the other in order to gain mutual security.

The Peace Treaty also remains quite influential today. Indeed, its preface contains admirable references to the United Nations Charter, internal stability and well-being in Japan, and fair trade practices that enter the bargained basis of bilateral security cooperation[3]:

> Whereas Japan for its part declares its intention to apply for membership in the United Nations and in all circumstances to conform to the principles of the Charter of the United Nations; to strive to realize the objectives of the Universal Declaration of Human Rights; to seek to create within Japan conditions of stability and well-being as defined in Articles 55 and 56 of the Charter of the United Nations and already initiated by post-surrender Japanese legislation; and in public and private trade and commerce to conform to internationally accepted fair trade practices;

In fact, the bases-for-rearmament deal was actually written into the text of this much sought-after Peace Treaty as Japan's preferred option. The government of Japan literally signed up to: (a) follow certain post-surrender Occupation legislation for domestic stability and well-being, (b) voluntarily enter into collective security arrangements; and (c) allow the retention or stationing of U.S. troops in Japan on the basis of other agreements. One could convincingly argue that the acceptance of UN norms of international behavior, domestic stability and prosperity in Japan, and acceptable trading practices are precisely what post Meiji Japan's search for "comprehensive security" was all about. Post-war Japan's military security has been an adjunct to these broader goals, pursued firmly within the American military relationship, and has achieved a degree of military autonomy only since the 1980s.

The transformation of the security bargain reveals continuity and change in the basis for bilateral cooperation. Each modification of the security bargain consists of political, economic, and military parameters, or dimensions. Viewed as a sequence of interrelated bargains, the postwar U.S.–Japan security relationship has periodically adjusted to its environment as it appears to move toward a more equivalent relationship of unlike contributions. The sources of change are complex and varied; a mix of domestic and international forces which security policy makers deemed important enough to act upon. The following summary characterizes each of the four major cases of change in three ways: (1) the change in the basis for cooperation, (2) the forces that led to the change in the security bargain, and (3) the dimensions of the new security bargain.

SUMMARY OF SECURITY BARGAIN TRANSFORMATION

1954 Basis for Cooperation: a military—economic quid pro quo whereby U.S. military protection, aid for re-industrialization, and defense assistance are exchanged for U.S. bases in Japan and Japan's promise to rearm.

1960 Security Treaty

Basis for Cooperation:
  A broadened military—economic quid pro quo: U.S. regional military guarantee exchanged for bases in Japan and Japan's rearmament progress

Forces Producing Bargain:	*Dimensions of Bargain:*
Political -	
Japan domestic turbulence	"Seikei-bunri" separation of political affairs from economic issues
Occupation-era institutional reforms	
Economic -	
Japan monetary and trade imperatives	Collaboration without burden-sharing
U.S. economic predominance	
Military -	
Absence of military factors	U.S. military guarantee is made more explicit U.S. internal military security role is deleted Japan's rearmament is re-promised

1981 Reagan-Suzuki Communiqué

Basis for Cooperation:
  Tightened military—economic quid pro quo; a limited JSDF regional defense role

Forces Producing Bargain: *Dimensions of Bargain:*

Political -
U.S. pressure to contribute militarily
Defense Agency empowerment

"Sei iki" separation of military affairs from economic issues

Economic -
Substantial change in relative economic growth

Japan's burden-sharing increased

Military -
Increased Soviet military capabilities

Division of military roles, expansion of combined plans and exercises

Decreased credibility of U.S. military commitment
Increases in military technology

1987 FS-X-CO-Development

Basis for Cooperation: Aggravated military — economic quid pro quo; integrated military-technological initiatives

Forces Producing Bargain: *Dimensions of Bargain:*

Political -
U.S. pressure for enhanced military performance

Merger of military and economic issues at the political level

New capability based on 1981 division of roles
Defense Agency push for autonomy

Economic -
Capital gap
Complex interdependence

Japan's burden-sharing increased Technology transfer issues

Military -
Increased Soviet military capabilities
Regional modernization
Increases in military technology

Military-technological competition
Expansion of plans and exercises based on roles

1997 Defense Guidelines

Basis for Cooperation: Clarified military-economic quid pro quo; expectation of mutual military commitments

Forces Producing Bargain:	Dimensions of Bargain
Political - U.S. pressure for credible military Japan domestic support for marginal increases in JSDF capabilities	Separation of military and economic issues Japan's case-by-case regional commitment
Economic - Recession in Japan U.S. economic growth	Maintained burden-sharing
Military - Collapse of Soviet military threat	Regional contingency planning and coordination of operations U.S. post Cold War draw-down of forces Persian Gulf War North Korea nuclear crisis

In light of these four historic cases of alliance change, the long-term dynamic of U.S.–Japan alliance transformation has been mainly the work of economic and military-technological forces filtered through domestic political constraints that define what national security is, and seek relative national advantage based on that conception. The cases support the view that economic and military-technological factors are forces of change, while institutional structures are forces for stability (or rigidity) that attempt to dampen the effects of change. Institutional arrangements, themselves products of historical circumstances, clearly erode over time. But their institutional remnants continue to constrain future policy options. Institutionalized departures from the previous security bargain have not been frequent. However, when such changes have transpired, such as in the 1976 National Defense Program Outline and 1978 U.S.–Japan Guidelines, they have been quite pivotal to subsequent "first-ever" mutual changes in alliance relations. Institutions can and do initiate national change which in later years enable significant bilateral adaptation. These points become evident as we examine the dynamics of alliance transformation in each case.

Treaty Revision

In the 1960 case of treaty revision, political-economic forces, filtered through different domestic systems of relative security priorities, produced a new security treaty that codified the 1954 quid pro quo and acquired Japanese domestic legitimacy. From the perspective of the Kishi administration, the major motivations for revising the Treaty were similar to what had driven prewar Japanese state officials to seek national economic advantage — basic monetary needs (dollar reserves and a positive balance of payments) and trade requirements (stable export markets and secure sources of raw materials).[4] However, Eisenhower administration officials viewed matters of national security through traditional American lenses that suppressed state-led economic security initiatives in favor of containing the ubiquitous communist threat. Therefore, genuine military burden-sharing against that common threat was sought, with the goal of including a regional Japanese military role.

In the interaction of these two competing sets of national security priorities, military considerations of security were screened out by two political factors — Japanese domestic turbulence and American fears of Japanese neutrality. Domestic political opposition to both rearmament and continuation of the 1951 Security Treaty pressured the newly unified Liberal Democratic Party ruling coalition. As a result, Prime Minister Kishi needed a new treaty that would remove its more unpopular aspects yet preserve the "economics first" security strategy. For their part, American officials initially rejected treaty revision in an effort to compel Japan to credibly rearm against the presumed common communist threat. The Eisenhower administration ultimately relented to all of Kishi's treaty revision goals after mounting Japanese domestic opposition appeared to threaten the U.S.–Japan security relationship itself. This second failure by U.S. security policy makers to institutionalize the Japanese rearmament promise,[5] in contrast to the success of Japanese officials in reemphasizing national economic priorities, reinforced Japan's dependence on the U.S. military guarantee.

Division of Military Roles

In the case of the 1981 military role-sharing agreement, two factors provided the fundamental impetus for alliance change: military technology, and the marked shift in relative economic potential. As in 1960, the forces of change worked their way through different national priorities of economic and military security. Elements of the original 1954 framework had eroded, but the Suzuki administration still operated within the confines of persistent constitutional limits as well as new policy proscriptions. The 1967 and 1976 arms export bans, the three non-nuclear principles, and the 1 percent GNP military spending restriction continued to suppress military means to achieving national security. In contrast, the Reagan administration embarked on a large-scale defense buildup, continued to eschew industrial policy, and relentlessly pressured allies to contribute to the common defense.

The interaction of the major forces of change was markedly different from the 1960 case. In 1981, American pressure and internal Japanese institutional changes such as the 1976 National Defense Program Outline and the 1978 Guidelines for U.S.–Japan Defense Cooperation enabled the Defense Agency to overcome domestic constraints to bilateral military cooperation. Compared to the domestic turbulence of 1960, there was a relative lack of concern about challenges to Liberal Democratic Party rule, internal instability or nascent neutralism. In 1960, the Kishi government was forced to focus on economic priorities of security by a swell of political factors such as the unpopular aspects of the 1951 treaty, a Japan Socialist Party with over one-third of Diet seats, organized strikes on a large-scale, and the rise of foreign policy neutralists focused the Kishi government on economic priorities of security. This domestic tsunami rolled back U.S. pressure for Japanese rearmament. In 1981, such internal concerns paled in comparison to other considerations — the presence of a rapidly increasing Soviet threat and reduced American credibility coincided with significant advances in military technology, thereby increasing the incentives for military role sharing. In addition, a long period of sustained Japanese economic growth provided noise abatement of domestic political opposition, enabling increases in JSDF capabilities and size, and financial compensation for USFJ. The combination of military role sharing and increased Japanese compensation produced a satisfactory, if vague, equivalence of alliance contributions. However, the political cost of simultaneously deepening military ties and increasing financial payments to adhere the U.S. military guarantee was rather poisonous, elevating uncertainty about the nature and cross-purposes of the security relationship. The passing domestic shock in Japan over the 1981 announcement that the security relationship was in fact an "alliance" contrasted to American incredulity that this could really be an issue. Ambiguity over the details of cooperation seemed necessary to declare bilateral agreement. Apparently it was permissible for the security arrangement to change, but it should not appear to change very much. After the resignation of the Foreign Minister and toppling of the Prime Minister, Japan's domestic crisis subsided. Subsequently, military security ties deepened with more bilateral planning, military exercises, information exchanges and burden sharing. As military-to-military ties continued to develop smoothly, the delicate policy line walked by public affairs offices illustrates the pervasive uncertainty about what, in fact, the basis for U.S.–Japan security cooperation is.

Co-Development of Military Technology

In the 1987 FS-X transition to co-development, military technology and economic interdependence aggravated the quid pro quo in a complex way, opening up new areas for cooperation and competition. Military technological advances and the need to replace an obsolete Japanese fighter aircraft presented a difficult choice. Japan could pursue autonomous development, purchase an American aircraft, or enter into a joint development project. Autonomous development would increase Japan's military contribution to the alliance, while the other alternatives would more or less preserve the military-economic quid pro quo.

As in the 1981 case, political institutions played the critical role in determining how and when security relations change. The Defense Agency's bid for autonomy was countered with DoD pressure to buy American. JDA's ultimate failure to gain domestic allies forced a mutually distasteful compromise. The Defense Agency was able to garner the FS-X program and retain Japanese industrial leadership over the co-development project, but under forced concessions that benefited U.S. aerospace industrial titans. The Department of Defense was able to gain access to leading Japanese military technologies, but felt piqued over the lost sales of objectively superior U.S. fighter aircraft. In the aftermath of the negative lessons of FS-X, steering groups were established to manage the bargaining over the fruits of military technologies. This effectively broadened the scope of the security bargain to include more potentially divisive technology transfer issues. The dilemma for Japan was that part of the original deal was its promise to incrementally develop defense capabilities, yet the process of bargaining undercut autonomous development because in the case of high technology fighter aircraft, Japan's defense industry could not yet compete. FS-X was indeed a stretch for the relationship with respect to producing a high technology weapons system. At best, the agreement transformed the relationship from one of acquisition dependence to getting Japan to rearm itself. But more than a few Japanese still felt occupied by American military hubris. Many Americans still saw Japan the insular free-rider. In a way, the allies had reversed roles albeit temporarily. Japan initially sought to develop an autonomous fighter aircraft, but it had done so for economic reasons and failed. The U.S. had pushed for the superior performing aircraft but in the end adopted an economic approach with congressional intervention that locked in American work shares. Both sides digested the negative lessons of FS-X and vowed to avoid a repeat performance. Under strain and forced consultations, the core quid pro quo of promised unlike capabilities held. At least until a real world crisis tested the determination to actually implement alliance capabilities.

Allied Military Commitment

The revision of the Defense Guidelines stemmed from U.S. pressure to obtain tangible defense assistance and Japan's need to retain the U.S. military guarantee in the uncertain post–Cold War security environment. Insufficient Japanese will to provide military support to clear threats in the Persian Gulf War of 1991 and the potential North Korean crisis of 1994 questioned the alliance's credibility. U.S. expectations of military support were higher than Japan's ability to deliver. In contrast to the FS-X case, sustained recession in Japan and economic growth in the U.S. reinforced Japan's strategic dependence on the United States. In this context, a merger among political conservatives in Japan created a domestic coalition that supported greater coordination with U.S. forces, if controlled on a case by case basis. While the American side generally viewed the Guidelines as a framework for what Japan could do in the region, Japan's negotiators tended to focus on what Japan could not do. These divergent negotiating stances perpetuated the fundamental quid pro quo — American military for Japanese economic security — while allowing incremental increases of military contributions by Japan.

Overall, changes in the dimensions of the security bargains indicate movement toward a complex strategic partnership composed of more equivalent commitments. The trend is illustrated by steadily increasing Japanese rearmament, substantial increases of Japanese non-military burden-sharing contributions, the expansion of military ties and greater mutual commitment, and economic interdependence.[6] These interests find their institutional expression in the 1960 Treaty, numerous co-production agreements, host nation support accords since the late 1970s, the 1981 military role-sharing communiqué and joint arrangements, the 1983 technology transfer procedure agreement, the 1987 FS-X co-development/co-production accord, and the 1997 defense guidelines.

The practical impact of the defense guidelines, themselves a product of nearly a half-century of persistent postwar security cooperation, became evident when the United States was attacked by Al Qaeda on September 11, 2001. In the next three days, Japanese Prime Minister Koizumi used unprecedented language in a crescendo that expressed Japan's anger, outrage and commitment to fight terrorism. The following month, Liberal Democratic Party leaders invoked the Defense Guidelines to win Diet approval of JSDF combat support of U.S. counterterror operations. JMSDF destroyers, minesweepers and supply ships joined U.S. and UK forces in the Persian Gulf, and JASDF C-130 flew to Pakistan for refugee relief missions. On December 22nd, Japan used lethal force for the first time when a Japan Coast Guard patrol boat sunk a North Korean spy boat in Japan's territorial waters. Mutually supportive U.S.–Japan military operations increased rapidly, including the domestically controversial step of placing JSDF troops on the ground in Iraq to conduct humanitarian relief operations in a combat zone.

Significant Post 9/11 Defense Policy and Operations:

2001 JGSDF deployed overseas to support counter-terrorism in a combat zone
2003 JASDF AWACS + USAF air refuel JASDF F-15 aircraft in long-range force capability exercise
Diet approves JSDF deployment to Iraq
Japan joins Proliferation Security Initiative (PSI)
Japan–U.S. multilateral talks with DPRK
Diet eases ban on arms exports to allow U.S.–Japan missile defense cooperation
2004 JGSDF troops deployed to Samawah, Iraq
Japan hosts PSI Maritime Interdiction Exercise
2005 JGSDF in Iraq extended to June 2006

Do these examples of cooperation indicate a shared common threat, or simply practical preservation of the asymmetry that has served as the basis for continued security cooperation? This is a long-term question at the heart of the nature of the U.S.–Japan security relationship, and the answer is likely to continue to be a blend of mixed motives. However, if the future of the U.S.–Japan security relationship is to include such expansions in military cooperation that test domestic policy limits, then policy makers ought to be prepared for complexity. The road ahead is likely to be a familiar, problematic progression of continuity and change, cooperation and competition.

One method to detect increases in Japan's potential to commit to alliance in the security bargain is to look for adjustments in fundamental defense policies. While it is less likely to expect policies to anticipate changes in threats, reactive policy changes are a normal means for states to adapt to a changing environment. Three examples of incremental changes in Japan's fundamental defense policies (1957) bear watching.[7] First is the modification of the long-standing vow to "avoid becoming a military power." Subsequent qualifiers to this vow are the addition, "that could threaten others," and the most recent verbal stretch, "to avoid becoming a major military power." A robust self-defense is made more palatable and therefore acceptable by bringing in the goal of not threatening others, which all states tend to claim anyway. The subsequent self-allowance of military power status, as long as Japan is not a *major* military power, adds more flexibility to the original rigid interpretation of self-defense. A second incremental yet fundamental change in Japan's defense policies is the addition of the clause, "to firmly maintain the Japan–U.S. security arrangements." The absence of referring to the revised

Security Treaty by name leaves open the possibility of another bilateral treaty revision. It is not reasonable to assume the current treaty will continue to absorb increasingly significant changes in military roles and missions. Indeed the 1951 Security Treaty was alternately expected to: (a) be a provisional arrangement to achieve allied acceptance of a Peace Treaty with Japan, and (b) enable a temporary U.S. military presence until Japan could rearm. Then the 1960 revised Treaty increased U.S. expectations that Japan would take on a degree of responsibility for regional security, but also acknowledged Japan's constitutional limitations. A third change to watch is the addition of Japan's intent "to build up defense capabilities within moderate limits." As in the previously example, this policy reiterates an historic element of the founding U.S.–Japan security bargain. However, "moderate limits" contains more flexibility than "constitutional limits." Should the constitution be revised through democratic Japan's political process, a "moderate" defense capability will surely take on a new meaning. In states unfettered by domestic policy constraints on war potential, collective security, and offensive forces, whether defense capabilities are minimal or moderate or extreme is defined a bit more by the external threat environment.

What if large changes in the relationship were to occur, such as a revision of Japan's Constitution to openly allow collective defense, collective security and offensive options? Would this lead to an alliance of mutual military commitments or a more independent Japanese security policy? A formal alliance with regional responsibilities would require some level of American basing in Japan, or at least access to Japanese bases, to preclude Japan's diplomatic isolation. It is difficult to imagine how Japan would independently address peace and security in the region without being seen by its neighbors as a potential threat. Strategic alternatives to going it alone, or bilateralism with the United States, would require security relationships with other powerful partners (rising China) or active engagement in an effective regional security organization (Northeast Asian Treaty Organization). Dramatic changes in the U.S.–Japan relationship must not be ruled out simply because the alternatives are unclear or likely, as there are opportunities for security bargains among China, the Koreas, and Japan that deserve to be explored. As revealed in the FS-X case of this book's bilateral study, movement toward strategic similarity with partners may open up new areas for cooperation, but also introduces new potential rivalries.

What is clear from the succession of changes to the founding U.S.–Japan security bargain is that there has been a gradual erosion of the original military-economic quid pro quo. What started out for Japan as utter dependence on U.S. military protection and defense assistance in exchange for bases, economic reconstruction and a promise of re-armament, has evolved into a generally equivalent albeit asymmetric alliance under certain conditions. The gradual improvement in Japan Self-Defense Force military capabilities, division of bilateral military roles, and emergence of mutual commitments involving operational roles are cooperative developments that just so happen to erode the military-economic quid pro quo.

As remnants of the original framework fade away, the relationship holds the promise of becoming a more symmetrical alliance if it can build reciprocal military commitments. The 1997 defense guidelines increased the U.S. expectation of military support from Japan in the next crisis, but the Japanese commitment is not formalized as in agreements such as NATO and the U.S.–South Korean alliance. Yet, Japan sent forces to Iraq in support of Operation Iraqi Freedom almost a year before regional ally South Korea dispatched its brigade. The promise to consider rear area support on a case-by-case merely formalized what any government would do: wait and see. Compared to other formal allies of the United States, Japan's recent decisions seem to clarify the terms of the security bargain as a conditional military alliance. According to the defense guidelines, this kind of rear area support of combat operations can continue, but on a case by case basis. Will national publics like what they see, or will they demand change?

Theoretical and Policy Implications

The history of U.S.–Japan alliance origins demonstrates that different national security concepts can arise from different values or different conceptions of threat based on historical conditions. Despite the often cited agreement on general values, there are specific differences regarding individual and rights, government intervention in the economy, and the legitimate use of force that matter. Differences about the relative importance of military, economic, and ideological threats may account for differences in security policy priorities that seek relative advantage over those threats. Regardless of the cause of these differences, security concepts can interact in patterns described in terms of the scope of national security matters — narrow-narrow, broad-broad, and broad-narrow. A narrow-narrow interaction of state definitions of security seems ideal for harmonious security relations. Economic competition can occur outside the official realm of national security as defined by the state, according to the rules of the market. Certainly the rules and processes of "globalization"— the integration of economies through relatively open trade and financial flows — are regarded as both opportunities and threats. But theoretically, with closer attention paid to differences among security priorities, more states and associated organizations (bilateral, multilateral, regional or global) could accept common norms and processes by which to adjust to international changes without elevating internal adjustments to matters of national security. The U.S.–Japan case suggests that the ability of alliance partners to cooperate without serious discord is enhanced by separating military matters from economic activities. However, such an idyllic state of affairs requires mutual willingness to embrace the common rules (such as the global market) and share a commitment to them.

It is difficult to imagine reaching a narrow-narrow interaction without Japanese constitutional revision and a new Security Treaty in which defense obligations are genuinely reciprocal, and mutual, non-discriminatory and open economic access. While the former is still deadlocked in Japan, there has been progress on the latter. Japanese policy makers can claim progress eliminating non-tariff barriers to trade and finance, while the U.S. government as of late has avoided blaming Japanese protectionism for American economic failures. To the extent that reforms promote open access, security relations can move forward toward this ideal type of narrow-narrow interaction. However, until and unless military obligations are truly reciprocal rather than dependent, the partnership will be exceptionally prone to misunderstandings and require constant monitoring for health. Instead, a vestigial framework of unlike contributions will cultivate perceptions among both allies that the other partner is intentionally, perhaps strategically, reaping unfair benefits from an unequal arrangement.

At the other extreme of security concept interactions, a broad-broad mix of state definitions where both states actively pursue relative military and economic advantage over each other. This interaction implies increased potential for serious tensions, even between two democracies. A broad-broad state of affairs could emerge from events that trigger an American embrace of illiberal economic security and failed Japanese economic liberalization with a return to seeking independent military security. These conditions could arise from a widely defined Commerce-Defense industrial policy, or national integrated strategy that strengthens the hands of the Ministry of Economy, Trade and Industry and the Japan Defense Agency. Or, it could result from events that drastically reduce the credibility of the U.S. military commitment to Japanese defense — a massive weakening of the dollar, long-term failure to reduce the U.S. federal deficit, or large-scale American protectionism against Japanese products. Cross-national linkages that frustrate broad domestic definitions of security, such as Department of State-Ministry of Foreign Affairs common interests in open trade, militate against a broad-broad state of affairs.

In this regard, issues such as technology transfer that merge economic and military considerations of national security are inherently explosive. When state security institutions are not involved in technology transfer issues, private firms can simply collaborate or compete for new technology. But when such issues become elevated to the mantle of national security, state concerns (including national pride) replace market considerations, and the potential for conflict at the political level rises. Ironically, the increased potential for broad policy coordination that comes with government involvement in military-economic issues includes a greater risk that such issues become nationalistically politicized, leading to wide-ranging policy antagonism. The aftermath of FS-X provides a useful example of a broad-broad interaction at lower levels of management to reach agreements before they become political issues. If military technological issues come to dominate U.S.–Japan relations and nationalistic coalitions held, both Japan and the United States theoretically could consider the broad pursuit of economic and military advantage as vital matters of national security. This situation, the prewar experience has shown, leaves scant room available for compromise and legitimate competition. Even with the close military relationship of today, the danger of a broad-broad interaction of security concepts is that Japanese and American security policy makers could view each other as national security threats rather than as legitimate economic competitors.

The asymmetric exchange of relative security priorities can become unstable as the basis for security cooperation. Rising American intolerance of lopsided economic benefits favoring Japan and growing Japanese displeasure with an increasingly expensive and noisome U.S. military guarantee are signs of instability. But the old framework has adapted over time, so a sudden change in the basis for cooperation toward a mutually acceptable alliance division of labor, or integration of labor, requires persistence and patience. Scrapping the 1960 Security Treaty or negotiating a new one is not yet considered acceptable. Even the incremental improvements in military coordination of the Defense Guidelines were weakened by laws supposedly passed to implement the guidelines.

We know from this historical analysis that two factors have been present in each major change in the U.S.–Japan security bargain: domestic institutional change in Japan, and a substantial gap in bilateral economic performance. External military change was usually present, either in the form of increased regional capabilities or reduced credibility of either partner's commitment. Various types of recent domestic changes or feasible incremental changes in Japan illustrate how the bargain is likely to change next:

1. An alternative Japanese coalition consisting of Minshuto and defectors from LDP and Jiyuto advocate looser interpretations of constitutional restrictions or simply empower the Defense Agency to take on new capabilities for offensive (preemptive) self-defense
2. Increase in public support for reasonable defense items such as the reconnaissance satellite, the U.S. theater missile defense system, air-to-air refueling capability for deep strike aircraft, longer-range destroyer capability for fast reaction against incursions

3. Sudden rise in anti–U.S. base presence due to a high profile crime committed by a U.S. service member, forcing central government concessions to local governments

The recent persistent Japanese recession and steady growth in the U.S. economy constitutes a gap in bilateral economic performance. If this trend were to continue, Japan's military dependence on the U.S. could increase, with Japan having to make more military contributions to avoid over-dependence. External changes that trigger alliance change could take various forms:

1. A reunified Korea, unconstrained by constitutional prohibitions against offensive forces, which could be perceived in Japan as a regional competitor
2. A modernizing China with power projection capability seizes more Spratly islands currently in dispute with Vietnam, Taiwan, Malaysia, Brunei, the Philippines, raising Japanese concerns about Chinese territorial ambitions with respect to the Senkaku islands, in dispute with China
3. Resolution of Northern Territories issue with Russia, leading to development opportunities and defense cooperation
4. Self-Defense Forces fail to perform well against North Korean special operations forces or terrorist attacks, revealing SDF vulnerability to offensive forces

The credibility of the U.S. guarantee might drop due to global over extension, or lack of support in the United States for overseas bases. Japan's credibility could again be seen as inadequate in the event of failing to support U.S. actions in a regional contingency that merely affects Japan's security.

Managing an Asymmetric Alliance

In view of these theoretical concerns, the current security bargain can best adapt to a changing environment with three types of limited policy adjustments.

First, military-economic agreements can retain the U.S. military guarantee in exchange for Japanese financial compensation, effective basing arrangements, and economic contributions to security. The limits to these adaptations are American reluctance to provide mercenary services, reduced Japanese ability to pay, and the exclusive benefits of economic aid. Yet even this option of the status quo can accommodate change if we focus on the types of bases provided to U.S. forces. With enhanced civil-military cooperation, some bases in Japan could essentially become local economies for surrounding neighborhoods. Bases might be transformed or transferred from large, concentrated footprints of American forces and capabilities to leaner 'reception" bases for expeditionary operations. Advanced logistic support for U.S. and JSDF forces, state-of-the art command centers for planning and directing operations, combined military education and training schools, and dual-use bases are other possibilities. Constraints to these options are domestically set, and subject to change by agitated publics or economic conditions. But as long as military technological issues can be managed at relatively low levels and sensitivity to local concerns is adequate, military-economic agreements can continue to provide some flexibility in the relationship.

Second, enhanced military cooperation can replace the military-economic quid pro quo with mutual commitments against clear threats such as terrorism, drug trafficking, external aggression, or severe internal repression such as in Kosovo. The limits are Japan's constitutional and political restrictions on its military role, and the ability of the JSDF to develop integrated, joint forces.[8] The constitutional constraint on the use of force to settle disputes, and prohibition against war potential have been single-mindedly applied to Japan's self-defense forces, not other forces that might present a threat to Japan. This was due to the assumption that Japanese militarism was the cause of the Pacific War. If militarism were indeed the cause of war, then regime change in Japan, a fact for over 50 years, should have ameliorated these concerns by now. If the militarism assumption is not valid by itself and instead, different security priorities arising from historical circumstances with associated threat perceptions were the causes of the war, these have changed, too. Therefore, by confining military cooperation to situations that involve threats widely regarded as offensive, contemporary Japanese plans and responses could be justified today as defensive. Japanese offensive capabilities could be viewed as acceptable if the motivation to use those capabilities is to protect Japan against forces deemed hostile by today's standards. Such threats could reasonably include: ballistic missiles ranging Japan; naval, amphibious or airborne forces capable of seizing Japanese territory, embedded terrorist cells with the means to conduct devastating urban or infrastructural attacks, and the proliferation of weapons of mass destruction. In cases such as these, political decisions in the future might enable collective self-defense and offensive actions. These advances in military cooperation could be eased by the recent JSDF initiative to develop a joint system so allied collective action could be more effective. A functional joint Japanese command and control system, under trusted civilian control, could enable external integration for an effective allied response.

Third, technological advances can produce new areas of security cooperation within existing structures and restrictions. The limits are residual national differences over security and non-security competition in technology transfer issues. Examples of expanded cooperation include: cyberspace defense operations; multiple sensor intelligence, surveillance and reconnaissance; command & control software and procedures; integrated disaster relief planning and operations; incident management and response database sharing and exercises; and robust air and missile defense systems. As we have seen in the security bargain's major cases of change, new areas of cooperation can generate new missions that involve new technologies applied to maritime or air forces. Operations in Iraq may be seeding new technologies and human competencies for enhanced effectiveness of security missions. Policies tend to change as they become driven by interests and incentives that grow more complex. The prospects of systems integration and military advantage impel bilateral cooperation. Through realistic, incremental adjustments that stretch domestic limits and seek opportunities for equivalent exchanges of interests, the security bargain can continue to build reciprocal benefits and meet new challenges.

How likely are these types of change? In the first type of adjustment, domestic support for the security relationship in both countries is a key ingredient to success. Subject to economic conditions and mutuality of exchanged interests, deepening economic interdependence and increased equality of contributions in kind are positive trends. Military cooperation based on common threats has increased due to global terrorism and the vulnerability of modern societies to asymmetric warfare and weapons of mass destruction. Combating terrorism is a mission that can deepen mutual benefits if both nations invest in putting forth an adequate effort. Another arena for adjustment includes strategic missile defense and information and cyberspace defense, although the line between defense and offense will be prone to dueling definitions. Given increased lethality of weapons and the presence of committed terrorists to use them, an exclusively defensive mindset may be utterly ineffective in the new security environment.

Both partners need to be sensitive to differences rather than presume shared similarities of security priorities. At the same time, there must be sustained dialogue and periodic agreement over what constitutes legitimate state-to-state competition and what should be left to individuals or groups outside the rhetoric of national security. Common values promote such understanding and help maintain a stable security bargain.

What are the prospects that the security bargain will become a formal alliance of mutual military commitment? Several regional considerations need to be taken into account. First, unprecedented JSDF actions in support of U.S. military operations during the war on terrorism raise U.S. expectations of partnership as they increase Japan's freedom of action. Radical Islam or other forms of violent extremism may pose a sufficient long-term threat to forge an alliance out of the security bargain, if the United States does not demonstrate itself to be an unreliable or dangerous ally. Bilateral consultations are profoundly important, but during crises, time can run out before a Japanese commitment emerges and the U.S. takes action. U.S. actions taken without consultation could elicit support in Japan for a more multilateral approach to security. But there is no viable multilateral security organization in East Asia yet. In extreme cases of U.S. unilateral action, Japan could conceivably abrogate the 1960 security treaty, followed by neutralism or independence. This course of action would likely isolate Japan from its neighbors. Compared to the differentiated exchange of unlike interests at the heart of the U.S.–Japan security bargain, mutual military commitment is a significant promotion of the relationship that does not automatically follow from increases in military capabilities. It will require a common view of the military threat that is simpler to understand, but much more difficult to attain.

Second, recurring North Korean nuclear crises and the drives for peninsular reunification are important regional challenges for the U.S. to address in a responsible manner if it is to earn the trust of Japan the ally. Japan's historical role in Korea places it at a disadvantage when it comes to playing a political role in resolving the dispute, although the Six-Party Talks (U.S., China, Russia, the Koreas, Japan) and other multilateral opportunities facilitate Japan's engagement in regional efforts. The Korean price the U.S. needs to pay for a mutual alliance with Japan is to maintain a delicate balancing act. North Korea must be deterred from military intimidation of South Korea or Japan, and the peaceful reunification of the peninsula must be promoted. When reunification does occur, stable Korean-Japanese relations will be critical to regional security. Chinese ambitions may attempt to draw a reunified Korea away from alignment with the United States and closer relations with Japan. This would likely reinforce U.S.–Japan incentives for a formal alliance. Or, Chinese leaders might use the existence of a formal U.S.–Japan alliance to stoke anti–Japanese fears in the region. A U.S.–Japan alliance also presents Beijing an incentive to cooperate with the United States and Japan. Either way, a coordinated U.S.–Japan approach to Korean crises is important to maintaining balance on the peninsula and with respect to China.

Third, there is the nearly certain rise of China to great power status, with attendant questions about what its regional influence will be and whether the leadership will value and act on the concept of political freedom. An authoritarian China is a problem for regional security. In its present state, China is more likely to continue the party line that any increase in Japan's security role is inherently hostile, even with increased China-Japan economic ties. Incremental U.S.–Japan alliance building is a realistic way Japan can increase security capability and manage tensions with the rising one-party Chinese regime. A liberal China enhances regional security on key regional issues. A majority of Taiwan's citizens would vote to acknowledge Taiwan as part of China if the latter were democratic, or at least well on the way. A liberalizing China is still likely to be highly nationalistic, but not as hostile toward an expanded Japanese security role if arrangements included China-Japan military cooperation. Indeed, unless Northeast Asia is so disturbingly different from the rest of the planet that it precludes two democracies from establishing military ties, such cooperation will be a natural outcome of China's political development over time. To this end, U.S.-Japan alliance processes which are open, transparent and extendable to other countries (as collective security or defense) could promote the emergence of a consensus within China that Japan is not a threat. As in democratic South Korea, Japan's reputation in democratic China would still be shaded by Pacific War resentment and distrust of Japanese power. Ongoing territorial disputes between the Koreas and Japan, and China and Japan, reveal these tensions. However, just as properly managed U.S. security relations with South Korea and Japan promote stable relations among the three states, a positive U.S.-China relationship is key to avoiding a U.S.-Japan alliance that threatens China.

This study suggests that such a positive security relationship may not be based on happy agreement on a common threat, or on shared ideological pretenses. An alternative basis for bilateral cooperation is a differentiated exchange of military, economic and political interests. In the real world of diverse values and competition, a pragmatic bargain among relative security priorities can be the beginning of cooperative security relationships.

This security bargain approach may be useful beyond the U.S.-Japan case to others situations where diverse partners seek to manage complex relationships. Broad definitions of security that comprise economic, military, political, ideological or religious matters are risky if they contain opposed values. By approaching the concept of security in terms that include threats to different values, policy makers might address underlying fears and identify more possibilities to exchange interests. Key to such legitimate, non-security related competition resides in sharing a concept of security that is liberal enough to tolerate mutual differences.

Chapter Notes

Chapter 1

1. Richard Neustadt, *Alliance Politics* (New York: Columbia University Press, 1973), p. 56. This authoritative study of U.S.-British alliance crises uses a bureaucratic approach to explain a cycle of "muddled perceptions, stifled commissions, disappointed expectations, paranoid reaction. In turn, each 'friend' misreads the other, each is reticent with the other, each is surprised by the other, each replies in kind."
2. Data *from Defense of Japan 1995*, and *Defense of Japan 1996*.
3. Mancur Olsen, *The Logic of Collective Action: Public Goods and the Theory of Groups* (Cambridge: Harvard University Press, 1965), and Mancur Olsen and Richard J. Zeckhauser, *An Economic Theory of Alliances, Review of Economics and Statistics* 48, pp. 266–279.
4. Soviet incremental increases in naval, air and ground capabilities in the Far Eastern theater included weapons upgrades to destroyers, guided missile cruisers, and attack submarines; readiness and sustainability improvements of army coastal divisions; and increases in air regiments designed for ground attack and deep-strike missions.
5. Robert D. Putnam, "Diplomacy and International Politics," *International Organization* 42, No. 3 (Summer 1988), pp. 427–460.
6. John Herz, *Political Realism and Political Idealism* (Chicago: University of Chicago Press, 1951).
7. Robert Jervis, "Cooperation under the Security Dilemma," *World Politics* (January 1978), pp. 167–214. The four alternative worlds are defined by (a) whether an offensive military posture is distinguishable from a defensive military posture, and (b) whether offensive weapons have the advantage over defensive weapons.
8. Glenn H. Snyder, "The Security Dilemma in Alliance Politics," *World Politics* (January 1984), pp. 461–495.
9. Aaron L. Friedberg, *The Weary Titan: Britain and the Experience of Relative Decline, 1895–1905* (Princeton: Princeton University Press, 1988).
10. Neustadt, Alliance Politics, p. 56.
11. I.M. Destler, Priscilla Clapp, Hideo Sato, Haruhiro Fukui, *Managing an Alliance: The Politics of U.S.–Japan Relations* (Washington, D.C.: Brookings, 1976).
12. Graham T. Allison, *Essence of Decision: Explaining the Cuban Missile Crisis* (Boston: Little, Brown, 1971).
13. Gregory F. Treverton, *Making the Alliance Work* (Ithaca: Cornell University Press, 1985).
14. Douglas J. Murray and Paul R. Viotti, *The Defense Policies of Nations: A Comparative Study* (Baltimore: Johns Hopkins University Press, 1989).
15. E. H. Norman, *Japan's Emergence as a Modern State* (New York: Institute of Pacific Relations, 1940).
16. See Chapter 1, *E.H. Norman, Japan, and the Uses of History*, by John Dower, in E.H. Norman's *Origins of the Modern Japanese State: Selected Writings of E.H. Norman* (New York: Random House, 1975) edited by John Dower. The positivist attack on Norman's class-based

approach took place in the 1950s and 1960s and was anticommunist in its motivations.

17. For instance, pluralist Edwin Reischauer stressed the primacy of commerce to an island country bereft of natural resources, while class theorist E.H. Norman emphasized the perception of a foreign economic threat. Dower, *Origins of the Modern Japanese State*, p. 216.

18. John W. Dower, *Empire and Aftermath: Yoshida Shigeru and the Japanese Experience 1878–1954* (Cambridge: Harvard University Press, 1979); Chalmers Johnson, *MITI and the Japanese Miracle: The Growth of Industrial Policy 1925–1975* (Stanford: Stanford University Press, 1982), p. 20.

19. Ronald Dore, *Flexible Rigidities: Industrial Policy and Structural Adjustment in the Japanese Economy 1970–1980* (Stanford: Stanford University Press, 1986). Three economic challenges which demanded structural adjustment, for example, were (a) the increase in energy prices, (b) the increase in inflation and decrease in competitiveness, and (c) the rise of the newly industrialized countries.

20. Peter J. Katzenstein, *Cultural Norms and National Security: Police and Military in Postwar Japan* (Ithaca: Cornell University Press, 1996).

21. Walter LaFeber, *The Clash: U.S.–Japanese Relations Throughout History* (New York: W.W. Norton & Co., 1997).

22. Richard J. Samuels, *The Business of the Japanese State: Energy Markets in Comparative and Historical Perspective* (Ithaca: Cornell University Press, 1987).

23. Daniel I. Okimoto, *Between MITI and the Market: Japanese Industrial Policy for High Technology* (Stanford: Stanford University Press, 1989).

24. Karel van Wolferen, *The Enigma of Japanese Power: People and Politics in a Stateless Nation* (London: Macmillan, 1989), p. 375.

25. Kent E. Calder, *Crisis and Compensation: Public Policy and Political Stability in Japan, 1949–1986* (Princeton: Princeton University Press, 1988), p. 175.

26. Gerald L. Curtis, *The Japanese Way of Politics* (New York: Columbia University Press, 1988).

27. Masaru Kohno, *Japan's Postwar Party Politics* (Princeton: Princeton University Press, 1997).

28. Dr David Lai, China's Grand Strategy, presentation at Colorado Council of International Organizations Conference, 4 October 2002. Dr Lai was a career diplomat of the Chinese foreign ministry serving in Chicago before defecting to the United States after the Tiananmen Square incident of June 1989.

29. Dr Lai, China's Grand Strategy presentation, 4 October 2002.

30. Howard M. Krawitz, *China's Trade Opening: Implications for Regional Stability*, Strategic Forum No. 193 (Washington, D.C.: National Defense University, August 2002), p. 2.

31. See David M. Lampton, *Same Bed Different Dreams: Managing U.S.–China Relations 1989–2000* (Berkeley: University of California Press, 2001), Chapter 7, *The Seamless Web*, pp. 279–309, on the increasing domestic constraints on China's Communist Party Chairman.

32. The Five Principles of Peaceful Coexistence are: mutual respect for territorial integrity and sovereignty, mutual non-aggression, non-interference in each other's internal affairs, equality and mutual benefit, and peaceful coexistence. *China's National Defense, Section I, the International Security Situation* (Beijing: Office of the State Council, July 1998), english. peopledaily.com.cn/whitepaper/2(1).html.

33. In his speech at the West Point graduation exercise in June 2002, President George W. Bush announced: "And our security will require all to be forward-looking and resolute, to be ready for preemptive action when necessary to defend our liberty and to defense our lives."

34. See Andrew Scobell's *China and Strategic Culture* (Carlisle, PA: U.S. Army War College Strategic Studies Institute, May 2002), an excellent analysis of China's dualistic views on war and peace. Scobell identifies four "guiding principles" of China's external security policy: Chinese just war theory, the primacy of national unification, a siege mentality threat perception, and the concept of active defense.

35. Border agreements with India in since 1993 have formalized the cease-fire in existence since the 1962 border war in the Himalayas. The 1962 war resulted in India's recognition of Chinese rule in Tibet.

36. India's substantial indigenous missile program includes development of the third generation Agni-3 intermediate-range ballistic missile capable of reaching Beijing. See Swaine, *Ballistic Missiles and Missile Defense in Asia*, p. 25.

37. Brett Benson and Emerson Niou, *Public Opinion and the Taiwan Strait Conflict*, Duke University, February 2002, p. 8.

38. *Convergence of Cross-Straits Economic Interests and Implications for Singapore*, Singapore Ministry of Trade and Industry, Economics Division, www.mti.gov.sg/public/EDA/..\PDF\CMT\EDA_crossstraits.pdf.

39. *Cross-straits trade rising*, People's Daily,

http://english.peopledaily.com.cn/200009/13/eng20000913_50452.html.

40. Hwan C. Lin, *Taiwan has overinvested in China, Taipei Times*, October 31st, 2002, www.taipeitimes.com.

41. Tang Yao-ming, *The 2002 National Defense Report* (Taipei: Ministry of National Defense, July 2002), Preface, pp. 1–2. www.mnd.gov.tw/report/REPORT/revised/bb/Preface.htm

42. An excellent review of South Korean reforms is found in Jiyul Kim and Michael Finnegan, *The Republic of Korea Approaches the Future, Joint Force Quarterly* No. 30, (Washington, D.C.: Government Printing Office, Spring 2002), pp. 33–40.

43. See the Ministry of Unification's home page, Frequently Asked Questions, http://152.99.76.131/en/.

44. *National Security Concept of the Russian Federation*, full English translation from *Rossiikaya Gazeta*, 18 January 2000, www.fas.org/nuke/guide/russia/doctrine/gazeta012400.htm.

45. For example, the Russian Foreign Ministry expressed resentment over the tone of the Russian Democracy Act of 2002 which authorized $50 million to promote journalism and cultural exchanges for the purpose of democratizing Russia. *Russia assails 'pedantic' tone of U.S. Russian Democracy Act, The Russian Journal Daily*, 4 November 2002, www.russiajournal.com/news/cnewswire.html.

46. Wolfers, Arnold. National Security as an Ambiguous Symbol, Political Science Quarterly 67 (December 1952), pp. 481–502.

47. This definition of Arnold Wolfers views security as one of several competing values in international relations.

Chapter 2

1. Payson J. Treat, *Diplomatic Relations Between the United States and Japan, 1853–1895* (Stanford: Stanford University Press, 1932), p. 58.

2. Ryusaku Tsunoda, Wm. Theodore de Bary, and Donald Keene, compilers, *Sources of Japanese Tradition* (New York: Columbia University Press, 1958), p. 671.

3. Japan's military inferiority was not inevitable, as cannon and muskets had been introduced by Portuguese in 1542, and were used by Japan's first shogun, Oda Nobunaga, in the decisive battle of Nagashino in 1575. However, subsequent shoguns, Toyotomi Hideyoshi and Tokugawa Ieyasu, forbade this samurai-threatening technology after the use of firearms by Japanese Christians in the Shimbara Rebellion of 1637. John Keegan, *A History of Warfare* (New York: First Vintage Books, 1994), PP. 40–46.

4. Treat, *Diplomatic Relations Between the United States and Japan, 1853–1895*, pp. 8–9. The single most important individual that served as the catalyst for the Perry mission is Aaron Haight Palmer. Over a period of nine years, Palmer lobbied Congress and State to open Japan to trade, presenting a "Plan for Opening Japan" to the Secretary of State in 1849. See Aaron Haight Palmer, Documents and Facts Illustrating the Origin of the Mission to Japan, first published in 1857 and available as Origins of the Mission to Japan (Wilmington: Scholarly Resources, 1973).

5. Perry's four warships were "the largest naval force and the first steamers ever seen in Japanese waters...." Payson J. Treat, *Diplomatic Relations Between the United States and Japan 1853–1895*, p. 11.

6. Diary of an official of the Bakufu, in Transactions of the Asiatic Society of Japan, 2d Series, Vol. 7, p. 98, cited in Treat, p. 15.

7. Historian Charles E. Neu, in *The Troubled Encounter: The United States and Japan* (Krieger: Malabar, FL, 1981), p. 8, says of Perry's method: "His tactics were typical of the era. He warned the Japanese of the fate of Mexico, threatened to assemble an even larger force, and made it clear that he intended to achieve his aims at whatever cost."

8. *Foreign Relations of the United States, 1879*, pp. 631–634. Statement made to Japanese Commissioners by the first American Consul-General to Japan, Townsend Harris.

9. For a rich source of internal debates going on in Japan see Ryusaku Tsunoda, Wm. Theodore de Bary and Donald Keene, compilers of *Sources of Japanese Tradition* (New York: Columbia University Press, 1958).

10. Captain M. D. Kennedy, *Some Aspects of Japan and Her Defence Forces* (London: Kegan Paul, Trench, Trubner, 1928), pp. 20–22.

11. See Edwin O. Reischauer, *Japan: Past and Present* (New York: Knopf, 1958), Chapter 9, "The Creation of a Modern State."

12. Official concern over Japan's response to the foreign presence is plainly evident in public speeches and national journals of the time. See: Kamekichi Takahashi's *The Rise and Development of Japan's Modern Economy: The Basis for 'Miraculous' Growth* (Tokyo: Jiji Tsushinsha, 1969), *Policies of Meiji Government Toward Production Industries; issues of Meiroku Zassi* [Journal of the Japanese Enlightenment] (Tokyo: University of Tokyo Press, 1976); and Yukichi Fukuzawa's *Keio Gijuku*

Hensan [Compilation of Keio Era Style], 22 vols. (Tokyo: University of Tokyo Press, 1958–1964).

13. E.H. Norman, *Japan's Emergence as a Modern State: Political and Economic Problems of the Meiji Period* (New York: Institute of Pacific Relations, 1940), pp. 40–42.

14. The electorate in 1890, at the time of the first national elections to the Diet, amounted to 1 percent of the population. Reischauer, Japan, p. 126. For a history of the centralized feudalism of pre-Meiji Tokugawa rule, see Takahashi, "Relation of Tokugawa Feudal Structure to Post-Restoration Economic Development," Chapter One in *The Rise and Development of Japan's Modern Economy*, pp. 48–57 (Book One).

15. See Yoshi Tsurumi, *Japanese Business: A Research Guide with Annotated Bibliography* (New York: Praeger, 1978), pp. 19–21.

16. Increased nationalism associated with the interaction of foreign external threat and domestic flux are described in many works. See Marius Jansen, "Tokugawa and Modern Japan" John W. Hall and Marius B. Jansen, *Studies in the Institutional History of Early Modern Japan* (Princeton: Princeton University Press, 1968), pp. 317–330; and Albert Craig, "The Restoration Movement in Choshu," in Hall and Jansen, pp. 363–373.

17. The first, in 1870, borrowed 1 million pounds at 9 percent interest from Great Britain to finance Tokyo-Yokohama railway construction. The second, in 1873, was a 2.4 million pound British loan to buy bonds to support samurai pensions. Takahashi, The Rise and Development of Japan's Modern Economy, pp. 184–185.

18. Of the reasons cited for such a paucity of foreign loans by Sakatani Yoshiro in 1897, Director of the Bureau of Computation in the Department of Finance, the most important was a late industrializing nation's fear of dependence on foreign capital. External dependence was feared to invite foreign intervention—Egypt and Turkey were cited as historical examples. Ibid., pp. 222–224.

19. Akira Iriye, *Across the Pacific*, p. 46. The Iwakura mission also attempted revision of the unequal treaties of the 1850s, but failed. U.S. insistence on bilateral revision and Japanese demands for a general revision conference in Europe prevented a U.S.–Japan revision. On this point see Chapter 18 in *Treat*.

20. The classic work is that of Alfred T. Mahan, *The Influence of Seapower on History 1660–1783* (Boston, 1890). "Naval isolationism" is a term coined by Stephen B. Jones in "Global Strategic Views," *The Geographical Review*, 492–508.

21. See William H. McNeill, *The Pursuit of Power: Technology, Armed Force, and Society since A.D. 1000* (Chicago: The University of Chicago Press, 1982), Chapter 7.

22. James N. Buck, *Civilian Control of the Military in Japan* (Buffalo, NY: State University of New York at Buffalo, 1975), p. 13.

23. In 1880, gold specie comprised 90.7 percent of the world's official international reserves, compared to approximately 50 percent today. Peter H. Lindhert, *Key Currencies and Gold, 1900–1913* (Princeton: Princeton University Press, 1969), Chapter 2.

24. Tsurumi, *Japanese Business*, p. 43.

25. On the historical origins of the norm of consensus, as well as its impact on the public policy making process in Japan, see Bradley M. Richardson and Scott C. Flanagan, *Politics in Japan* (Boston: Little, Brown, 1984), pp. 333–336.

26. Samuels, *The Business of the Japanese State*, Chapters 3, 4, and 5.

27. See Jeff Frieden, "Sectoral conflict and U.S. foreign economic policy, 1914–1940," in Ikenberry, Lake and Mastanduno, *The State and American Foreign Economic Policy* (Ithaca: Cornell University Press, 1989), p. 63.

28. This most clearly began with President Monroe's warning in 1823 against the Holy Alliance interfering in Spanish-American republics. It is also apparent in subsequent American resistance to British, Spanish, and French territorial designs in Mexico and Central America in the latter half of the 1800s. See John W. Foster, *A Century of American Diplomacy, 1776–1876* (New York: Houghton and Mifflin, 1900).

29. See Chapter 9 in James M. Callahan, *American Foreign Policy in Mexican Relations* (New York: Macmillan Press, 1932).

30. See Foster, *A Century of American Diplomacy*, pp. 456–457, for a review of American expectations of British restraint.

31. Dana G. Munro, *Intervention and Dollar Diplomacy in the Caribbean, 1900–1921* (Princeton: Princeton University Press, 1964), p. 4.

32. In 1866 the American ship "General Sherman," loaded with European wares, was set afire as it attempted to sail up the Taedonggong River to Pyongyang. Five years later, another American attempt to land on Kanghwa Island was repulsed by the Korean garrison there. *A Handbook of Korea* (Seoul: Seoul International Publishing House, 1987), p. 84.

33. Neu, *Troubled Encounter*, p. 24.

34. compiled from M.D. Kennedy, *Some Aspects of Japan and Her Defence Forces* (London: Kegan Paul, Trench, Trubner, 1928), pp.

45–46; and *Historical Statistics of the United States, Colonial Times to 1970* (Washington, D.C.: Bureau of the Census, 1975), p. 1114.

35. The Treaty of Nanking of 29 August 1842, and Treaty of the Bogue of 18 October 1843, extracted eight main conditions: (1) a $21 million indemnity; (2) abolition of Chinese monopolistic trade practices; (3) opening of five ports to British consuls, merchants, and warships; (4) cession of Hong Kong; (5) equality in official correspondence; (6) a fixed import duty (13 percent ad valorem) and export duty (10.75 percent); (7) extraterritoriality; (8) most-favored-nation status for Great Britain. Immanuel C. Y. Hsü, *The Rise of Modern China* (London: Oxford University Press, 1975), p. 243.

36. By negotiating the revision of the unequal treaties (the joyaku kaisei movement) Japan in 1899 became the first Asian nation to rid itself of extraterritoriality. Tariff autonomy was finally gained in 1911.

37. Bong-youn Choy, *Korea: A History* (Tokyo: Charles E. Tuttle, Co., 1971), pp. 106–107.

38. Peter Duus, *Economic Dimensions of Meiji Imperialism: The Case of Korea, 1895-1910*, in Myers and Peattie, *The Japanese Colonial Empire, 1895–1945*, pp. 128–171, p. 132.

39. See Morinosuke Kajima, *The Diplomacy of Japan, 1894–1922*, Vol. I (Tokyo: Kajima Institute of International Peace, 1980), p. 44.

40. This was the Tonghak [Eastern Learning] Rebellion of 1894, a peasant uprising with strong religious and anti-foreign elements.

41. James W. Christopher, *Conflict in the Far East* (Leiden, The Netherlands: Brill, 1950), p. 35.

42. The Sino-Japanese War Peace Treaty was concluded on 17 April 1895 at Shimonoseki, Japan.

43. Hisahiko Okazaki (Japanese Ambassador to the United States), *The U.S.–Japan Alliance in Historical Perspective*, in Dora Alves, ed., *Evolving Pacific Basin Strategies: The 1989 Pacific Symposium* (Washington: National Defense University Press, 1989), pp. 78–84.

44. See Friedberg, *The Weary Titan*, pp. 180–182.

45. This was reportedly accomplished in secret negotiations between Ambassador Yamagata and Russian Foreign Minister Lobanov in 1896. See Kajima, *The Diplomacy of Japan 1894–1922*, Vol. III, p. 439.

46. For example, consumption of foreign crude oil in 1925 was 43 times greater than in 1916. Kennedy, *Some Aspects of Japan and Her Defence Forces*, p. 209.

47. For details of the planning for the strike on Port Dairen and in particular tactics used in naval battles, see Chapters 13–19 in Edwin A. Falk, *Togo and the Rise of Japanese Sea Power* (New York: Longman's, Green: 1936).

48. Michael A. Barnhart, *Japan Prepares for Total War: The Search for Economic Security, 1919–1941* (Ithaca: Cornell University Press, 1987), pp. 51–52.

49. There were bitter divisions between the Imperial Army and Navy over an "army first" or "navy first" approach to achieving state power and prosperity not considered here. The roots of these rivalries can be traced to the initial Meiji strategy of industrial catch-up. See Marius B. Jansen, *Japanese Imperialism: Late Meiji Perspectives*, in Myers and Peattie, *The Japanese Colonial Empire, 1895–1945*, pp. 1–79.

50. *Foreign Affairs*, October 1925, p. 158.

51. Barnhart, *Japan Prepares for Total War*, p. 30.

52. Ibid.

53. Dower, *Empire and Aftermath*, p. 49.

54. Dower, *Empire and Aftermath*, pp. 69–70.

55. The Nine-Power Treaty was signed by the United States, Japan, China, Great Britain, France, Italy, Portugal, the Netherlands and Belgium. Article one declared: "The Contracting Powers, other than China, agree: (1) to respect the sovereignty, the independence, and the territorial and administrative integrity of China." Cited in Herbert Feis, *The Road to Pearl Harbor: The Coming of the War Between the United States and Japan* (Princeton: Princeton University Press, 1971), p. 9.

56. Barnhart, *Japan Prepares for Total War*, p. 57.

57. *Foreign Relations of the United States, Japan: 1931–1941*, volume I (Washington: U.S. Government Printing Office, 1943), p. 242.

58. *Foreign Relations of the United States, Japan: 1931–1941*, p. 243.

59. *Japan's Policies and Purposes: Selections from Recent Addresses and Writings* (Boston: Marshal Jones, 1935), p. 100.

60. For example, when German-Soviet hostilities broke out in 1941, Foreign Minister Matsuoka and Army officials advocated attacking Russia, and dispatched troops for "special maneuvers." Prince Konoe had been unable to prevent the dispatch of troops, although a subsequent Imperial Conference limited the troops to use in China "to secure the basis for self-sufficiency and self-defense." Togo, The Cause of Japan, pp. 79–80.

61. Factors working against liberalism in Japan were several, some of the most often noted being:

(1) The weakness of the Diet in the Meiji Constitution.
(2) Competing centers of power outside public control (the military services, "genro" informal senior statesmen council, the bureaucracy, Privy Council, and Imperial Household members
(3) State control over education
See *The High Tide of Prewar Liberalism*, in Ryusaku Tsunoda, Wm. T. de Bary, and Donald Keene, ed., *Sources of the Japanese Tradition* (New York: Columbia University Press, 1958), pp. 718–724.

62. The proposals can be found in Foreign Relations of the United States, Japan 1931–1941, pp. 608–609 and 656–661.

63. See Feis, *The Road to Pearl Harbor*, p. 277, on the significance of the Japanese proposals of 6 September and Hull's reply of 2 October.

64. Statement by Secretary of State Hull to Ambassador to Great Britain Yoshida Shigeru on 12 June 1936. *Foreign Relations of the United States, Japan 1931–1941*, Vol. I, p. 243.

65. *Foreign Relations of the United States, Japan 1931–1941*, Vol. II, p. 658. These principles were: (1) Respect for territorial integrity and sovereignty of each and all nations; (2) Support of the principle of non-interference in the internal affairs of other countries; (3) Support of the principle of equality, including equality of commercial opportunity; (4) Non-disturbance of the status quo in the Pacific except as the status quo may be altered by peaceful means.

66. *Foreign Relations of the United States, Japan 1931–1941*, Vol. II, p. 66.

67. Dean Acheson, *Present At The Creation: My Years in the State Department* (New York: W.W. Norton, 1969), p. 36.

68. In this report the "gunbatsu" included not only top military officers but leading industrialists, large landowners, Imperial Household members and top government officials. Papers of Harry S. Truman, Official File 197, Box 685, Truman Library.

69. Belief in the inevitability of a Soviet invasion of Manchuria was widespread throughout the government, but whether to encourage or dissuade Soviet action against Japanese forces was a subject of disagreement. Joseph Grew, for example, advocated delaying Soviet entry into the war while offering conditional surrender terms to Japan. General MacArthur advocated early Soviet entry into the war to facilitate the American invasion of Japan. Neither individual knew about the development of the atomic bomb.

70. Memo to President Truman from Admiral Leahy, speaking one behalf of the Joint Chiefs, cited in Herbert Feis, *Japan Subdued: The Atomic Bomb and the End of the War in the Pacific* (Princeton: Princeton University Press, 1961), p. 69.

71. Frederick S. Dunn, *Peacemaking and the Settlement with Japan* (Westport, CN: Greenwood, 1963), p. 37.

72. Dunn, *Peacemaking and the Settlement with Japan*, pp. 2–3.

73. See former Foreign Minister Togo Shigenori, *The Cause of Japan* (New York: Simon and Schuster, 1956) for this perspective. In addition, naval intelligence officer Kinoaki Matsuo's *How Japan Plans to Win* (Boston: Little and Brown, 1942)—originally published in Tokyo as *The Three-Power Alliance and a United States-Japan War*, provides militarist viewpoints on: the righteousness of the co-prosperity sphere, China as the lifeline of Japan, the Washington Conference, and anti-Japanese treatment in the United States.

74. See Dower, *Empire and Aftermath*, pp. 231–252, on the "Yohansen" anti-war movement in Japan.

75. Butow, *Japan's Decision to Surrender*, pp. 14–16.

76. Robert M. Spaulding, Jr., discusses the impact of the bureaucratic "revisionist-military coalition" in *The Bureaucracy as a Political Force, 1920-45* in Morley, *Dilemmas of Growth in Prewar Japan*, pp. 33–80.

Chapter 3

1. Yoshida, *Yoshida Memoirs*, p. 456.
2. Cited in Tetsuya Kataoka and Ramon H. Myers, *Defending an Economic Superpower: Reassessing the U.S.–Japan Security Alliance* (Boulder: Westview Press, 1989), p. 16.
3. Harry S. Truman, *Memoirs by Harry S. Truman* (New York: Doubleday, 1955), pp. 455–456.
4. Mamoru Shigemitsu, *Japan and Her Destiny: My Struggle for Peace* (London: Dutton, 1958).
5. Yoshida, *Yoshida Memoirs*, p. 246.
6. Yoshida, *Yoshida Memoirs*, p. 457.
7. As in the case of other Foreign Ministry officials, Yoshida's and Ashida's anti-communist credentials absolved them from Occupation purges. They became important intermediaries between SCAP and the Japanese populace. See Drifte, *The Security Factor in Japan's Foreign Policy*; Dower, *Empire and Aftermath*; Weinstein, *Japanese Defense Policy*; and Sakeda Sekai, Kowa to kokunai seiji [the Peace Conference and domestic politics], in Hosoya

Watanabe, *San Furanshisuko e no michi* [the road to San Francisco] (Tokyo: Chuo Koronsha, 1984), pp. 88–112.

8. See Sekai, Kowa to kokunai seiji [The Peace Conference and domestic politics] in Watanabe, *San Furanshisuko e no michi*. The question of trade with China and Taiwan is cited as the most tense issue with Washington at the time. This disagreement complicated obtaining a Peace Treaty and establishing stable postwar security relations. The Japanese goal of economic independence included China in a Peace Treaty, which the U.S. government opposed. Following the outbreak of the Korean War, a compromise was reached — inviting neither China nor Taiwan to the Peace Conference, and leaving Japan to decide the matter afterwards.

9. Watanabe Shofu, Kowa mondai to Nihon no sentaku [The Peace Conference problem and Japan's options], in Akio Watanabe and Seigen Miyasato, *San Furansisuko Kowa* [The San Francisco Peace Conference] (Tokyo: Tokyo University Press, 1986), pp. 17–56.

10. Takafusa Nakamura, *The Postwar Japanese Economy: Its Development and Structure* (Tokyo: University of Tokyo Press, 1981), p. 14.

11. Transcript of a Recorded Interview with Shigeru Yoshida, interviewer Spencer Davis (Princeton University Mudd Library: The John Foster Dulles Oral History Project, 1964), pp. 3–5.

12. *James Forrestal Diaries*, Princeton University Library, Vol. II, Box 1, 4 April 1945 telegram to Secretary of State.

13. Eisenhower Library Dulles Files "JFD-JMA," Princeton Mudd Library, Box 2, A Commentary upon the terms of the United States-Japan security treaty, 19 September 1951, p.1.

14. Melvyn P. Leffler, *The American Conception of National Security and the Beginnings of the Cold War, 1945-48*, The American Historical Review 89, No. 2 (April 1984), pp. 346–400, p. 351. This unique article analyzes differences in the ways U.S. security policy makers thought about intentions and capabilities of other powers during this formative postwar period (sources are declassified official documents and memoranda).

15. Michael Schaller has emphasized the role of the Central Liaison Office, staffed mostly by former Japanese diplomats who came to interpret and implement reforms. Schaller, *The American Occupation of Japan*, p. 28.

16. Theodore Cohen, *Remaking Japan: The American Occupation as New Deal* (New York: The Free Press, 1987), p. 101.

17. July 1990 interview with former legal counsel of the Anti-Trust Division, SCAP, during the American Occupation of Japan.

18. The Department of State's permanent electronic archive of Foreign Relations of the United States 1945–1950 is a useful source for this topic. See *Foundings of the National Intelligence Structure, August 1945-January 1946*, http://www.state.gov/www/about_state/history/intel/intro.html.

19. "The History of the Government Section, GHQ, SCAP," in *Supreme Commander for the Allied Powers, The Political Reorientation of Japan, September 1945–September 1948*, Report of the Governmental Section of SCAP (Washington, 1948), p. 792.

20. Roger N. Baldwin, *Civil Liberties in Japan*, Baldwin Papers, Box 11, Mudd Library. The Baldwin Collection at Princeton University's Mudd Library remains a largely unexamined source about civil liberties reforms in American-occupied Japan.

21. JCS Directive 1380/15, Basic Directive for Post-Surrender Military Government in Japan Proper, in Political Reorientation of Japan, p. 432.

22. Economic organizations included a variety of financial organizations, aircraft, munitions, iron and steel, heavy industrial, chemical, transportation, communications and mining companies. See *The Political Reorientation of Japan*, Appendix B.

23. *The Political Reorientation of Japan*, p. 557.

24. Papers of Harry S. Truman, Official File 197, Truman Library.

25. Yoshida, *Yoshida Memoirs*, p. 159.

26. Dower, *Empire and Aftermath*, p. 333.

27. Yoshida, *Yoshida Memoirs*, pp. 171–172.

28. See Cohen, *Remaking Japan*, Chapter 19, on the classic liberal economic outlook of Professor Corwin Edwards, head of the State Department's mission to evaluate zaibatsu dissolution.

29. See *Report of the Mission on Japanese Combines: A Report to the Department of State and the War Department* (Washington, D.C.: U.S. Government Printing Office, 1946), p. 21.

30. This decision caused friction with wartime allies. The British and French governments advocated severe restrictions on Japanese shipping and commercial activity even after economic recovery, while the U.S. protected Japanese shipping preferences on the basis of "external financial position and balance of payments." Papers of John Foster Dulles, 26 June 1951 Allison to Dulles message, "JFD-JMA" Box 1, Princeton University Mudd Library.

31. Central Intelligence Agency Situation Report 38, "Japan," 14 Sept 48, Papers of Harry

S. Truman, Central Intelligence Reports, Box 261, Truman Library.

32. Papers of Dean Acheson, Memoranda of Conversations, Box 65, Truman Library.

33. Dunn, *Peacemaking and the Settlement with Japan*, pp. 58–61.

34. *Foreign Relations of the United States*, Vol. VI (Washington, D.C.: U.S. Government Printing Office, 1972), p. 185.

35. Papers of Harry S. Truman, Presidential Secretary Files 1948–1953, Box 220, Truman Library.

36. From 1951–1958, MSP's economic assistance for Far East and Pacific states, including defense support, totaled $4.89 billion. Papers of D.D. Eisenhower, Mutual Security Program, Far East and Pacific, White House Central Files, Box 43, p. 2, Eisenhower Library.

37. 10 July 1946 conversation between James V. Forrestal and Douglas MacArthur. Forrestal Diaries, Volume 4, Mudd Library, Princeton University.

38. Reference to wartime Secretary of Treasury Henry Morganthau's plan to reduce Germany to a group of agrarian states.

39. Acheson, *Present at the Creation*, p. 541.

40. Dulles Files, JFD-JMA series, Box 2, Princeton University Mudd Library.

41. Walter Mills, ed., *The Forrestal Diaries* (New York: Viking Press, 1951), p. 187.

42. Memorandum from Army Secretary Royall to Defense Secretary Forrestal, 18 May 1948, "Limited Military Armament for Japan," with appendices, Papers of Harry S. Truman, Box 182, File PSF/Japan, Truman Library. This study contained 12 conclusions, citing strategic, economic and political considerations for armament.

43. SR-38, "Japan," 14 September 1948 concluded, "The future political stability and orientation of Japan depend largely on the attainment of a viable economy." NSC-19, 15 June 1949, and NSC-49/1, Current Strategic Evaluation of the U.S. Security Needs in Japan, cited similar concerns. National Intelligence Estimate-19, 20 April 1951, Feasibility of Japanese Rearmament in Association with the United States, predicted that "if Japan were accorded sovereignty under a treaty of peace, and if the U.S. provided military protection and economic support, the Japanese Government would move toward reconstituting its armed forces in strength sufficient to defend Japan and could gain popular support for this program." National Intelligence Estimate-52, 29 May 1952, predicted a continued "pro-Western orientation," as long as Japan is able to solve its economic problems. NSC 125/2, 7 August 1952, continued this line of thinking.

Papers of Harry S. Truman, Boxes 198 and 253, PSF/CI Rpts, Truman Library.

44. Congressman Charles B. Deane noted "several disturbing questions" discussed behind the scenes during the Peace Conference of 1951 in a letter to President Truman:

(1) How far has Japan progressed toward democracy?

(2) Do the Japanese have the unity and stability to throw in their lot wholeheartedly with the West in the world ideological struggle?

(3) Can Japan increase her exports and administer her domestic affairs sufficiently wisely so that she can in due course stand on her own feet?

Papers of Harry S. Truman, Official Files 197-C, Truman Library.

45. Dulles Papers, Acheson's memoirs, and Dunn's work clearly establish that these separate security pacts were deemed necessary by U.S. policy makers to obtain allied acceptance of a liberal peace treaty with Japan. See "A commentary upon the terms of the Philippine-U.S. Mutual Defense Treaty," "Commentary on the Terms of the Tripartite Security Treaty, signed by Australia, New Zealand and the United States of America at San Francisco, California, September 1, 1951," "Negotiations Leading to Conclusion of Australia-New Zealand-U.S. Security Treaty," "Summary of Negotiations Leading to the Conclusion of the U.S.-Japan Security Treaty," Eisenhower Library Dulles Files, Box 2, Mudd Library; Acheson, Present at the Creation, pp. 687–688; Dunn, Chapter IX, "Security in the Pacific," in *Peace-making and the Settlement with Japan*, pp. 187–204.

46. Ikeda had been a career official in the Ministry of Finance for over 35 years before serving as Minister from 1949 to 1952, and 1956–7. He later became Minister of International Trade and Industry.

47. Army Secretary Royall, in a February 1949 Tokyo press conference, suggested American forces in Japan should be withdrawn, due to the difficulty of defending Japan against Soviet attack. This instilled Japanese fear of abandonment, as an American presence was preferable to Russian imperialism. Harry E. Wildes, *Typhoon in Tokyo: The Occupation and its Aftermath* (New York: Macmillan, 1954), p. 291— a readable, personal and informative account.

48. Terminology of groups compiled from analysis by Kataoka and Myers, *Defending an Economic Superpower*, pp. 9–23.

49. Kennan preferred to wait out Soviet behavior — if the Soviets "changed for the better," demilitarization of Japan would be accept-

able. If the Soviets became a threat, "limited remilitarization" of Japan would be prudent. In either case, delaying the signing of a peace treaty was seen to give the U.S. control over Japan's rearmament option. The JCS advocated delaying a peace treaty for similar reasons of control. See *Foreign Relations of the United States 1947*, Vol. 5, p. 691.

50. John Foster Dulles papers, Box 304, Princeton University Firestone Library.

51. A joint intelligence estimate conducted by the CIA, Air Force, Army, Navy, and Joint Staff, concluded that an attack against Japan was unlikely due to the damage U.S. forces could inflict in such an attack: "The majority concludes, therefore, that a Soviet assault on Japan in 1951 is unlikely except in the event of a major war." Special Intelligence Estimate 11, p. 4, Box 258, Papers of Harry S. Truman, Truman Library.

52. In the Lower House national elections prior to the signing of the peace and security treaties, the Japan Communist Party, the party most vehemently opposed to rearmament, had boosted its share from 4 to 35 seats.

53. A secret memo, undated in 1951, titled "Probable Effects on Soviet Intentions of Arming the Japanese National Police Reserve as Four Fully Equipped Divisions," estimated: "The creation of four fully-equipped, combat-efficient, and tactically-disposed Japanese divisions would limit but could not in itself effectively reduce Soviet capabilities to invade Japan." Memorandum for the President, Box 258, President's Secretary's Files, Papers of Harry S. Truman, Truman Library.

54. Cited in John Dower, *Empire and Aftermath*, p. 426.

55. Dower, *Empire and Aftermath*, p. 427.

56. *Far East Data Book, Economic Cooperation Administration* (Washington, D.C.: U.S. Government Printing Office, 1951), p. 51.

57. "NSC Policy Paper on Asia," 10 January 1950, President's Secretary's Files, Box 198, Papers of Harry Truman, Truman Library, p. 2.

58. Nakamura, *The Postwar Japanese Economy*, p. 42. This sudden dollar income erased a negative balance of payments.

59. The National Safety Agency (Hoancho) was responsible for "security" or "safety" forces until the Defense Agency (Boeicho) was created in 1954.

60. The total included 18 patrol frigates and 50 large support landing ships. See United States Treaties and Other International Agreements, Vol. 9, 1958, pp. 55–56.

61. *Foreign Relations of the United States*, Vol. 14, Part 2, 1952–1954, pp. 1550.

62. "Memorandum For The President," 3 August 1950, Papers of Harry Truman, White House Central Files, Box 41, Truman Library.

63. The United States would pay dollars to purchase the agricultural produce and the Japanese government would deposit a yen equivalent in the Bank of Japan on behalf of the U.S. government. This deposit would be applied as yen grants and a MAP support account. Department of State Press Release No. 117, 8 March 1954.

64. Japan's share of military assistance rose from $65 million in 1956 to $170 million in 1958, second behind South Korea's $286 million of military assistance and $270 million of defense support. Other Far East nations that received MDA funds were Burma, Cambodia, Indonesia, Laos, Philippines, Taiwan, Thailand, and Vietnam. Mutual Security Program 1958, White House Central Files, Box 43, Eisenhower Library, p. 7.

65. Yoshida, *Yoshida Memoirs*, p. 188.

66. *Foreign Relations of the United States*, Vol. 14, Part 2, p. 1455.

67. See "MSA taisei to jieiryoku zenzo," [MSA system and gradual increase of self-defense forces]in *Nihon no Boei to Keizai* [Japan's Defense and Economy], Vol. 9 of *Nihon no Anzen Hosho* [Japan's Security] (Tokyo: Asahi Shinbun Sha, 1967) pp. 168–171.

68. Mutual Security Program 1958, White House Central Files, Box 43, Eisenhower Library, p. 11.

69. *Economic Cooperation Division's Far East Data Book*, No. 3, (Washington, D.C.: USGPO, 1951), p. 51.

Chapter 4

1. The ANZUS (Australia–New Zealand–U.S.) Treaty of 1951 does not include U.S.–N.Z. commitments due to a 1984 dispute over nuclear-powered or armed U.S. ships visitation rights in N.Z. ports. The U.S.–Philippines Mutual Defense Treaty remains in effect although the Bases Treaty was rejected by the Philippine Senate in 1991. The 1954 U.S.–ROK Mutual Defense Treaty is still in effect. The U.S. abrogated the 1954 Mutual Defense Treaty with Taiwan (Republic of China) in 1979 to recognize the People's Republic of China. The Taiwan Relations Act of 1979 promises arms and assistance to Taiwan. The 1954 Manila Pact of the now defunct Southeast Asia Treaty Organization remains in force, supplemented by the 1962 Thanat-Rusk Communiqué, to form a bilateral alliance. The 2005 Strategic Framework Agreement between the U.S. and Singa-

pore formalizes a relationship of defense and security cooperation.

2. For an argument of the U.S. role in elevating Kishi to replace Yoshida, see Michael Schaller, *America's Favorite War Criminal: Kishi Nobusuke and the Transformation of U.S.-Japan Relations*, Japan Policy Research Institute Working Paper No. 11, July 1995, http://www.jpri.org/publications/workingpapers/wp11.html.

3. George R. Packard, *Protest in Tokyo: The Security Treaty Crisis of 1960* (Princeton: Princeton University Press, 1966), p. 56.

4. Http://www.eisenhower.utexas.edu/Korea/documents/postarmisticepolicy1554.html.

5. The UN Charter's Article 51 begins: Nothing in the present UN Charter shall impair the inherent right of individual or collective self-defense if an armed attack occurs against a Member of the United Nations, until the Security Council has taken measures necessary to maintain international peace and security.

6. *Defense of Japan 1998* (annual white paper), trans. *The Japan Times* (Tokyo: Japan Defense Agency, 1998), pp. 68-70.

7. Ibid.

8. Japan 1960, p. 2, Ann Whitman Files/International Series, Box 31, Eisenhower Library.

9. Mutual Security Program Year 1958, White House Central Files/Subject Series, Eisenhower Library, pp. 6-7 and 11-12.

10. *Asahi Shinbun*, 2 September 1955, p. 1.

11. In a later interview, Kishi explained Dulles' rejection of Shigemitsu's revision proposal in terms of the fragmented domestic situation in Japan. Transcript of a Recorded Interview with The Honorable Nobusuke Kishi, interviewer Spencer Davis, The John Foster Dulles Oral History Project, Mudd Library, p. 11.

12. *Mainichi Shinbun*, 31 August 1955, p. 1.

13. Background Paper on the Bonins, American Military Bases in the Bonin and Volcano Islands, 1957, Subject Files Relating to the Ryukyuu Islands, 1952-58, Box 14, National Security Archive Electronic Briefing Book No. 23, http://www.gwu.edu/nsarchv/NSAEBB/NSAEBB22/index.html.

14. Telegram from U.S. Ambassador in Japan to the Department of State, 13 Oct 52, U.S. Department of State, Foreign Relations of the United States 1952-1954, Vol. XIV (Washington, D.C.: 1985, p. 1341.

15. Chairman's Staff Group to Admiral Radford, Dispersal of Atomic Weapons in the Bonin and Volcano Islands, 4 June 57, National Archives, Records of the JCS, Record Group 218, Chairman's Files, Admiral Radford, Box 44, National Security Archive Electronic Briefing Book No. 23, Http://www.gwu.edu/nsarchv/NSAEBB/NSAEBB22/index.html.

16. Okinawa Chronology 1945-72, http://faculty.tamu-commerce.edu/sarantakes/Time.html.

17. Kurzman, *Kishi and Japan: The Search for the Sun*, , pp. 274-276.

18. This is corroborated in another Spencer Davis interview with Ichiro Kono, present with Shigemitsu and Kishi during these initial talks with Dulles. Transcript of a Recorded Interview with The Honorable Ichiro Kono, interviewer Spencer Davis, The John Foster Dulles Oral History Project, Mudd Library, pp. 20-21.

19. Compiled from Weinstein, *Japan's Postwar Defense Policy*; Dwight D. Eisenhower, Waging Peace 1956-1961 (New York: Doubleday, 1965); Dan Kurzman, *Kishi and Japan*; Packard, *Protest in Tokyo*, and Dulles-Eisenhower Memoranda, Ann Whitman Files, Box 31, Eisenhower Library.

20. For an excellent review of this era in American national security strategy, see Richard Smoke, *National Security and the Nuclear Dilemma: An Introduction to the American Experience* (New York: Random House, 1987), chapter 5, "The First Era of American Military Superiority."

21. Memorandum for General Goodpaster, 19 June 57, Eisenhower Library, Ann Whitman File, International Series, Box 34, National Security Archive Electronic Briefing Book No. 23, Http://www.gwu.edu/nsarchv/NSAEBB/NSAEBB22/index.html.

22. Given the global reach of American postwar security commitments, reliance on the relatively inexpensive nuclear edge allowed for affordable containment of communist aggression, while the free flow of liberalism presumably would destroy Communism in the long run.

23. The case of U.S. Army Specialist William S. Girard involved the shooting of Mrs. Sakai Naha with a blank grenade launcher cartridge in an army training area on January 30, 1957. Jurisdiction was ultimately given to Japanese authorities. Girard was tried in a Japanese court and given a three-year suspended sentence.

24. A rightist fanatic during a 1960 election debate later killed Asanuma over the Security Treaty in Hibiya Hall, Tokyo.

25. White Paper on Japan's Trade: 1956, Embassy of Japan Trade Report Summary, Vol. III, No. 11, 10 July 1957, p. 8. Despite record increases in exports, MITI White Papers expressed alarm over increased imports, and the

potential of industrialized countries' protectionism against exports. The promotion of exports and technological improvement of the export structure — away from more volatile commodity exports to heavy machinery and chemical products — received consistent emphasis as a way to improve dollar holdings and balance of payments.

26. *Department of State Bulletin*, Vol. 37, 8 July 1957, Joint Communiqué of June 21, 1957 issued by President Eisenhower and Prime Minister Kishi," pp. 51–53.

27. State Department officials also worked on invalidating laws in Alabama and South Carolina that discriminated against Japanese textiles, and in overcoming Dodd resistance against the repatriation of Bonin Islanders.

28. Dulles expressed these thoughts to Eisenhower in a letter one week before Kishi's visit to Washington: After a period of drift, sentiment in Japan is now beginning to crystallize, and we stand on the threshold of a new era in our relations with Japan. The Prime Minister's visit affords a unique opportunity to influence the pattern of this new era in the critical period of the next decade or more. A strong, cooperative Japan is fundamental and essential to our position, and the road that Japan chooses to follow will influence greatly the path which other free Asian nations take.
Memorandum for the President, Dulles-Eisenhower, 12 June 1957, Ann Whitman Files, International Series, Box 31, Eisenhower Library.

29. A later Foreign Minister maintained this separation. See Transcript of a Recorded Interview with Aiichiro Fujiyama, interviewer Spencer Davis, 23 October 1964, pp. 26–27.

30. *Kaitei no hokin*, [Settlement on a policy line] *Nihon Anzen Joyaku no Shoten*, pp. 58–59.

31. Telegram from MacArthur to Dulles, Ann Whitman Files/International Series, Box 30, Eisenhower Library.

32. See "For the Press" No. 528 and 533, Department of State notes on the Fujiyama-Dulles talks of 11 and 12 September 1958. Papers of John Foster Dulles, Box 130, Mudd Library.

33. For a detailed account of the origins and wartime activities of the Japanese Communist Party, see George M. Beckmann and Okubo Genji, *The Japanese Communist Party, 1922–1945* (Stanford: Stanford University Press, 1969).

34. *Asahi Shinbun*, 8 and 12 November 1959.

35. Kajima, *Modern Japan's Foreign Policy*, p. 296.

36. In addition, the cost sharing agreement (Article 25 of the Administrative Agreement to the 1951 Security Treaty), whereby Japan would subsidize the American military guarantee by providing transportation and services support, was discontinued. See Chapter 3, sixth element of the security framework: Administrative Agreement.

37. *Joint Statement of August 31, 1955*, *Department of State Bulletin*, Vol. 33, No. 846, pp. 419–420.

38. Agreement Under Article VI of the Treaty of Mutual Cooperation and Security Between the United States of America and Japan, Regarding Facilities and Areas and the Status of United States Armed Forces in Japan, Article XXIV, paragraph 2, Headquarters, United States Forces, Japan. In paragraph 1 of this Article, the United States agreed to "bear for the duration of this Agreement without cost to Japan all expenditures incident to the maintenance of the United States armed forces in Japan except those to be borne in paragraph 2." U.S. officials would later regret this SOFA clause when requesting cost sharing and host-nation support in the late 1970s.

39. It was not until July 1986 that the National Security Council under Prime Minister Nakasone's reforms replaced the National Defense Council. The 1980s also saw the formation of special Diet committees on defense, allowing for a broader discussion of defense needs. Interview with John E. Endicott, Director, Institute for National Strategic Studies, National Defense University, May 1988.

40. Transcript of a Recorded Interview with Nobusuke Kishi, interviewer Spencer Davis, 2 October 1964, pp. 3–5.

41. In 1960, while the Foreign Ministry affirmed the principles of liberalization, MITI worked to increase the number of items designated for protection by introducing such bills to the Diet. Agricultural commodities, automobiles, petro-chemicals, machinery, electronics, were among the sectors designated for "non-liberalization" in order to maintain international industrial competitiveness.

42. An international comparison of real GNP in 1960 is found in Nakamura, *The Postwar Japanese Economy*, p. 103 (in $U.S. millions): U.S. 511, West Germany 74, France 60, Great Britain 72, Japan 43, Italy 34.

43. On the dispersion of power in the American state, see Robert Pastor, *Congress and the Politics of U.S. Foreign Economic Policy, 1929–1976* (Berkeley: University of California Press, 1980).

44. Sources include: Papers of Harry S. Truman, President's Secretary's Files, Foreign

Affairs Files, Box 182; NSC Meetings, Box 220; Papers of John W. Snyder, Secretary of the Treasury, Box 20; White House Files, Boxes 41, 905–906, Truman Library.

45. The Papers of Dwight D. Eisenhower, Ann Whitman Files, NSC Series, Boxes 3, 10–12, Eisenhower Library.

46. Weinstein, *Japan's Postwar Defense Policy*, p. 87.

47. See *Nichi-bei anpo joyaku no shoten* [Focus on the Japan–U.S. Security Treaty] (Tokyo: Asahi Shinbun Sha, 1967), pp. 179–180.

48. Weinstein, *Japan's Postwar Defense Policy*, pp. 79–80.

49. See Ichiro Saito, *Anpo Toso Shi* [Security Struggle History] (Tokyo: Sanichi Shobo, 1962), for the view that mass demonstrations were directed at alignment with the U.S., and Packard, Protest in Tokyo, for view that political opportunism against Kishi was the prime motivation.

50 Http://www.country-data.com/cgi-bin/query/r-7328.html.

51. Three "shocks" of 1971 are typically mentioned: Nixon's abandonment of the gold standard allowed the dollar to float, increasing the value of yen; his temporary freeze of wages and price controls included a 10 percent surcharge on imports; and his announcement that Kissinger had conducted direct talks with China (without consulting Japan), to be followed by Nixon in 1972. See Walter LaFeber, *The Clash: U.S.–Japanese Relations Throughout History* (New York: W.W. Norton and Company, 1997), pp. 352–356.

Chapter 5

1. The 1960 Security Treaty required prior consultation before U.S. nuclear weapons were "introduced" (mochikomu) to Japan. By agreeing to different U.S. and Japanese definitions of what this verb meant (did it include port calls or did it require placement of such weapons on Japanese territory?) the ambiguous policy complicated Soviet war planning. However, it was politically explosive in Japan.

2. The Kennedy administration coined "flexible response" as a strategy due to the lack of credibility of massive retaliation to deter limited wars, as shown in Korea and deemed critically important after the Cuban Missile Crisis of 1962. Possessing a wide range of options from which a response to aggression would be selected would hopefully constrain any conflict to conventional weapons.

3. "Mutual assured destruction" (Johnson), "strategic sufficiency" (Nixon), "flexible targeting" (Ford), "countervailing" strategy (Carter), "prevailing" or "nuclear warfighting" strategy (Reagan). Smoke, National Security and the Nuclear Dilemma.

4. Foreign Minister Ito and Director of the Cabinet Legislation Bureau Tsunoda testified before the Diet that the "defense only" policy allows the SDF to engage the enemy only after Japan was attacked. Director General of the Defense Agency Omura testified that the SDF could take offensive action within the context of a strategic defensive posture, and that this included attacks on enemy forces outside Japanese territory. *Japan Times*, 29 March 1981.

5. See study by U.S. Senator Carl Levin which used the 1000-mile SLOC mission as the criterion: *U.S. Relationships with NATO and Japan—Sharing the Burdens of Common Defense, The Congressional Record*, 27 June 1983, p. S9217.

6. Tsurutani, *Japanese Security and East Asian Security*, and J.W.M. Chapman, R. Drifte, and L.T.M. Gow, *Japan's Quest for Economic Security: Defense, Diplomacy and Dependence* (London: Pinter, 1983), contain chapters which cite these and other general deficiencies.

7. Compiled from Rix, *Japan's Economic Aid*, p. 32; and *Japan 1987: An International Comparison* (Tokyo: Keizai Koho Center, 1987), p. 55.

8. Tied aid refers to stipulations that money received must be used to purchase Japanese goods and services; limited tied aid requires that a Japanese firm accomplish the feasibility study for an economic project.

9. Tomohisa Sakanaka, Kaijo *Jieitai no Senryaku Koso* [Strategic Plans of the Maritime Self-Defense Force] *Nihon no Jieiryoku* [Japan's Self-Defense Power] (Tokyo: Asahi Shinbunsha, 1967), pp. 52–61.

10. James Auer, in *The Postwar Rearmament of Japanese Maritime Forces, 1945–1971* (New York: Praeger, 1973), pp. 132–145, suggests that the 1000-mile SLOC responsibility was likely planned for in the early years of MSDF development.

11. Kataoka and Myers, *Defending an Economic Superpower*, p. 96.

12. This point was made in several separate interviews in Tokyo and Washington by senior Defense Agency officials, Headquarter U.S. Forces Japan military officers, and DoD officials.

13. Nakamura, *The Postwar Japanese Economy*, p. 243.

14. This contrasts to declines in real growth in defense spending among NATO allies (including -2.2 percent for the United States in 1980).

15. Throughout 1976–1981, the leading opposition party, JSP, never captured more than 24 percent of the lower house seats. This contrasts sharply to the situation in 1960, when the JSP alone owned nearly one-third of the seats.
16. Interview with Japan Defense Agency official, Bureau of Defense Policy, Tokyo, Japan, 10 August 1990.
17. Yasushi Kozai, *Kodo Seicho no Jidai* [Period of High Growth] (Tokyo: Nihon Hyoronsha, 1981).
18. Interview with DoD official, International Security Affairs, East Asia and Pacific Region, Washington, D.C., April 1990.
19. See the Agreement Under Article VI of the Treaty of Mutual Cooperation and Security Between the United States of America and Japan, Regarding Facilities and Areas and the Status of United States Armed Forces in Japan, Headquarters, United States Forces, Japan, p. 18.
20. *New York Times*, 5 May 1981.
21. *Defense of Japan* 1976, p. 79.
22. Standardization enhances "interoperability"—greater ease of joint maintenance and military operations.
23. See Boei Hakusho 1980 [Defense White Paper 1980] (Tokyo: Boeicho, 1980), p. 111.
24. For analyses of Japan's foreign aid process and the significance aid politics plays in U.S.–Japan relations, see Alan Rix, *Japan's Economic Aid: Policy-making and Politics* (New York: St. Martin's, 1980); and Robert M. Orr's *The Aid Factor in U.S.–Japan Relations*, Asian Survey, Vol. 28, No. 27, July 1988, pp. 740–756 and *The Emergence of Japan's Foreign Aid Power* (New York: Columbia University Press, 1990).
25. This term characterizes a Reagan/Weinberger administration policy to consider national defense matters as special areas to be insulated from political and economic disputes. Interview with Japan Defense Agency official, 10 August 1990, Tokyo.
26. *New York Times*, 16 May 1981.
27. *Japan Times*, 14 May 81.
28. *New York Times*, 18 May 1981.
29. Ministry of Foreign Affairs and Department of State and Defense spokesmen helped defuse this issue by offering different interpretations of what "introduction of nuclear weapons into Japan" meant. According to Reischauer, the 1960 Security Treaty had been supplemented by a secret, verbal agreement that allowed for the transit of U.S. nuclear weapons. The American interpretation at the time of the alleged nuclear weapons transit was that the 1960 agreement only prevented the loading and unloading of nuclear weapons. This position (confirmed in the press by Nathaniel B. Thayer, Reischauer's former Press Secretary) would be consistent with the international law of right of innocent passage, as opposed to being a matter of prior consultation under the 1960 Treaty. According to Foreign Minister Sonoda, Ito's replacement, no confidential 1960 agreement ever existed. Both sides agreed at a minimum that since the 1967 Sato government's Three Non-Nuclear Principles and the 1968 Miki government's explicit prohibition against the transit of nuclear weapons through Japanese territory, there has been no such movement. See *Japan Times* and *New York Times*, 19–25 May 1981.
30. Common Security Interests in the Pacific and How the Cost and Benefits of Those Interests Are Shared by the U.S. and its Allies, Hearing Before The Defense Burden sharing Panel of the Committee on Armed Services, House of Representatives, 100th Congress, 19 April 1988, p. 36.
31. See Boei Hakusho 1989, pp. 422–443 for detailed listing of joint exercises.
32. Masashi Nishihara, Japan's Changing Security Role, *Harvard International Review* X, No. 4, April/May 1988, p. 39.
33. One such modification is the outfitting of Lockheed C-130H transport aircraft with a mine release system. In JFY 1990, the JDA's Technical Research and Development Institute funded development with Kawasaki Heavy Industries and Kayaba Industry Co., Ltd., to design and fabricate a prototype to lay mines in strategic straits and harbors.
34. John O'Connell, "Strategic Implications of the Japanese SSM-1 Cruise Missile," *Journal of Northeast Asian Studies*, Vol. VI, No. 2, Summer 1987, pp. 53–66. Captain O'Connel (retired), served as Defense and Naval Attaché in Japan. The 100-kilometer range (estimated) SSM-1 is expected to give Japan the capability to interdict surface ships transiting the Sea of Japan.
35. Compiled from several Defense of Japan volumes.
36. Compiled from Defense of Japan 1987, 1989, 1990.
37. House Armed Services Committee Hearing No. 100-114, 10 May 1988, p. 18.
38. F-16 deployment began in 1985, accompanied by the creation of a first ever U.S.–Japan Joint Staff Council for long-range scenario planning and training.
39. Sources include Defense Burden sharing Panel Hearing, 10 May 1988, p. 10; United States Forces Japan Labor Cost Sharing Briefing, Yokota Air Base, Tokyo, Japan, 14 August

1990; *Japan Times* Weekly International Edition, 23 Jan-3 Feb 91, p. 2. On 14 Jan 91, Foreign Minister Nakayama and Secretary of State Baker signed a five-year agreement, effective April 1991, in which Japan will pay for all Japanese labor and utilities costs previously incurred by USFJ (¥84 billion in FY 1995) and other maintenance costs (estimated at ¥400 billion in 1995). This totals approximately one-half of all USFJ stationing costs.

40. Today, it some respects it is even a better deal for the United States, with Japan agreeing in January 2006 to pay 85 percent of utility costs of the USFJ bases and local employees' salaries for a total of $1.2 billion. Generally, facilities improvement costs increased after the 1981 agreement through the 1990's then decreased, while labor and utility costs have risen steadily. See Japan Facilities Defense Administration Agency homepage: http://www.dfaa.go.jp/en/enlibrary/how.html.

41. See Common Security Interests in the Pacific and How the Cost and Benefits of Those Interests are Shared by the U.S. and Its Allies, Hearing Before the Defense Burden sharing Panel of the Committee on Armed Services, House of Representatives, 100th Congress, 19 April 1988, p. 38.

Chapter 6

1. See Yoichi Funabashi and Eiichi Shindo, *FSX to nichibei miriteku masatsu* [FSX and U.S.-Japan military-technology friction], *Sekai*, Vol. 528, June 1989, pp. 74–88.

2. In the Agreement to Facilitate Interchange of Patent Rights and Technical Information for Purpose of Defense1956 Patent Secrecy Agreement, both states pledged to facilitate the flow of defense technology and protect ownership of classified patents.

3. In this commitment to encourage transfers, "military technologies" were defined as those in the design and production of 11 traditional "arms" as set forth in Japan's ban on military exports, including firearms, military vessels, vehicles aircraft and components, military-related biological, chemical and radiological agents.

4. In 1980, the Systems and Technology Forum was formed to coordinate defense technology projects between the JDA and DoD. But until the 1983 agreement, Japanese policy prohibited the export of military technology as well as equipment.

5. *Japanese Technologies for Cooperation with the United States*, U.S. Army Material Command, Science and Technology Center, Tokyo, 1990.

6. See the account of DSAA's main action officer for FS-X: Andrew J. Button, *Cooperation in the Development of the FS-X: An Analysis of the Decision Process*. Executive Research Project (Washington, D.C.: Industrial College of the Armed Forces, 1989).

7. Between 1980 and 1989, the number of Japanese semiconductor firms ranked in the top ten measured by global sales doubled, with Japanese-owned companies accounting for half of worldwide output.

8. Report Memorandum #167 on MITI's 1988 *Sangyo Gijutsu no Doko to Kadai* [Trends and Future Tasks in Industrial Technology] (Tokyo: Office of the U.S. National Science Foundation, 1988), p. 12.

9. FS-X was a "special operational requirement" rather than a broader and more politically vulnerable "general operational requirement." Kazuhisa Ogawa, *FSX no hamon* [The ripple of FSX] *Sekai*, Vol. 528, June 1989, pp. 63–73.

10. The Goldwater-Nichols Act of 1986, the most significant reorganization of the DoD since its establishment in 1947, increased jointness across the military services primarily by (a) increasing the authority of the Chairman of the Joint Chiefs of Staff at the expense of the individual service chiefs, and (b) strengthening the hand of the Secretary of Defense by giving him operational authority over the regional and functional combatant commanders.

11. In accordance with the Cabinet Law, the Security Council is headed by the Prime Minister and includes the Minister of Foreign Affairs, the Minister of Finance, the Chief Cabinet Secretary, the Chairman of the National Public Safety Commission, the Director General of the Japan Defense Agency, and the Director General of the Economic Planning Agency.

12. During the Korean conflict, for instance, the F-86's short combat radius (D model 600 mi, F model-900 mi) barely supported a two-way mission from Japan to North Korea, allowing about 10 minutes over a typical target. Although F-80's (and bombers) routinely flew from southern Japan to Korea early in the conflict, the conversion of F-80's to F-86's occurred in 1951. The availability of basing in South Korea meant that Japan-based F-86 operations in support of the Korean conflict was limited to rear area maintenance at Tsuiki. On this latter point, see Robert F. Futrell, *The United States Air Force in Korea 1950–1953* (Washington, D.C.: Office of Air Force History, 1983), pp. 394–400.

13. Modernization efforts are continually subject to political interpretations of what con-

stitutes self-defense and what exceeds self-defense. Examples include the procurement of air refuelable fighters, airborne tanker aircraft, and E-3A Airborne Warning and Control System (AWACS) aircraft.

14. *Washington Post* interview in January 1983. Nakasone was criticized from the left for "obediently following the United States anti-Soviet military strategy" and from the right for having "too small a force to make Japan an unsinkable aircraft carrier." *Nakasone's Frank Remarks Threaten Support in Japan, Washington Post,* 22 Jan 83.

15. The Defense Agency gave priority to three areas in the MTDP: (1) air defense, SLOC protection, and countering a landing invasion; (2) high quality defense buildup; and (3) efficiency and rationalization of defense forces. Defense of Japan 1986, pp. 145–147.

16. *Nihon Keizai Shinbun,* 12 April 1987.

17. Fueled by domestic defense development contracts, TRDI's proportion of overall defense-related expenditures doubled since the 1970s. See *Defense of Japan 1989,* p. 143.

18. Joint Staff Council Chairman Shigehiro Mori, quoted in *Tokyo Shinbun,* 29 June 87.

19. Interview with TRDI official involved in FS-X negotiations, 8 August 1990.

20. The counter air mission is fundamental to any air operation because it seeks to establish air superiority to enable other missions to succeed. An example of an offensive counter air mission is a "fighter sweep" to eliminate enemy air threats in advance of a friendly operation. An example of a defensive counter air mission would be the interception of enemy aircraft attempting to attack friendly forces.

21. Andrew J. Button, *Cooperation in the Development of the FS-X: An Analysis of the Decision Process* (Washington, D.C.: Industrial College of the Armed Forces, 1989).

22. *Mainichi Shinbun,* 14 September 1987, reported JDA estimates that modification costs of a U.S. aircraft would run 30 percent higher than autonomous development of a domestic Japanese fighter. GAO testimony estimated FS-X developments costs to be two or three times the price of an off-the-shelf F-16 (the latter is $26 million). Statement of Frank C. Conahan, Assistant Comptroller General, National Security and International Affairs Division, Before the Committee on Science, Space and Technology, House of Representatives, 11 May 1989, p. 12.

23. Interview with Mutual Defense Assistance official, Tokyo, Japan, 9 August 1990.

24. Interview with FS-X Steering Committee members, 25 July 1990, Tokyo.

25. *Japan's Aerospace and Aviation Weekly,* No. 842, 2 November 1987 (Tokyo: Koku Shinbun Sha, 1987), p. 2.

26. Compiled from assorted articles in Nihon Keizai, Mainichi, Asahi, and Yomiuri Shinbun, 1987–1989.

27. *Asahi Shinbun,* 28 May 1987.

28. Dan Graniter, *Multinational Corporate Power in Inter-state Conflict: The Toshiba Case,* Olin Institute Economics and National Security Program Paper 90-003, January, 1990.

29. *FSX no kettei o meguru 'ziguzegu' no haikai* [The FS-X decision zigzag's background], *Jiyu,* Vol. 29, November 1987, pp. 10–31.

30. *Yomiuri Shinbun,* 1 July 1987, and *Nihon Keizai Shinbun,* 21 May 1987. The meeting discussed the impact of independent development on the long-term future of Japan's defense industry, and the short-term military benefits of licensed and co-production.

31. *Yomiuri Shinbun,* 12 June 1987.

32. Interviews with JDA Bureau of Defense Policy and Ministry of Foreign Affairs officials.

33. Memorandum of Understanding Between the Government of the United States and the Government of Japan, No. 847, November 29, 1988, signed in Tokyo by Minister of Foreign Affairs Uno and Ambassador Mansfield.

34. The original plan was for flight testing in 1993 and service entry in 1995. By 1999, the program was 1 1/2 years behind schedule and double JDA's initial cost estimate.

35. 40 percent is calculated based on the total FS-X budget, subject to reviews by the joint FS-X Technical Steering Committee.

36. Technologies include active phased array radar, laser gyro inertial navigation, electronic countermeasures, and mission computer hardware.

37. By contrast, all F-16 aircraft versions use a GE or PW engine rated in the 23,000 lbs. thrust range, with the exception of the F-16XL or F-16E prototype, which is planned to use a GE F110-GE-100 rated at 29,000 lbs. thrust. Data taken from *The Defenders: A Comprehensive Guide to the Warplanes of the USA* (New York: Gallery, 1988).

38. For strongly held opposing views on both sides of the FSX deal, see technonationalists: Shintaro Ishihara, *FSX no zasetsu: sengo taisei matsushuen* [The collapse of FSX: the beginning of the death of the postwar structure], *Chuokoron,* Vol. 104, July 1989, pp. 194–198; and Clyde Prestowitz, *Giving Japan a Handout—Why Fork Over $7 Billion in Aircraft Technology?* in *Washington Post,* 29 January 1989.

39. United States Technology Transfer Structure, Defense Security Assistance Agency/Weapons System Division, Washington, D.C., p. 2.

40. Frank C. Carlucci, "The FS-X Project Is No Handout to Japan," *Washington Post*, 9 February 1989.
41. Thomas P. Griffin, *The FSX Debate: Implications for Future U.S. International Armaments Programs*, Master's Thesis, July 1989, Air Force Institute of Technology, Wright-Patterson Air Force Base, Ohio.
42. *The U.S.–Japan FS-X Fighter Agreement: Assessing the Stakes*, The Center for Security Policy, Washington, D.C., p. 5.
43. Between 1982 and 1988, MHI's percentage of total income derived from military equipment sales climbed from 6 percent to 15.4 percent.
44. *Nihon Keizai Shinbun*, 18 February 1988.
45. *Nihon Keizai Shinbun*, 24 August 1987.
46. *Aerospace Japan Weekly*, No. 848, 14 December 1987, p. 1.
47. *The Wing Newsletter*, 9 November 1988.
48. Nihon Keizai Shinbun, 22 December 1989.
49. *Defense Science Board Report on Defense Industrial Cooperation With Pacific Rim Nations*, 27 July 1989 Mutual Defense Assistance Office, U.S. Embassy, Tokyo.
50. An elaborate technology control procedure within DoD exists among the Defense Technology Security Administration, National Disclosure Policy Committee, Service Program Managers, and U.S. industry contractors. This process updates the Military Critical Technologies List.
51. *Facts and Figures: U.S.–Japan Relations*, compilation by the Consulate General of Japan, New York, 1989, p. 21.
52. The Kaifu administration's pledge to provide nearly $13 billion to support actions against Iraq was the largest financial contribution behind Saudi Arabia and the United States.
53. "Dual use" describes technologies with both commercial and military applications. In 1982, MITI announced a policy in which the nature of an export product, and not its ultimate use, determined its military status. DoD policy is to avoid using dual use as a category, and consider a technology "commercial" if there is any commercial application potential.
54. "Flow back" refers to the return of an improved technology to the original owner after it has been transferred to and modified by the other partner.
55. Although the 1956 agreement allowed technology to flow from the U.S. to Japan, there was no patent secrecy law in Japan until 1988. This meant that if Japanese firms could develop or acquire technology invented and classified in the United States, they could gain first rights by simply applying for a patent. Ownership in Japan is determined by time of application, not time of invention, creating an enormous array of technology ownership issues between 1956 and 1988.
56. Established in Tokyo in 1990, DTO's charter is to build armament cooperation, rather than sales, to increase combat capabilities through technology development. Interview with DoD official, 17 Feb 99, Tokyo, Japan.
57. Michael Green, MITJP 94-01, p. 3.
58. Matthew Rubiner, *U.S. Industry and Government Views on Defense Technology Cooperation with Japan: The MIT Japan Program Survey: March 1994* (MITJP 94-03). Naturally, Japanese industry officials viewed their government's ban on arms exports officials as the top obstacle in another study: Michael Green, *The Japanese Defense Industry's Views of U.S.–Japan Defense Technology Cooperation: Findings of the Japan MIT Program Study: January 1994* (MITJP94-01).
59. A comprehensive interpretation of the drift in the alliance relationship is found in: Yoichi Funabashi, *Domei Hyoryu* [Alliance Adrift] (Tokyo: Iwanami Publishing, 1998).
60. A 1990 Congressional report notes, "It is highly unlikely that any NATO country would permit a U.S. company to co-develop and produce a major weapons system, even one based on U.S. technology, if the U.S. government did not share in the development and procurement costs." U.S. Congress, Office of Technology Assessment, *Arming Our Allies: Cooperation and Competition in Defense Technology* (Washington, D.C.: U.S. Government Printing Office, May 1990), p. 12.
61. The current cost of an F-2 is well over $108m, compared to perhaps $40m for the best F-16C/D which unlike the F-2 is air refuelable. Takeoff weight is 48,700lb compared to an F-16C's 42,000 lb, allowing a greater payload to be carried, but both aircraft are powered by the same GE F110-129 engine rated at 29,000lb thrust (with afterburner). The 130-aircraft purchase plan is currently down to 90. htttp://www.aerospaceweb.org/aircraft/fighter/fsx/; http://www.airforce-technology.com/projects/f16/.
62. A survey of government and private sector individuals involved in FS-X concluded that both sides agreed the benefits of the program were inconclusive. Japanese participants tended to criticize FS-X's unequal partnership in terms of responsibilities, costs, benefits, and operational requirements. Americans complained about the diversity of objectives and the tedious nature of the ensuing negotiations. Thomas S.

Stumpf, *The FS-X Program—Insiders' Views* (Japan Defense Agency: National Institute for Defense Studies, May 1998), p. 38.

Chapter 7

1. See appendices A and B in *Maximizing U.S. Interests in Science and Technology: Report of the Defense Task Force* (National Research Council, Washington, D.C.: The National Academies Press, 1995). http://fermat.nap.edu/books/NX006023/html/R1.html.

2. The Mutual Defense Assistance Office (MDAO) is the successor to the Military Assistance Advisory Group established in 1954 to support the National Police Reserve, and later, the Japan Self-Defense Force. In 1969, the MAAG was reorganized as the MDAO to conduct foreign military sales and international armaments cooperation. Noboru Y. Flores, "International Armaments Cooperation Programs in Japan," *The Defense Institute of Security Assistance Management Journal* (Tokyo: Mutual Defense Assistance Office, 1999), pp. 63–67.

3. Lawrence Freedman and Efraim Karsh, *The Gulf Conflict 1990–1991* (Princeton: Princeton University Press, 1993), p. 67.

4. Courtney Purrington and A.K., "Tokyo's Policy Responses During the Gulf Crisis," *Asian Survey* (April, 1991), p. 308. Purrington and A.K. also point out that Kaifu failed to convene and chair the Security Council, relying instead on ad hoc collections of ministerial inputs during the crisis.

5. Purrington and A.K., p. 308.

6. Jordan was not committed against Iraq but was likely to lose 30 percent of its national income due to the economic sanctions.

7. Freedman and Karsh, p. 123.

8. *Japan Times*, 30 September 1990.

9. Purrington and A.K., pp. 313–314.

10. The Senate vote was 52–47; the House vote was 250–183.

11. Freedman and Karsh, *The Gulf Conflict 1991–1992*, p. 359.

12. The distinction was that if the SDF were dispatched overseas under United Nations command rather than Japan Self-Defense Force command, this would constitute collective security rather than collective defense, and therefore be constitutionally permitted.

13. *Defense of Japan 1997*, p. 68.

14. In a study initiated by former Secretary of Defense Les Aspin, the Clinton administration's Bottom Up Review reassessed "all of our defense concepts, plans, and programs from the ground up." Following the review, U.S. forces still planned for two simultaneous Major Regional Contingency (MRC) operations in the post Cold War threat environment.

15. For a comparison of American and Japanese views on UN operations, see the volume edited by Selig S. Harrison and Masashi Nishihara: *UN Peacekeeping: Japanese and American Perspectives* (Washington, D.C.: Carnegie Endowment for International Peace, 1995).

16. Two 600-member strong engineering battalions were sent for successive six-month duty from September 1992 to September 1993. Missions included repairing roads and bridges, and supplying UNTAC with water, fuel, food, medicine and tents. *Paths to Peace: Japan's Contributions to World Peace* (Tokyo: Jiji Gaho Sha, 1996), pp. 3, 6.

17. Illustrating the high cost of peace enforcement was the comprehensive plan of retired Lt Gen William Odom, which laid out an invasion to reduce the violence, prevent conflict from spreading, allow for negotiations to occur, stop ethnic cleansing, and deny territorial predation. To accomplish these aims, he estimated 300,000 to 400,000 troops would be required to destroy Serb tanks and artillery, and establish adequate fortifications throughout Yugoslavia. Wayne Bert, *The Reluctant Superpower: United States' Policy in Bosnia, 1991–95* (New York: St Martin's Press, 1997), pp. 179–180

18. Byung-joon Ahn, "The Man Who Would Be Kim," *Foreign Affairs*, November/December 1994 (pp. 94–108), p. 97.

19. If constructed, the three facilities reportedly could reprocess the plutonium to make 20–30 bombs a year. Byung-joon Ahn, pp. 102–3.

20. In 1990 Japan's annual real GDP growth rate was 5.5 percent, then plummeted to an annual average rate of 0.5 percent. Asahi Shimbun, *Japan Almanac 1999* (Tokyo: Toppan Printing, 1998), p. 81.

21. Japan's first Socialist prime ministership since the 1950's was made possible by Hosokawa's March 1994 reform of the 1947 electoral law. The reforms replaced the exclusive multi-member district system with a combination of single-member plurality and multi-member proportional representation in larger sized districts. These changes increased political competition and led to the rise of more new parties.

22. The public use of the term "defense" rather than "military" reflects the political restrictions on Japan's military capability, even though (or perhaps because) it confuses the analytical distinction between political, economic, and military tools of security policy.

23. The continued informal budgetary limit of 1 percent of GNP is believed by many

observers to provide politicians and bureaucrats civilian control of the military.

24. In December 1994, the Defense Agency's National Institute for Defense Studies held the first annual Asia-Pacific Defense Symposium of regional military officers.

25. Over the years, widespread local opposition to any military presence has produced numerous restrictions that damage combat readiness such as port city bans on military vessels, reductions in aircraft night landing practice, and the absence of any large-unit ground maneuver training. Without realistic public appreciation of the need to maintain fighting skills, knowledgeable officials worry that military skills in Japan may be suffering the death of a thousand cuts.

26. See Chapter 4, p. 6.

27. The total return of six facilities (Futenma Air Station, Aha Training Area, Ginbaru Training Area, Sobe Communication Site, Yomitan Airfield, Naha Port) and partial return of five facilities (Northern Training Area, Senaha Communication Site, Camp Kuwae, Makimanato Service Area, Camp Zukeran) constitute a return of 21 percent of the total land used by U.S. forces on Okinawa. However, Okinawa still bears the burden of 70 percent of all U.S. forces facilities in Japan.

28. "Lack of Decision-making Holds Security Hostage," *The Daily Yomiuri On-line* (7 March 1999).

29. Negotiators operated under the authority of the Security Consultative Committee (U.S. Secretary of State and Secretary of Defense, and Japan Foreign Minister and Minister of State for Defense) and managed by the Subcommittee for Defense Cooperation (U.S. Assistant Secretary of State, Assistant Secretary of Defense, and U.S. Embassy officials, Joint Chiefs of Staff representative, U.S. Pacific Forces, U.S. Forces Japan, and Japan Foreign Ministry's Director General of the North American Bureau and Joint Staff Council representative). Meetings between U.S. deputy assistant secretaries and Japan deputy director generals oversaw detailed discussions. *Defense of Japan 1998* (Tokyo: Japan Defense Agency, June 1998), p. 192..

30. The 1996 ACSA permitted Japanese support of U.S. military activities only during peacetime.

31. Since 1993, the U.S. Navy has worked on a Theater-wide Missile Defense system to shoot down ballistic missiles threatening fleet operations. JDA's decision to conduct feasibility studies of TMD were subject to government concerns over its high cost, estimated at $10 billion over 10 years, questions about how effective it could be, and China's opposition to any defensive system that could protect Taiwan from Chinese attack.

32. Interview with involved Department of Defense and Defense Agency officials, Washington and Tokyo, February-March 1999.

33. The final section of the 1978 Guidelines, overlooked until the review, left the door wide open to a regional reorientation: "The governments of Japan and the United States will consult together from time to time whenever changes in the circumstances so require. The scope and modalities of facilitative assistance to be extended by Japan to the U.S. forces in the case of situations in the Far East outside of Japan which will have an important influence on the security of Japan will be governed by the U.S.-Japan Security Treaty, its related arrangements, other relevant agreements between Japan and the United States, and the relevant laws and regulations of Japan." *Defense of Japan 1997*, p. 323.

34. This defense line was generally agreed within the Government of Japan to include Taiwan and South Korea, but not North Korea. Areas of the Russian Far East were outside the defense line, even though Japan had programmed its force posture against a Soviet threat from the north. Interviews with Defense Agency and U.S. Forces Japan officials, Tokyo, March-May 1999.

35. This Ministry of Foreign Affairs position on the defense line and the U.S.-Japan Security Treaty includes Japanese territory and areas under the administrative control of Japan. This interpretation excludes the disputed Northern Territories but includes the Senkaku Islands as falling under the U.S. alliance obligation to defend Japan.

36. The October 1996 national election was the first time since 1958 that an opposition party, Shinshinto, garnered enough Lower House positions (156 seats) to deny the Liberal Democratic Party (239 seats) a single-party majority in the 500-seat Diet.

37. *The New Guidelines For Japan–U.S. Defense Cooperation* (Tokyo: Defense Agency, 1998).

38. A contingency plan is one which is "on the shelf" waiting to be implemented. After being quickly tailored to fit a developing world situation, a contingency becomes an operational plan (OPLAN), complete with scheduled flow of forces and support material.

39. Attentive watchdogs of security policies were keen to identify differences between the Japanese and English translations of the Guidelines. Their general argument is that intentional ambiguities in the Japanese version conceal

constitutionally questionable SDF military activity. Much of the debate turns on fine distinctions such as the difference between "additional mobility and strike power," which is in the English version as a U.S. responsibility, and "seidodakeiryoku" [power projection capability], which is in the Japanese version as a U.S. responsibility. The idea is that the Japanese version more clearly assigns offensive missions to U.S. forces, while the English version assigns less offensive responsibilities to U.S. forces. This would set the SDF up to take on offensive missions if one assumes U.S. forces would avoid any responsibility that is not specified in the English version of the Guidelines. See Kobayashi, *Nichi Bei Shin Guidorain* [Japan–U.S. New Guidelines] (Tokyo: Nihon Heironsha, 1999).

40. When the main opposition party (Shinshinto) leader Ichiro Ozawa disbanded the party in December 1997 to create a loyal core renamed the Liberal Party, its Diet membership dropped from 173 seats to 54 seats. The Democratic Party of Japan (Naoto Kan) became the largest opposition with 138 seats, while former Shinshinto members began a sequence of small party formation and disintegration that further fractured opposition to the LDP.

41. Budget decisions were further sharpened by the contracting economy. By the summer of 1998, Japan's economy had recorded GDP contraction for four consecutive quarters. Quarterly corporate capital spending had fallen 2.7 percent, on the way to a 5.7 percent decline by the fall, the third largest decline on record.

42. The SDF had been participating in RIMPAC since 1980 based on the need to train for the defense of Japan by protecting sea lines of communication. The division of military roles was publicly codified in the 1978 Guidelines for U.S.–Japan Defense Cooperation, and further emphasized in the Reagan-Suzuki Communiqué of 1981.

43. North Korea reportedly has three missiles under development with increasing ranges: Nodong (620 miles), Taepodong I (1250 miles), and Taepodong II (3700 miles).

44. Japan Foreign Minister Komura later reversed the suspension to achieve the longer term goal of buying North Korean agreement to abandon nuclear weapons development.

45. Director-General Norota replaced Fukushiro Nukaga after the Diet passed a resolution criticizing the latter to take the blame for a cover-up in a Defense Agency procurement scandal. Nukaga's 19 November resignation was announced the same day that the Liberal Democratic and Liberal parties announced their "Ji-Ji" alliance for the 1999 Diet session.

46. The study council would consist of Diet members, administrative vice ministers, chiefs of the Defense Policy Bureau and Defense Operations Bureau, Chairman of the Joint Staff Council, chiefs of the Ground, Air and Naval Self-Defense Forces, and head of the Defense Intelligence Headquarters. *Yomiuri Shimbun*, 9 January 1999.

47. U.S. officials were actually briefing Ministry of Foreign Affairs officials from the Intelligence and Assessment section when news of the Taepodong missile launch broke.

48. The group consists of members from the Liberal Democratic Party, Liberal Party, Democratic Party of Japan, New Komeito, and Kaikaku Club — 640 out of 742 Diet seats. *The Japan Times*, 10 February 1999.

49. Prime Minister Koizumi statements during the three days after the terrorist attacks on the United States: "I am shocked to hear the news about the tragic incidents at the World Trade Center buildings and the Pentagon... I share your anger... I offer my heartfelt condolences" (12 Sept 01). "The terrorist acts are extremely heinous and outrageous and cannot be forgiven. It is not only a challenge to the United States but also to democracy" (13 Sept 01). "Japan will support the United States to fight against the terrorism" (14 Sept 01).

50. Japanese patrol vessels botched the first attempt prior to 9/11 when on 23 March 99, two vessels disguised as Japanese fishing boats were found in Japan's territorial waters. By the time Japanese patrol boats received permission to fire, the North Koreans were able to escape. They were later seen anchored in the North Korean port of Wonsan. Based on this incident, the SDF Law and Maritime Safety Law were revised to allow JMSDF and Japan Coast Guard to fire on suspicious vessels inside Japan's territorial waters. By December 2001, patrol boats were fitted with the 20mm Remote Firing System gun, too.

51. Brad Glosserman, *Planning Ahead*, *Comparative Connections*, Pacific Forum CSIS, 22 Oct 05 (http://www.csic.org/pacfor/cc/0404Qus_japan.html).

52. Yuki Tatsumi, *Japan's First Step Toward a National Security Strategy: Assessing the Araki Commission Report*, PacNet 47A, 22 Oct 05 (http://www.csic.org/pacfor/pac0447A.pdf).

53. Brad Glosserman, *Planning Ahead*, *Comparative Connections*, Pacific Forum CSIS, 22 Oct 05 (http://www.csic.org/pacfor/cc/0404Qus_japan.html).

Chapter 8

1. In *Economic Backwardness in Historical Perspective*, Alexander Gerschenkron argues that late industrializers will have more concentrated financial and industrial institutions. Chalmers Johnson, in *MITI and the Japanese Miracle*, applied this argument to Japan: "In states late to industrialize, the state itself led the industrialization drive and it took on developmental functions" (p. 19).

2. This assumes the alternative of unarmed neutrality never has been seriously considered by those in power. On this point, the Japan Socialist Party's recent reversal against unarmed neutrality and in favor of a U.S.–Japan security tie is instructive.

3. Treaty of Peace with Japan, Japanese Peace Conference, San Francisco, September, 1951. From the Papers of Myron M. Cowen, Box 21, Truman Library.

4. Prime Minister Kishi's own ambition to unify the Liberal Democratic Party clearly benefited from these economic security priorities.

5. The verbal commitment to rearm was originally made by Prime Minister Yoshida during the 1951 Security Treaty negotiations (see Chapter 3, "Staying the Rearmament Promise").

6. This is not to deny increasing regional interdependence among Japan, China, Taiwan and Korea. Foreign Direct Investment from the U.S. still accounts for 40 percent of Japanese inward FDI, the largest of any country, and Japanese FDI in the U.S. (12 percent of total U.S. inward FDI) is second only to Great Britain (17 percent).

7. Overview of Japan's Defense Policy, Japan Defense Agency, May 2005, p.2. http://www.jda.go.jp/e/index_.htm.

8. Comments made by Joint Staff Office Chief Massaki indicate the importance placed on the joint operations system reform effort underway in the JSDF: "Under the present system, basically each service of the SDF carries out operations independently, coordinating operations when necessary. And the chief of staff of each service assists the minister of state of defense separately. There are three reasons for the shift to a new posture for joint operations... swift and effective response, ... unification of assistance to the minister from the viewpoint of military expertise, ... smooth conduct of bilateral actions with the U.S. military...." *Japan Defense Focus*, No. 1, Japan Defense Agency, March 2006, p.4.

Bibliography

Acheson, Dean. *Present at the Creation: My Years in the State Department.* New York: Norton, 1969.
Akao, Nobutoshi. *Japan's Economic Security.* New York: St. Martin's Press, 1983.
Allison, Graham T. *Essence of Decision: Explaining the Cuban Missile Crisis.* Boston: Little, Brown, 1971.
Alves, Dora. *Evolving Pacific Basin Strategies: The 1989 Pacific Symposium.* Washington, D.C.: National Defense University Press, 1990.
Asai, Kibun. "Nichi-bei anpo taisei ni kawaru koso" [Toward setting up a U.S.–Japan security structure]. *Sekai,* No. 543 (July, 1990), pp. 57–68.
Auer, James. *The Postwar Rearmament of Japanese Maritime Forces, 1945–1971.* New York: Praeger, 1973.
Barnett, Robert W. *Beyond War: Japan's Concept of Comprehensive Security.* New York: Pergamon-Brassey's International Defense Publishers, 1984.
Barnhart, Michael A. *Japan Prepares for Total War: The Search for Economic Security, 1919–1941.* Ithaca: Cornell University Press, 1987.
Bean, R. Mark. *Cooperative Security in Northeast Asia.* Washington, D.C.: National Defense University Press, 1990.
Binder, Leonard, James S. Coleman, Joseph LaPalombara, Lucian W. Pye, Sidney Verba, and Myron Weiner. *Crises and Sequences in Political Development.* Princeton: Princeton University Press, 1971.
Borden, William S. *The Pacific Alliance: United States Foreign Economic Policy and Japanese Trade Recovery, 1947–1955.* Madison: University of Wisconsin Press, 1984.
Buck, James N. *Civilian Control of the Military in Japan.* Buffalo: State University of New York at Buffalo, 1975.
Butow, Robert J.C. *Japan's Decision to Surrender.* Stanford: Stanford University Press, 1954.
Button, Andrew J. "Cooperation in the Development of the FS-X: An Analysis of the Decision Process." Executive Research Project. Fort McNair, Washington, D.C.: Industrial College of the Armed Forces, 1989.
Calder, Kent E. *Crisis and Compensation: Public Policy and Political Stability in Japan, 1949–1986.* Princeton: Princeton University Press, 1988.
_____. "The Emerging Politics of the Trans-Pacific Economy." *World Policy Journal* 2, No. 4 (Fall 1985).

_____. "International Pressure and Domestic Policy Response: Japanese Informatics Policy in the 1980s." Princeton University Research Monograph No. 51. Princeton: Center of International Studies, 1989.
_____. "Japan in 1990: Limits to Change." *Asian Survey* 31, No. 1 (January 1991), pp. 21–35.
_____. "Japanese Foreign Economic Policy Formation: Explaining the Reactive State." *World Politics* (July 1988), pp. 517–541.
_____. "The North Pacific Triangle: Sources of Economic and Political Transformation." *Journal of Northeast Asian Studies* 7, No. 2 (Summer 1989), pp. 3–16.
_____. "The Rise of Japan's Military-Industrial Base." *Asia-Pacific Community*, No. 17 (Summer 1982), pp. 26–41.
Callahan, James M. *American Foreign Policy in Mexican Relations.* New York: Macmillan, 1932.
Calleo, David. *Beyond American Hegemony.* New York: Basic Books, 1987.
Carlucci, Frank C. "The FS-X Project Is No Handout to Japan." *Washington Post* (9 February 1989).
Chapman, J.W.M., R. Drifte, and L.T.M. Gow. *Japan's Quest for Economic Security: Defense, Diplomacy and Dependence.* London: Pinter, 1983.
Choy, Bong-youn. *Korea: A History.* Tokyo: Charles E. Tuttle, 1971.
Christopher, James W. *Conflict in the Far East.* Leiden, The Netherlands: Brill, 1950.
Cohen, Jerome B. *Japan's Economy in War and Reconstruction.* London: University of Minnesota Press, 1949.
Cohen, Theodore. *Remaking Japan: The American Occupation as New Deal.* New York: The Free Press, 1987.
Collins, John M. *U.S.–Soviet Military Balance, 1960–1980.* New York: McGraw-Hill, 1981.
Common Security Interests in the Pacific and How the Cost and Benefits of Those Interests Are Shared by the U.S. and Its Allies. Hearing Before the Defense Burdensharing Panel of the Committee on Armed Services, House of Representatives, 100th Congress (19 April 1988).
Currie, Malcolm R., Chairman, Defense Science Board Task Force. *Defense Science Board Report on Defense Industrial Cooperation With Pacific Rim Nations.* Washington, D.C.: Department of Defense, 1989.
Curtis, Gerald L. *The Japanese Way of Politics.* New York: Columbia University Press, 1988.
"The Decision for Peace: Interrogation of Sakomizu Hisatsume." *The ONI Review* 1, No. 8 (June 1946), p. 14.
Defense of Japan (annual White Paper). Tokyo: Japan Defense Agency.
Destler, I.M., Priscilla Clapp, Hideo Sato, and Haruhiro Fukui. *Managing an Alliance: The Politics of U.S.–Japanese Relations.* Washington, D.C.: Brookings Institution, 1976.
Destler, I.M., Haruhiro Fukui, and Hideo Sato. *The Textile Wrangle.* Ithaca: Cornell University Press, 1979.
Destler, I.M., and Michael Nacht. "Beyond Mutual Recrimination: Building a Solid U.S.–Japan Relationship in the 1990s." *International Security* 15, No. 3 (Winter 1990/91), pp. 92–119.
Destler, I.M., and Hideo Sato, eds. *Coping with U.S.–Japan Economic Conflict.* Lexington, MA.: Lexington Books, 1982.
Detrio, Richard T. *Strategic Partners: South Korea and the United States.* Washington, D.C.: National Defense University Press, 1989.
Dore, Ronald. *Flexible Rigidities: Industrial Policy and Structural Adjustment in the Japanese Economy 1970–1980.* Stanford: Stanford University Press, 1986.
Dower, John W. *Empire and Aftermath: Yoshida Shigeru and the Japanese Experience, 1878–1954.* Cambridge, MA.: Harvard University Council on East Asian Studies, 1979.
_____, ed. *Origins of the Modern Japanese State: Selected Writings by E.H. Norman.* New York: Random House, 1975.

Doyle, Michael. "Kant, Liberal Legacies and Foreign Affairs." *Philosophy and Public Affairs* 12, Nos. 3/4, pp. 205–353.
———. "Liberalism and World Politics." *American Political Science Review* (December 1986).
Drifte, Reinhard. *Japan's Foreign Policy*. New York: Council on Foreign Relations Press, 1990.
———. *The Security Factor in Japan's Foreign Policy, 1945–1952*. East Sussex: Saltire Press, 1983.
Duffield, John S. "International Regimes and Alliance Behavior: Explaining NATO Conventional Force Levels." Paper presented at American Political Science Association Conference, San Francisco Hilton, 1 September 1990.
Dunn, Frederick S. *Peace-Making and the Settlement with Japan*. Westport, Conn.: Greenwood, 1963.
Economic Cooperation Division. *Far East Data Book, No. 3*. Washington, D.C.: USGPO, 1951.
Economics and Pacific Security: The 1986 Pacific Symposium. Washington, D.C.: National Defense University Press, 1987.
Eisenhower, Dwight D. *Waging Peace: 1956–1961*. New York: Doubleday, 1965.
Endicott, John. "Can the U.S.–Japanese Security Partnership Continue into the 21st Century?" Paper prepared for National Defense Symposium at Fort McNair, Washington, D.C., "The Coming Decade in the Pacific Basin: Change, Interdependence, and Security." 1–2 March, 1990.
Evans, Peter B., Dietrich Rueschemeyer, and Theda Skocpol, eds. *Bringing the State Back In*. Cambridge: Cambridge University Press, 1985.
Falk, Edwin A. *Togo and the Rise of Japanese Sea Power*. New York: Longmans, Green: 1936.
Feis, Herbert. *Japan Subdued: The Atomic Bomb and the End of the War in the Pacific*. Princeton: Princeton University Press, 1961.
———. *The Road to Pearl Harbor: The Coming of the War Between the United States and Japan*. Princeton: Princeton University Press, 1950.
Finifter, Ada W., ed. *Political Science: The State of the Discipline*. Washington, D.C.: The American Political Science Association, 1983.
Flanagan, Scott C., and Bradley M. Richardson. *Politics in Japan*. Boston: Little, Brown, 1984.
Foreign Relations of the United States (selected issues). Washington, D.C.: Department of State.
Foster, John W. *A Century of American Diplomacy, 1776–1876*. Cambridge: Riverside, 1900.
Freeman, Christopher. *Technology Performance and Economic Performance: Lessons from Japan*. New York: Pinter Publishers, 1987.
Friedberg, Aaron L. "The Political Economy of American Strategy." *World Politics* 16, No. 3 (April 1989), pp. 381–406.
———. *The Weary Titan: Britain and the Experience of Decline, 1895–1905*. Princeton: Princeton University Press, 1988.
Frost, Ellen. "Strengthening the U.S.–Japan Alliance." In Robert E. Hunter, ed., *Structuring Alliance Commitments*. Washington, D.C.: The Center for Strategic Studies, 1988, pp. 16–34.
"FSX no kettei o meguru 'ziguzegu' no haikai" [The FS-X decision zigzag's background]. *Jiyu* 29 (November 1987), pp. 10–31.
Funabashi, Yoichi, and Eiichi Shindo. "FSX to nichibei miriteku masatsu" [FSX and U.S.–Japan military-technology friction]. *Sekai* [World] 528 (June 1989), pp. 74–88.
Gambles, Ian. *Prospects for West European Security Co-operation*. Adelphi Paper 244. London: International Institute for Strategic Studies, 1989.
Gerschenkron, Alexander. *Economic Backwardness in Historical Perspective*. Cambridge, MA: Harvard University Press, 1960.

Gibney, Frank. *Japan: The Fragile Superpower*. New York: Norton, 1975.
Gilbert, Felix. *To the Farewell Address: Ideas of Early American Foreign Policy*. Princeton: Princeton University Press, 1961.
Gilpin, Robert. "The Asia-Pacific Region in the Emergent World Economy." *Analysis: The National Bureau of Asian and Soviet Research*, No. 4 (April, 1990), pp. 15–20.
_____. *The Political Economy of International Relations*. Princeton: Princeton University Press, 1987.
_____. *War and Change in World Politics*. Cambridge: Cambridge University Press, 1981.
_____. "Where Does Japan Fit In?" *Millennium* 18, No. 3 (1989).
Gourevich, Peter A. "The Second Image Reversed." *International Organization* (Autumn 1978).
Granirer, Dan. *Multinational Corporate Power in Inter-State Conflict: The Toshiba Case*. Olin Institute Paper 90-003. Cambridge, MA: Harvard University Center for International Affairs, 1990.
Grew, Joseph C. *Ten Years in Japan: A Contemporary Record Drawn from the Diaries and Private and Official Papers of Joseph C. Grew, United States Ambassador to Japan, 1932–1942*. New York: Simon and Schuster, 1944.
Griffin, Thomas P. "The FSX Debate: Implications for Future U.S. International Armaments Programs." Master's Thesis. Wright-Patterson Air Force Base, Ohio: The Air Force Institute of Technology, 1989.
Hall, John A., and G. John Ikenberry. *The State*. University of Minnesota Press, 1989.
Hall, John W., and Marius B. Jansen. *Studies in the Institutional History of Early Modern Japan*. Princeton: Princeton University Press, 1968.
Handbook of Korea. Seoul: Seoul International Publishing House, 1987.
Hanreider, Wolfram F. *Germany, America, Europe: Forty Years of German Foreign Policy*. New Haven: Yale University Press, 1989.
Herz, John. *Political Realism and Political Idealism*. Chicago: University of Chicago Press, 1951.
Historical Statistics of the United States: Colonial Times to 1970, Part 1. Washington, D.C.: Department of Commerce, 1975.
Horton, Frank B., III, Anthony C. Rogerson and Edward L. Warner III, ed., *Comparative Defense Policy*. Baltimore: Johns Hopkins University Press, 1974.
Hsü, Immanuel C. Y. *The Rise of Modern China*. London: Oxford University Press, 1975.
Hundred-Year Statistics of the Japanese Economy. Tokyo: Bank of Japan, 1966.
Huntington, Samuel P. *Political Order in Changing Societies*. New Haven: Yale University Press, 1968.
Iida, K. *Nihon kindai Seitetsugijutsu Hattatsushi* [Development of Japan Modern Iron Technology]. Tokyo: Toyo Keiai Shinpo, 1957.
Ikenberry, G. John. "The Irony of State Strength: Comparative Responses to the Oil Shocks." *International Organization* 40 (Winter, 1986), pp. 105–137.
_____. *Reasons of State: Oil Politics and the Capacities of American Government*. Ithaca: Cornell University Press, 1988.
Ikenberry, G. John, David A. Lake, and Michael Mastanduno, eds. *The State and American Foreign Economic Policy*. Ithaca: Cornell University Press, 1988.
Inoguchi, Takashi, and Daniel I. Okimoto. *The Political Economy of Japan: The Changing International Context*. Stanford: Stanford University Press, 1988.
Iriye, Akira. *Across the Pacific: An Inner History of American-East Asian Relations*. New York: Harcourt, Brace & World, 1967.
_____. *After Imperialism: The Search for a New Order in the Far East, 1921–1931*. New York: Atheneum, 1969.
Ishihara, Shintaro. "From Bad to Worse in the FSX Project." *Japan Echo* 16, No. 3 (Autumn, 1989), pp. 59–65.

_____. "FSX no zasetsu: sengo taisei matsushoen" [The collapse of FSX: the beginning of the death of the postwar structure]. *Chūō Kōron* 104 (July 1989), pp. 194-198.
Ito, Kan. "Trans-Pacific Anger." *Foreign Policy*, No. 78 (Spring 1990), pp. 131-152.
James Forrestal Diaries. Princeton University Mudd Library.
Japan's Policies and Purposes: Selections from Recent Addresses and Writings. Boston: Marshal Jones, 1935.
"Japan's White Paper on Science and Technology." Report Memoranda 62, 65, 88, 102, 115. Tokyo: U.S. National Science Foundation.
Jervis, Robert. "Cooperation under the Security Dilemma." *World Politics* (January 1978), pp. 167-214.
Johnson, Chalmers. *MITI and the Japanese Miracle*. Stanford: Stanford University Press, 1982.
Jordan, Maria Rowan. "Two Case Studies of U.S. Policies Toward Dependent Allies." Master's Thesis. Georgetown University, 1986.
Kajima, Morinosuke. *Modern Japan's Foreign Policy*. Tokyo: Charles E. Tuttle Company, 1969.
Kamikawa, Hikomatsu. *Japan-American Diplomatic Relations in the Meiji-Taisho Era*. Tokyo: Pan-Pacific Press, 1958.
Karnow, Stanely. *In Our Image: America's Empire in the Philippines*. New York: Ballantine Books, 1989.
Kataoka, Tetsuya, and Ramon H. Myers. *Defending an Economic Superpower: Reassessing the U.S.-Japan Security Alliance*. Boulder: Westview Press, 1989.
Katzenstein, Peter J. *Small States in World Markets: Industrial Policy in Europe*. Ithaca: Cornell University Press, 1986.
_____, ed. *Between Power and Plenty*. Madison: University of Wisconsin Press, 1978.
Kennedy, M. D. *Some Aspects of Japan and Her Defence Forces*. London: Kegan Paul, Trench, Trubner, 1928.
Kennedy, Paul. *The Rise and Fall of the Great Powers*. New Haven: Yale University Press, 1987.
Keohane, Robert O. *After Hegemony: Cooperation and Discord in the World Political Economy*. Princeton: Princeton University Press, 1984.
Kim, Yu Nam Kim. "Perestroika and the Security of the Korean Peninsula." *Korean Journal of Defense Analysis* I, No. 1, p. 149.
Kotani, Hidejiro. *Boeiron to Ajia* [Defense Issues and Asia]. Tokyo: Koseisha, 1968.
Kozai, Yasushi. *Kodo Seicho no Jidai* [Period of High Growth]. Tokyo: Nihon Hyoronsha, 1981.
Krasner, Stephen D. "Approaches to the State: Alternative Conceptions and Historical Dynamics." *Comparative Politics* 16, No. 2 (January 1984), pp. 223-246.
_____. *Defending the National Interest: Raw Materials Investments and U.S. Foreign Policy*. Princeton: Princeton University Press, 1978.
Kurzman, Dan. *Kishi and Japan: The Search for the Sun*. New York: Obolensky, 1960.
Langdon, F.C. *Japan's Foreign Policy*. Vancouver: University of British Columbia Press, 1973.
La Palombara, Joseph, ed. *Bureaucracy and Political Development*. Princeton: Princeton University Press, 1963.
Leffler, Melvyn P. "The American Conception of National Security and the Beginnings of the Cold War, 1945-48." *The American Historical Review* 89, No. 2 (April 1984), pp. 346-400.
Levin, Carl. "U.S. Relationships with NATO and Japan — Sharing the Burdens of Common Defense." *The Congressional Record* (27 June 1983), p. S9217.
Lindhert, Peter H. *Key Currencies and Gold, 1900-1913*. Princeton: Princeton University Press, 1969.

Liska, George. *Nations in Alliance: The Limits of Interdependence*. Baltimore: Johns Hopkins University Press, 1962.
Lowi, Theodore J. "American Business, Public Policy, Case Studies, and Political Theory." *World Politics* 16, No. 4 (July 1964).
Massaki, Hajime. Interview in *Japan Defense Focus*, No.1. Japan Defense Agency: March, 2006.
Matsuo, Kinoaki. *How Japan Plans to Win*. Boston: Little, Brown, 1942.
Matsusaki, Hajime, and Brian Y. Shiroyama. "Japanese Military Burdensharing." In Thomas C. Gill, ed. *Essays on Strategy VI*. Washington, D.C.: National Defense University Press, 1989, pp. 119–166.
McIntosh, Malcolm. *Japan Re-armed*. London: Pinter, 1986.
McNeill, William H. *The Pursuit of Power: Technology, Armed Force and Society Since A.D. 1000*. Chicago: University of Chicago Press, 1982.
The Military Balance. London: The International Institute for Strategic Studies, annually since 1960.
Mills, Walter, ed. *The Forrestal Diaries*. New York: Viking, 1951.
"Ministry of International Trade and Industry (MITI) R&D Budget." Report Memoranda 60, 76, 81, 107, 132, 172, 196. Tokyo: U.S. National Science Foundation.
"MITI's White Paper: Trends and Future Tasks" [Sangyo Gijutsu no Doko to Kadai]. Report Memorandum 167 (December 1988). Tokyo: U.S. National Science Foundation.
Mochizuki, Mike. "Japan's Search for Strategy." *International Security* 8, No. 3. (Winter 1983/84), pp. 152–179.
Morley, James C. *Dilemmas of Growth in Prewar Japan*. Princeton: Princeton University Press, 1971.
_____, ed. *Security Interdependence in the Asia Pacific Region*. Lexington, MA: Lexington Books, 1986.
Morse, Ronald A. "Japan's Drive to Pre-Eminence." *Foreign Policy* 69 (Winter 1987–88), pp. 3–21.
Munro, Dana G. *Intervention and Dollar Diplomacy in the Caribbean, 1900–1921*. Princeton: Princeton University Press, 1964.
Murray, Douglas J., and Paul R. Viotti, eds. *The Defense Policies of Nations: A Comparative Study*. Baltimore: Johns Hopkins University Press, 1989.
Mutual Defense Assistance Office. *Japanese Military Technology: Procedures for Transfers to the United States*. Tokyo: MDAO, 1985.
Myers, Ramon H., and Mark R. Peattie. *The Japanese Colonial Empire, 1895–1945*. Princeton: Princeton University Press, 1984.
Nagai, Yonosuke, and Akira Iriye, eds. *The Origins of the Cold War in Asia*. Tokyo: University of Tokyo Press, 1977.
Nakada, Yasuhisa. "Japan's Security Perceptions and Military Needs." In Onkar Marwah and Jonathon D. Pollack, eds. *Military Power and Policy in Asian States: China, India, Japan*. Boulder: Westview, 1980, pp. 147–180.
Nakamura, Takafusa. *Economic Growth in Prewar Japan*. New Haven: Yale University Press, 1983.
_____. *The Postwar Japanese Economy: Its Development and Structure*. Tokyo: University of Tokyo Press, 1981.
Nakane, Chie. *Japanese Society*. Berkeley: University of California Press, 1970.
Neu, Charles E. *The Troubled Encounter: The United States and Japan*. Malabar, FL: Krieger, 1975.
Neustadt, Richard, and Ernest May. *Thinking in Time: The Uses of History for Decision Makers*. New York: Wiley, 1986.
Neustadt, Richard E. *Alliance Politics*. New York: Columbia University Press, 1973.
The New Guidelines for Japan–U.S. Defense Cooperation. Tokyo: Defense Agency, 1988.

Nichi-bei Anpo Joyaku no Shoten [Focus on the Japan–U.S. Security Treaty]. Tokyo: Asahi Shinbun Sha, 1967.
Nihon no Anzen Hosho [Japan's Security]. Tokyo: Asahi Shinbun Sha, 1967.
Nihon no Boei 1989 [Defense of Japan 1989]. Tokyo: Boeicho, 1989.
Nishihara, Masasashi. "Japan's Changing Security Role." *Harvard International Review* X, No. 4 (April/May 1988).
Norman, E. H. *Japan's Emergence as a Modern State.* New York: Institute of Pacific Relations, 1940.
O'Connell, John. "Strategic Implications of the Japanese SSM-1 Cruise Missile." *Journal of Northeast Asian Studies* VI, No. 2 (Summer 1987), pp. 53–66.
Ogawa, Kazuhisa. "FSX no hamon: tekunonajonarisuto no tojo" [The ripple of FSX: the technologist enters the stage]. *Sekai* 528 (June 1989), pp. 63–73.
———. "Joint Fighter Development: Security Sacrificed Again." *Japan Echo* 16, No. 3 (Autumn 1989), pp. 66–69.
Okawara, Yoshio. *To Avoid Isolation: An Ambassador's View of U.S./Japanese Relations.* Columbia: University of South Carolina Press, 1990.
Okazaki, Hisahiko. "Magarikado ni kita nichi-bei domei" [The upcoming U.S.–Japan alliance]. *Bungei Shunju* 66, No. 8 (July, 1988), pp. 94–111.
Okimoto, Daniel I. *Between MITI and the Market: Japanese Industrial Policy for High Technology.* Stanford: Stanford University Press, 1989.
Olsen, Mancur. *The Logic of Collective Action: Public Goods and the Theory of Groups.* Cambridge: Harvard University Press, 1965.
Olsen, Mancur, and Richard J. Zeckhauser. "An Economic Theory of Alliances." *Review of Economics and Statistics* 48, pp. 266–279.
Orr, Robert M., Jr. "The Aid Factor in U.S.–Japan Relations." *Asian Survey* 28, No. 27 (July 1988), pp. 740–756.
———. *The Emergence of Japan's Foreign Aid Power.* New York: Columbia University Press, 1990.
Packard, George R, III. *Protest in Tokyo: The Security Treaty Crisis of 1960.* Princeton: Princeton University Press, 1966.
Palmer, Aaron Haight. *Origin of the Mission to Japan* (first published in 1857 as *Documents and Facts Illustrating the Origin of the Mission to Japan*). Wilmington: Scholarly Resources, 1973.
Papers of Dean Acheson. Truman Library, Independence, Missouri.
Papers of Dwight D. Eisenhower. Eisenhower Library, Abilene, Kansas.
Papers of Harry S. Truman. Truman Library, Independence, Missouri.
Papers of John D. Sumner. Truman Library, Independence, Missouri.
Papers of John Foster Dulles. Princeton University Mudd Manuscript Library, Princeton, New Jersey.
Papers of Myron M. Cowen. Truman Library, Independence, Missouri.
Papers of Roger N. Baldwin. Princeton University Mudd Manuscript Library, Princeton, New Jersey.
Papers Relating to the Foreign Relations of the United States, Japan: 1931–1941. Vol. I. Washington, D.C.: U.S. Government Printing Office, 1943.
Pastor, Robert. *Congress and the Politics of U.S. Foreign Economic Policy, 1929–1976.* Berkeley: University of California Press, 1980.
Pempel, T. J. "The Unbundling of 'Japan, Inc.': The Changing Dynamics of Japanese Policy Formulation." *Journal of Japanese Studies* 13, No. 2 (1987), pp. 217–306.
———, and Keiichi Tsunekawa. "Corporatism without Labor? The Japanese Anomaly." In Philippe Schmitter and Gerhard Lehmbruch, eds. *Trends Toward Corporate Intermediation.* Beverly Hills: Sage, 1979.
Polomka, Peter. "U.S.–Japan: Beyond the Cold War." *Asian Perspective* 14, No. 1 (Spring 1990), pp. 171–186.

Prestowitz, Clyde. "Giving Japan a Handout — Why Fork Over $7 Billion in Aircraft Technology?" *The Washington Post* (29 January 1989).
Prestowitz, Clyde V., Jr. *Trading Places: How We Are Giving Our Future to Japan and How to Reclaim It*. New York: Basic Books, 1989.
Putnam, Robert D. "Diplomacy and Domestic Politics." *International Organization* 42, No. 3 (Summer 1988), pp. 427–460.
Pyle, Kenneth B. *The Trade Crisis: How Will Japan Respond?* Seattle: Society for Japanese Studies, 1987.
Reed, John A., Jr. *Germany and NATO*. Washington, D.C.: National Defense University Press, 1987.
Regional Pacific Security: The 1985 Pacific Symposium. Washington, D.C.: The National Defense University Press, 1988.
Reischauer, Edwin O. "The Broken Dialogue with Japan." *Foreign Affairs* 39 (October 1960), pp. 11–29.
_____. *Japan: Past and Present*. New York: Knopf, 1958.
Report of the Mission on Japanese Combines: A Report to the Department of State and the War Department. Washington, D.C.: U.S. Government Printing Office, 1946.
Rhea, John. "Silicon's Speedier Cousins." *Air Force Magazine* (November 1989), pp. 102–106.
Rix, Alan. *Japan's Economic Aid: Policy-making and Politics*. New York: St. Martin's, 1980.
Rubenstein, Gregg A. "Emerging Bonds of U.S.–Japanese Defense Technology Cooperation." *Strategic Review* (Winter 1987), pp. 43–50.
Saito, Ichiro. *Anpo Toso Shi* [Security Struggle History]. Tokyo: Sanichi Shobo, 1962.
Sakanaka, Tomohisa. "Kaijō Jieitai no Senryaku Kōsō: Nihon no Jieiryoku" [Strategic Plans of the Maritime Self-Defense Force: Japan's Self-Defense Power]. Tokyo: Asahi Shinbunsha, 1967.
Samuels, Richard J. *The Business of the Japanese State: Energy Markets in Comparative and Historical Perspective*. Ithaca: Cornell University Press, 1987.
Samuels, Richard J., and Benjamin C. Whipple. *Defense Production and Industrial Development: The Case of Japanese Aircraft*. M.I.T.–Japan Science and Technology Program Paper 88-09. Cambridge: Massachusetts Institute of Technology, 1988.
Sato, Seizaburo. "Ima koso nichi-bei domei no kyuka o" [The current Japan–U.S. alliance partnership]. *Chuo Koron*, No. 3 (June 1988), pp. 110–119.
_____, and Tetsuhisa Matsuzaki. *Jiminto Seiken* [The Liberal Democratic Party regime]. Tokyo: Chuo Koronsha, 1986.
Schaller, Michael. *The American Occupation of Japan: The Origins of the Cold War in Asia*. Oxford: Oxford University Press, 1985.
Seki, Kenji. *Nihon Mengyoron* [Japan Cotton Industry]. Tokyo: Tokyo University Press, 1954.
Shigemitsu, Mamoru. *Japan and Her Destiny: My Struggle for Peace*. London: Dutton, 1958.
Skowronek, Stephen. *Building a New American State: The Expansion of National Administrative Capacities, 1877–1920*. Cambridge: Cambridge University Press, 1982.
Sloan, Stanley R. *NATO's Future: Toward a New Transatlantic Bargain*. Washington, D.C.: National Defense University Press, 1985.
Smoke, Richard. *National Security and the Nuclear Dilemma: An Introduction to the American Experience*. New York: Random House, 1987.
Snyder, Glenn H. "Alliances, Balance, and Stability." *International Organization* 45, No. 1 (Winter 1990/91), pp. 121–142.
_____. "The Security Dilemma in Alliance Politics." In *World Politics* (January 1985), pp. 461–495.
_____, and Paul Deising. *Conflict Among Nations: Bargaining, Decision-Making, and System Structure in International Crises*. Princeton: Princeton University Press, 1977.

Solomon, Richard H. "Asian Security in the 1990s: Integration in Economics, Diversity in Defense." *Dispatch* 1, No. 10. Washington, D.C.: United States Department of State Bureau of Public Affairs, 5 November 1990.
Soviet Military Power. Washington, D.C.: U.S. Government Printing Office, annually.
Spencer, Edson W. "Japan as Competitor." *Foreign Policy*, No. 78 (Spring 1990), pp. 153–171.
Strayer, Joseph R. *On the Medieval Origins of the Modern State.* Princeton: Princeton University Press, 1970.
Suleiman, Ezra N., ed. *Bureaucrats and Policymaking.* New York: Holmes and Meier, 1984.
Supreme Commander for the Allied Powers. *The Political Reorientation of Japan, September 1945-September 1948, Report of the Governmental Section of SCAP.* Washington, D.C., 1948.
Taharasu, Ichiro. "Nichi-bei anpo ga omochya ni saredashita" [U.S.–Japan security is not treated seriously]. *Bungei Shunju* (June, 1990), pp. 164–181.
Takahashi, Kamekichi. *The Rise and Development of Japan's Modern Economy: The Basis for "Miraculous" Growth.* Vols. 1 and 2. Tokyo: Jiji, 1969.
Tessmer, Arnold Lee. *Politics of Compromise: NATO and AWACS.* Washington, D.C.: National Defense University Press, 1988.
Thayer, Nathaniel B. *How the Conservatives Rule Japan.* Princeton: Princeton University Press, 1969.
Tilly, Charles, ed. *The Formation of National States in Western Europe.* Princeton: Princeton University Press, 1975.
Togo, Shigenori. *The Cause of Japan.* New York: Simon and Schuster, 1965.
Tokinoya, Atsushi. *The U.S.–Japan Alliance: A Japanese Perspective.* Adelphi Paper 212. London: The International Institute for Strategic Studies, 1986.
"Transcript of a Recorded Interview with Aiichiro Fujiyama." Interviewer Spencer Davis. The John Foster Dulles Oral History Project, Princeton University Mudd Library, 1964.
"Transcript of a Recorded Interview with Ichiro Kono." Interviewer Spencer Davis. The John Foster Dulles Oral History Project, Princeton University Mudd Library, 1964.
"Transcript of a Recorded Interview with Katsuo Okazaki." Interviewer Spencer Davis. The John Foster Dulles Oral History Project, Princeton University Mudd Library, 1964.
"Transcript of a Recorded Interview with Nobosuke Kishi." Interviewer Spencer Davis. The John Foster Dulles Oral History Project, Princeton University Mudd Library, 1964.
"Transcript of a Recorded Interview with Shigeru Yoshida." Interviewer Spencer Davis. The John Foster Dulles Oral History Project, Princeton University Mudd Library, 1964.
Treat, Payson J. *Diplomatic Relations Between the United States and Japan, 1853–1895.* Stanford: Stanford University, 1932.
Treaties in Force: A List of Treaties and Other International Agreements of the United States in Force on January 1, 1988. Washington, D.C.: U.S. Government Printing Office, 1988.
Treverton, Gregory F. *Making the Alliance Work.* Ithaca: Cornell University Press, 1985.
Truman, Harry S. *Memoirs.* Vol 1, *Year of Decisions.* New York: Doubleday, 1955.
_____. *Memoirs.* Vol 2, *Years of Trial and Hope.* New York: Doubleday, 1956.
Tsunoda, Ryusaku, Wm. T. de Bary, and Donald Keene, eds. *Sources of the Japanese Tradition.* New York: Columbia University Press, 1958.
Tsurumi, Yoshi. *Japanese Business: A Research Guide with Annotated Bibiography.* New York: Praeger, 1978.
Tsurutani, Taketsugu. "Japan's Security, Defense Responsibilities and Capabilities." *Orbis* 25, No. 1 (Spring 1981), pp. 89–106.
U.S. Congress, Office of Technology Assessment. *Arming Our Allies: Cooperation and Competition in Defense Technology.* Washington, D.C.: U.S. Government Printing Office, 1990.
"The U.S.–Japan FS-X Fighter Agreement: Assessing the Stakes." Washington, D.C.: The Center for Security Policy, 1989.

U.S. National Science Foundation Report Memoranda on: Ministry of International Trade and Industry (MITI) R&D Budget, Science and Technology Agency (STA) R&D Budget, MITI White Paper, and STA White Paper for Japan Fiscal Years 1984–1990. Tokyo: U.S. National Science Foundation.

van Wolferen, Karel. *The Enigma of Japanese Power: People and Politics in a Stateless Nation.* London: Macmillan, 1989.

Viner, Jacob. "Power versus Plenty as Objectives of Foreign Policy in the Seventeenth and Eighteenth Centuries." *World Politics* 1 (1948), pp. 1–29.

Wagner, R. Harrison. "Economic Interdependence, Bargaining Power, and Political Influence." *International Organization* 42 (Winter 1988), pp. 460–490.

Walt, Stephen M. *The Origins of Alliances.* Ithaca: Cornell University Press, 1987.

Waltz, Kenneth N. *Theory of International Relations.* Reading, MA: Addison-Wesley, 1979.

Ward, Michael Don. *Research Gaps in Alliance Dynamics.* Denver: University of Denver Graduate School of International Studies, 1982.

Watanabe, Akio, and Seigen Miyasato. *San Furansisuko Kowa* [The San Francisco Peace Conference]. Tokyo: Tokyo University Press, 1986.

Watanabe, Hosoya. *San Furanshisuko e no michi* [The road to San Francisco]. Tokyo: Chuo Koronsha, 1984.

Weinstein, Martin E. *Japan's Postwar Defense Policy, 1947–1968.* New York: Columbia University Press, 1971.

White Paper on Japan's Trade: 1956. Embassy of Japan Trade Report Summary. Vol. III, No. 11 (10 July 1957).

Wildes, Harry E. *Typhoon in Tokyo: The Occupation and Its Aftermath.* New York: Macmillan, 1954.

Wolfers, Arnold. "National Security as an Ambiguous Symbol." *Political Science Quarterly* 67 (December 1952), pp. 481–502.

Yasusuke, Murakami. "The Age of New Middle Mass Politics: The Case of Japan." *Journal of Japanese Studies* (Winter 1982), pp. 29–72.

Yoon, Young-Kwan. "The Political Economy of Transition: Japanese Foreign Direct Investment in the 1980s." *World Politics* 43, No.1 (October 1990), pp. 1–27.

Zycher, Benjamin. "A Generalized Approach for Analysis of Alliance Burden-Sharing." RAND Note 3047-PCT (September 1990).

Index

Acheson, Dean 38, 46, 52
Acquisition and Cross-Servicing Agreement 140
Administrative Agreement 56, 63
Afghanistan 9, 103
Agreed Framework 137, 147
Air Staff Office, Defense Agency 113, 117–20
Albright, Madeline 143
Alliance: change 10, 163, 168–9; as security bargain 21; theories and challenges 7, 11; transformation 157; US–Japan use of term 104, 106, 109, 165
American–Japanese Treaty of Commerce 23, 30
Anami, Korechika 41
Anglo-Chinese Treaty 30
Anglo-Japanese Alliance 31, 32, 34
Anti-terrorism Special Measures Law 149
Araki Commission Report 150
Aritomo, Yamagata 25
Armitage, Richard 122–3
Arms Export Control Act 127
Asanuma, Inejiro 79
Ashida, Hitoshi 44; memoranda 50, 56, 58, 92
Asian Development Bank 81
Association of Southeast Asian Nations (ASEAN) 103
Asymmetric exchange 153–4, 172
Australia 53, 56, 71, 81

Basic Policy for National Defense 73, 104, 112, 138
Basis of cooperation 6, 21, 22, 154, 160–3
Bikini Islands 78
Bilateral Coordination Mechanism 144–6
Blaine, James G. 29
Bonin Islands 61, 75–8, 80, 82
Borton, Hugh 51
Boxer Rebellion 32
Brunei 173
Burden-sharing 63, 80–1, 105, 108, 127, 132, 167
Bureau of Defense Policy, Defense Agency 117
Bush, George H. 127, 131, 132
Byrd, Robert 127
Byrnes, James F. 39

Cambodia 135
Capital Flight Law, 1932 34
Carter, James E. 95, 101–2
Central Asia 13, 18
Central Intelligence Agency (CIA) 54
Central questions 5, 6
Charter Oath 24
Charter Party Agreement, 1952 56, 65–6
Chechnya 18
China: naval capability, response to 9; postwar concerns 53; prewar roles 23, 30–41; rising power issue 6, 141, 169; security priorities, threats, interests 12–14; Taiwan live-fire exercises 139–40;

Territorial Waters Act 15, 135; trade with Japan 70
Choi, Sae-chang 136
Churchill, Winston 38
Clark, Mark W. 66
Clinton, William J. 130, 135–6, 140, 143
Clinton–Hashimoto Joint Declaration on Security 140–1
Cohen, William S. 143, 146
Collective defense 73, 84, 89, 133, 138, 144
Comparative studies 10
Comprehensive Mechanism 145–6
Constitution of Japan 56–8, 60, 68, 82, 96, 104, 108, 111, 132, 148, 159, 169, 171
Cope Thunder Exercise 149
Culture 11, 20, 43

Dagestan 18
Deconcentration Review Board 49
Defense Advanced Research Projects Agency (DARPA) 127
Defense Production Act 67
Defense Security Assistance Agency 118
Defense spending 7, 9, 49, 90, 98–9, 100, 108
Defense Technology Office 130
Demilitarization 38–9, 44, 54, 57, 62
Democratization 14, 16, 17, 46–50, 55, 57, 142, 156
Differentiated exchange 20, 176–7
Disarmament 61
Dixon, Larry 127
Dodge, Joseph 59, 159
Dodge-Suto Exchange 56, 63–5
Draper, William H. 51
Dulles, John Foster 52, 55–6, 59, 68–9, 75–8, 81–2
Dulles-Yoshida Dialogues 56, 59–61

Economic security, vulnerability 11, 23
Education Reform Council 49
Egypt 108, 132
Eisenhower, Dwight D. 76, 80, 88–9, 164
Equipment Bureau, Defense Agency 117
Etajima Naval Academy 25

F-1 aircraft 114–15
F-2 aircraft 111, 115, 128
Fahd, bin Abdulaziz al Saud 131
Fillmore, Millard 23
Flexible Response 92
Foreign Military Sales (FMS) 112, 116, 118
Forrestal, James 52, 54

France 53
Free-riding 7, 101, 153, 166
FS-X (fighter support-experimental) aircraft 110, 166–7
Fudesaka, Hideyo 146
Fujiyama, Aiichiro 76, 82
Futenma Air Station 148

Gast, Philip 122
Global Defense Posture Review 149–50
Gorbachev, Mikhail 130
Government Appropriation for Relief in Occupied Areas (GAROIA) 101
Great Britain 10, 23–5, 28, 32–3, 39, 51, 53
Greater East Asian Co-Prosperity Sphere 39
Grew, Joseph 37, 39
Guam 75
Guidelines, Defense, 1997 140, 167, 170, 172
Guidelines for US-Japan Defense Cooperation, 1978 99, 130, 139, 144, 163

Han, Sung-joo 137
Hashimoto, Ryutaro 136, 139–40
Hatoyama, Ichiro 48, 72, 89
Higuchi, Hirotaro 138–9
Hirohito 40, 41, 42
Hiroshima 22, 41, 71
Hoover, Herbert C. 35
Hosokawa, Morihiro 135, 138
Host Nation Support (HNS) *see* burden-sharing
Hull, Cordell 35, 36, 155

Ikeda, Hayato 50, 56, 58–9, 61, 159
Ikeda-Robertson Communique 66–7
Imperial Rescript 25, 27
Inamine, Keiichi 148
Income-doubling plan 89
India 6, 13
Industrial Association Law, 1934 34
Industrial policy 11
Intelligence 46
International Atomic Energy Agency 136–7
International Wheat Agreement 51
Iraq 9, 149, 168, 170
Ishihara, Shintaro 127
Ishii, Mitsujiro 86
Ito, Hirobumi 106
Iwo Jima 75

Jamaica 108
Japan Defense Agency Law 67
Japan defense strategy 92–6

Japan National Safety Force 65, 68
Japan Security Council 115
Japan security priorities, threats, interests 18–20
Japan Self-Defense Force 67–9, 74–5, 81, 95–8, 105, 107, 146, 159
Joint Chiefs of Staff (JCS) 43, 49, 60–2, 75–6, 88, 119
Joint Military Planning Board 65
Joint Military Technology Commission 113, 115, 127
Joint Staff Council 106
Jordan 108, 122

Kagoshima Bay 23
Kaifu, Toshiki 131–4
Kan, Naoto 143
Kanagawa, Treaty of 23
Kawai, Yasunari 48
Kennan, George 51, 60
Kennedy, John F. 92
Kido, Koichi 40, 41
Kim, Dae-jung 13
Kim, Il-sung 16
Kim, Jong-il 16
Kim, Young-sam 137
Kishi, Nobosuke 48, 72, 76–7, 79–83, 86–8, 164
Knox, Philander C. 29
Koizumi, Junichiro 149, 167
Konoe, Fumimaro 36, 37, 40
Korean-American alliance 42–3
Korean Energy Development Organization 147
Korean Strait 55
Korean War 30–2, 56, 59, 60, 72, 74, 130, 136–8
Korean Strait 55
Korean unification 16, 19
Kuihara, Yuko 122–3
Kuwait 130
Kyuma, Fumio 143

La Perouse Strait 54
Legitimate competition 37, 155
Liaotung Peninsula 31
Liberalism 25, 27–8, 34–5, 37, 43–7, 50, 54–5, 78, 142, 155–6
London Disarmament Conference, 1934 35

MacArthur, Douglas 43–4, 46–7, 78, 85
MacArthur, Douglas, II 82
Malaysia 173

Massive Retaliation 92
Matsumoto, Joji 57
Meiji Constitution 26
Meiji reaction to the West 24–5, 27, 30
Mercantilism, state 25
Mid-Term Defense Program/Plan 117, 139
Midway, Battle of 40
Miike mines 83
Miki, Takeo 104
Military Assistance Program 67, 89
Military Technology, issues 12, 108, 112–16, 123–6, 128, 164, 171
Ministry of International Trade and Industry (MITI) 79, 113–114
Misawa Air Base 108, 12
Mitsubishi 48
Mitsui 48
Miyazawa, Kiichi 135
Mondale, Walter F. 140
Monroe Doctrine 26
Morganthau, Henry 39, 53
Mozambique 135
Mukden Incident 34, 35
Murayama, Tomiichi 136, 138
Mutual Assistance Program 69
Mutual Defense Assistance Act 54, 67
Mutual Defense Assistance Agreement 56, 67–8, 91
Mutual Defense Assistance Office 113
Mutual Defense Laws 56
Mutual Security Act 48, 67, 69
Mutual Security Program 52, 66–7, 75

Nagasaki 22, 23, 41, 71
Nakasone, Yasuhiro 90, 107, 116, 122
Nakayama, Taro 131
National Defense Council 86–7, 115–16
National Defense Program Guidance 150
National Defense Program Outline 99, 107, 117, 139, 163
National Police Bill 83
National Police Force 85
National Security Council (NSC) 52, 54, 65, 75, 87, 131
National Security Resources Board 88
National Stockpile Administration 88
NATO see North Atlantic Treaty Organization
New Look Policy 77–8
New Zealand 53, 56
Nine-Power Treaty 34
Nishihiro, Seiki 122–3
Nixon, Richard M. 95, 101

Nixon Shocks 90
Norota, Hosei 148
North Atlantic Treaty Organization (NATO) 11, 18, 54, 99, 101, 136
North Korea 6, 9, 13–16, 147, 149, 167, 176
NPT *see* Nuclear Non-Proliferation Treaty
NSC *see* National Security Council
Nuclear Non-Proliferation Treaty (NPT) 112, 136, 137
Nuclear weapons 77–8
Nukaga, Fukushiro 147
Nye, Joseph 139

Obuchi, Keizo 143, 146
Office of Strategic Services (OSS) 46
Official Development Assistance (ODA) 96–7, 105, 108, 127
Ohira, Masayoshi 102
Oil Embargo, 1940 36
Okinawa 55, 71, 75, 80, 139
Oman 108, 122, 148
Open Door notes 32, 34
Operation Enduring Freedom 149
Ota, Masahide 139, 148
Ozawa, Ichiro 132, 143

Pakistan 6, 14, 167
Panama Canal 28
Patent Rights Agreement 56
Pauley, Edwin W., mission 51
Peace Treaty (Multilateral, San Francisco, 1951) 50, 53, 56, 58–9, 61–2, 160
Pearl Harbor 22
Perry, Matthew C. 23
Perry, William J. 131
Persian Gulf: Gulf Crisis Countermeasures Headquarters 133; oil, Japan dependence on 9; war, 1990–1 130–4, 167
Petropavlovsk 54, 97
Philippines 29, 45, 53, 56, 71, 173
Poland 103
Political parties: Communist 77, 79, 106, 146–7; Democratic 72, 80, 143, 147; Democratic-Socialist 146; Komeito 133, 146, 148; Liberal 69, 72, 80, 148; Liberal-Democratic 72, 80, 82, 89, 109, 132, 143, 147–8, 159, 164, 167; New Komeito 148; Progressive 72; Reform 69; Sakigake 143; Shinshinto 143; Shinto Heiwa 148; Social-Democratic 143; Socialist 77, 79, 82, 89, 106, 165
Port Arthur 31, 32

Port Dairen 32
Potsdam Declaration 39, 41, 44, 53
Prior Consultation Clause 84
Protectionism 25
USS *Pueblo* 94
Purge 47–8, 72, 83

Quemoy and Matsu Islands 93
Quid Pro Quo 62, 68–70, 109, 125–6, 161, 164, 166–70, 174

Reagan, Ronald 91, 116
Reagan-Suzuki Communique 91, 100, 102–3, 105, 112, 167
Rearmament 53, 54–6, 60–6, 68–9, 72, 81, 85, 101, 111
Reischauer, Edwin O. 106
Reparations 51–3, 55
Rhee, Byoung-tae 136
RIMPAC (Rim of the Pacific) Exercise 106–7, 147
Robertson, Walter S. 66
Roosevelt, Franklin D. 35, 38, 46, 155
Roosevelt, Theodore 28, 39
Royall, Kenneth C. 52
Russia: decline and discord 6; North Korea ties 136; perception of China 13; post–Cold War drawdown 135; prewar roles 23, 33, 38; security priorities, threats and interests 17–18, 142
Russo-Japanese War 29, 32

Saito, Hiroshi 35
Sato, Eisaku 86, 90, 112
Saudi Arabia 133
Sawyer, Charles W. 52
SCAP *see* Supreme Commander Allied Powers 43, 45–7
Sea lanes of communication (SLOC) 97–8, 104–7, 117
Security: broad, narrow conceptions 12, 26–9, 155, 170–2; definition 20–21; economic and military 11, 24, 26–9, 30–7, 44–50, 57–8, 62, 65, 67, 70, 87, 89, 126, 154, 177; national concepts 24, 26–29, 37, 177; regional context 12–20
Security bargain: cooperation formula 56, 70; core bargain 20–21, 86; diplomatic adjustment—1960 83–88, 164; military adjustment—1981 102–6, 164–5; residual elements 158; strategic security bargain 153, 156; summary, basis for cooperation and transformative change

161–3; technology adjustment —1987 123–26, 127, 166; threat adjustment — 1997 140, 143–5, 167
Security Consultative Committee 85, 100
Security dilemma 10
Security Treaty, 1951 56, 61–2, 77
Security Treaty, 1960 71, 83–6, 100, 103, 150, 164, 167, 172, 176
Self-defense 73, 84, 159
Senaga, Kamejiro 76
Seward, William H. 28
Shantung territory 33
Shidehara, Kijuro 43
Shigemitsu, Mamoru 40, 43, 72, 75–7, 88
Shimonoseki, Straits of 23
Shoriki, Matsutaro 48
Shufeldt, Robert W. 29
Singapore 71
Sino-Japanese War 29, 30–1
Sinuiju 15
Six-Party Talks 176
SLOC *see* Sea lanes of communication
Snyder, John W. 52
Somalia 136
South Korea 16–17, 130, 134, 136–8, 142–3, 176–7
Sovetskaya Gavan 97
Soviet Union: expansionism as threat 54–5, 62; military capabilities 74, 100; Soviet Pacific Fleet increases, response to 9
Soya Strait 97
Stalin, Josef 38, 58
State-War-Navy Coordinating Committee (SWNCC) 38
Status of Forces Agreement (SOFA) 84, 86
Stimson, Henry L., Secretary of War 35, 39
Strategic Defense Initiative (SDI) 108
Strategic Denial 45
Strategic Frontier 45
Sudan 108
Sugamo Prison 72
Sullivan, Gerald 121
Sunakawa Incident 83
Supreme Commander Allied Powers (SCAP) 43, 45–7
Suto, Hideo 64
Suzuki, Kantaro 41
Suzuki, Zenko 91, 102–3, 105–6, 164
SWNCC *see* State-War-Navy Coordinating Committee

Taft, William H. 28
Taiwan: defense ties with U.S. 71; rise of nationalism 6; rogue province 13; security priorities, threats, interests 14–15
Tanimura, Tadaichiro 48
Technical Research and Development Institute 99, 113, 117–20, 119, 125
Territorial disputes: China-India, line of actual control 13; China-Russia 13, 135; China-Taiwan 13, 14, 15; Japan-China 19, 135, 177; Japan-Korea 19, 177; Japan-Russia 19, 76; Spratly Islands 6, 173
Terrorism 6, 149, 167
Thailand 71
Theater Missile Defense 140
Theory: alliance 7; balance of power 7, 10, 152; public goods 7–10, 153; rational choice 10; theoretical considerations 6, 170–3
Threat: conditions and agents 21; perceptions 24–26
Three Non-Nuclear Principles 13–14, 112
Tibet 13
Tojo, Hideki 38, 40, 72
Tokugawa Shogunate 24
Toshiba Incident 121, 123
Toyota, Sakichi 27
Trade issues 23, 78–80, 90, 101
Treaty of Friendship, Commerce and Navigation 84
Truman, Harry S. 39, 43, 46–7, 51–2, 72, 87
Tsugaru Strait 54–5
Tsushima Island 23
Tsushima Strait 55
Turkey 108, 132

Uchida, Yasuya 32
Unconditional surrender 37, 38, 39, 42–3, 46, 71
United Nations 19, 62, 77, 81–2, 112, 132; Operation in Mozambique 135; Operation in Somalia 136; Peace Cooperation Corps 133; Peacekeeping and Other Operations Bill 134–5; Transition Authority in Cambodia 135

Versailles Peace Treaty 52
Vietnam 89, 173
Vladivostok 97

Washington Naval Conference 34, 35, 155

Weinberger, Caspar W. 101, 123
World Trade Organization (WTO) 13

Xinjiang 13

Yalta agreement 38
Yasukuni 18
Yokosuka 25, 140, 149

Yokota Air Base 111
Yonai, Mitsumasa 41
Yoshida, Shigeru 34, 35, 40, 43, 48–9, 59, 60, 65, 69–70, 72

Zaire 136
Zimbabwe 108

www.ingramcontent.com/pod-product-compliance
Lightning Source LLC
Chambersburg PA
CBHW032054300426
44116CB00007B/730